THE WIND
IN THE REEDS

THE WIND
IN THE REEDS

A STORM, A PLAY, AND THE CITY
THAT WOULD NOT BE BROKEN

WENDELL PIERCE

WITH ROD DREHER

RIVERHEAD BOOKS
New York
2015

RIVERHEAD BOOKS
an imprint of Penguin Random House LLC
375 Hudson Street
New York, New York 10014

Library of Congress Cataloging-in-Publication Data

Pierce, Wendell.
The wind in the reeds : a storm, a play, and the city that would not be broken /
Wendell Pierce with Rod Dreher.
p.   cm.
ISBN 978-1-59463-323-2
1. Pierce, Wendell.   2. African American actors—Biography.   3. Hurricane Katrina,
2005—Social aspects—Louisiana—New Orleans.   I. Dreher, Rod.   II. Title.
PN2287.P5395A3   2015   2015024642
791.4302'8092—dc23
[B]

Printed in the United States of America
1   3   5   7   9   10   8   6   4   2

Book design by Lauren Kolm

Penguin is committed to publishing works of quality and integrity. In that spirit,
we are proud to offer this book to our readers; however, the story, the experiences,
and the words are the author's alone.

To my blessed mother, Tee

CONTENTS

ONE

A SONG OF RESURRECTION

I drove east across the Claiborne Avenue bridge on the first Friday night in November 2007, two years after the storm that devastated this city. My hometown. My New Orleans. As I came upon the Lower Ninth Ward, there was an extraordinary amount of traffic headed in the same direction as me. *They're coming to see the play,* I thought.

The play was *Waiting for Godot,* Samuel Beckett's immortal absurdist drama about two tramps, Vladimir and Estragon, living in a wasteland and waiting for a savior who may or may not come. The play, which Beckett wrote inspired by the agonies of Nazi-controlled Paris, deals with abandonment and the struggle inside all of us between hope and despair.

Paris had the Nazi occupation; New Orleans had Hurricane Katrina. We New Orleanians knew abandonment. We knew what it was like to struggle for a lifeline of hope in the midst of a maelstrom of despair. God knows that we who had to deal with FEMA (the Federal Emergency Management Agency) knew absurdity.

Nobody in the city knew it more intensely than the people of the Lower Ninth Ward.

For a long time after the storm, if you drove over the Claiborne Avenue bridge into the neighborhood, you plunged into a void, both physical and existential. There was nothing but a sea of night where once a thriving neighborhood had been. It was the abyss, a black hole of death and desolation, and a darkness so intense that many in New Orleans feared no light could ever overcome it.

On the morning of August 29, 2005, Katrina gashed the levee in two places north of the bridge, which traverses the Industrial Canal, the economically vital artery for shipping from the Mississippi River to Lake Pontchartrain and, via two other man-made canals, out into the Gulf of Mexico. Millions of gallons of water washed through the Lower Ninth Ward, scores of houses were toppled from their concrete pillars. A barge barreled over or through the levee, nobody can say for sure, crushing houses and cars. Hundreds of people drowned as the twenty-foot wall of water flattened everything in its path. It was biblical.

In a single morning, a historic African American neighborhood of fourteen thousand souls, among them the city's poorest, ceased to exist. Gone were the places where people lived, worked, shopped, prayed, visited, loved. Days later, after the water receded, there was nothing left but ruins, and corpses. In the heat and moisture of south Louisiana, weeds, vines, and trees rapidly consumed the desolate lots and sidewalks. Rattlesnakes and cottonmouths moved in, chasing the rats that overran backyards where children once played and stoops where families used to barbecue. Sometimes, packs of wild dogs owned the streets. The few residents able to return not only had to fight nature just to hold their ground, but also lived in fear of predatory rapists and other savages lurking in the rotting ruins and dark thickets that used to be a neighborhood.

This happened in one of the great American cities, or what was left of it. I knew intimately the agony of the people of the Lower Ninth Ward. Six miles north of the neighborhood, where the Industrial Canal meets the lake, the district of the city where I grew up— Pontchartrain Park, the first African American middle-class subdivision in New Orleans—had been virtually annihilated when a breach in a different canal to the west caused the neighborhood to fill with water up to the rooftops.

Built in the mid-1950s as the wall of segregation was beginning to crack, Pontchartrain Park symbolized the opening of the American dream to black folks in New Orleans—people like Althea and Amos Pierce, my schoolteacher mother and my photographer father, who in 1955 bought a modest ranch home there and started a family. Like their neighbors, Daddy and Tee, as we called our mother, lost everything in the flood. Like so many New Orleanians, from the upscale white enclave of Lakeview to the hardscrabble black Lower Ninth Ward, Daddy and Tee washed up on solid ground far from home, mourning and weeping in their Baton Rouge refuge, wondering if they would ever make it back.

The world post-Katrina was a hard time for my city. The hardest time. For people who didn't live through it, no words can fully express the pain, the rage, the grief, and the futility we New Orleanians felt. For the people who did, words seemed like a feeble protest against a relentless night without end.

How do you go on when you are bone-tired and broken down by a world where nothing makes sense, and there's no direction forward that leads to anywhere but the ditch or the grave? How do you embrace a life in which everything and everyone you knew and loved has been taken away, and may never return—and nobody else cares? How do you live through today when you fear there's no tomorrow?

These are the questions *Waiting for Godot* explores. In 2006, New York visual artist and publisher Paul Chan visited New Orleans, and when he saw the catastrophic ruin of the Lower Ninth Ward, he thought of *Godot* and conceived of staging the play for free in one of the neighborhoods most damaged by the ravages of Katrina. A year later, I played Vladimir in the Classical Theatre of Harlem's New York production of the Beckett play, one that Chan eventually brought to the Crescent City. We did two performances on an intersection near vacant Lower Ninth Ward street corners covered by grass and weeds as high as a man's chest. We did two more in the Gentilly neighborhood, which, like 80 percent of the city, had also taken cruel licks from the flood.

That night—November 2, 2007—was the first performance. More than six hundred people came and, before the show, ate free gumbo ladled out at the door. When showtime arrived, the Rebirth Brass Band burst into song and led the audience into the bleachers under the floodlights in a classic New Orleans second-line parade. From two blocks away, J. Kyle Manzay, who played Estragon, and I stood in our thrift-store suits and shabby bowler hats, preparing for our entrance. From where we stood, the butt-shaking fanfare of the brass band and the rustle of the crowd taking its seats were the only signs of life in the great and oppressive silence that surrounded us. As close as the people were, it felt like they were a hallucination.

Robert Green, a Lower Ninth Ward resident who lost his mother and granddaughter in the flood, stood in the performance space near the very spot of their death and gave a solemn benediction. On this night, he said, *Let's remember them. Let's remember all of them.*

I did. We all did.

(When we repeated the *Godot* performance in the Gentilly neighborhood later that month, my mother gave the first night's benediction as I stood inside an abandoned house, waiting to enter. She ended with "Now, enjoy my son.")

By then, I could see the audience under the lights. There were people from all walks of life—longshoremen and lawyers, teachers and shopkeepers. People from the neighborhood and people who had never set foot there before that night. All of these people—my people, New Orleanians—gathered in the ruins, expecting . . . what? Comfort? Remembrance? Catharsis? Revelation?

I stood there in the shadows, watching, trying to penetrate the thick canopy of night. There were no houses around us; they'd all been washed away. There were only grassy knolls, weed-choked lots, concrete stumps like teeth in a half-buried jawbone, and matching concrete staircases leading to nowhere.

And there we were, two actors in the center of the darkness, not much more than a stone's throw from where the levee broke, about to walk forward, poor as we were in the face of so great a need, and give everything we had.

Lord, I prayed silently, *we are on sacred ground. I've come here to make sure that You are honored, so bless me, that I may honor You. And God, I ask You to bless me that I may honor those who lost their lives in this place.*

The lights went down and I got my cue to go. My microphone was on, allowing the audience to hear me breathing and running and mumbling, even before they saw me.

"Here we go," I whispered, huffing. *"This is happening . . . we're going to change things . . . I'm coming . . . for you . . . for you . . . for all of them. . . ."*

Those were not Beckett's words, but I wanted them to lodge in people's heads, to know that we were there for them, that we were coming for them, that we were going to do something very special for them.

What I didn't know was that I was running toward the most transcendent experience of my life, one that combined all I am as an actor, a child of Amos and Tee, and a son of New Orleans. On that night, in that field of death and despair, I saw the rebirth of life and hope. I witnessed the power of art to renew the vision of people in danger of perishing. And not just to renew vision, but to impart a spirit of resurrection that proclaims in the face of the hurricane, *Yes, these bones can live!*

The *Godot* experience breathed life into my bones, bleached dry by the relentless grief and humiliation of Katrina's aftermath. It gave me the power and resolve to help my neighborhood and my city. Decades from now, little kids will ask, "Mr. Pierce, what did you do in New Orleans's darkest hour?" and I will tell them about that play, written by an expatriated Irishman who had experienced Paris in the depths of Nazi occupation. I will tell them about that night in the Lower Ninth Ward, and how, like some kind of miracle, the play said everything that could be said about what it was like to live through the endless nightmare of our post-Katrina city. I will tell them how it taught me about the power of art within an individual and a community to galvanize us, to renew, redeem, and rebuild our lives together.

And maybe I'll tell them the story about a kid like them who grew up in New Orleans, in a little house with a hardworking mother and father and two brothers. That kid spent his young life working hard in school, eating dinner with his family, going to mass on Sunday, playing in the park with neighborhood kids, and reveling in all the ordinary joys and sorrows of an American life. One day, when he was a little older, that kid discovered he had a talent for acting. Though that boy's parents were of modest means, New Orleans made it possible for him to attend one of the best performing arts high schools in the country. When he graduated, the kid launched himself into the great big world, leaving for the Juilliard School in New York City to become an actor. Later, the kid from the little house in Pontchartrain Park would go on to a stage, film, and TV career, with a starring role in *The Wire*, widely acclaimed as one of the greatest television dramas ever made.

When the boy became a man, he began to understand that all those gifts he had been given by his mother and father had not come easily to them. They had been earned with sweat, study, and endless perseverance in the hope that, one day, their children would have more. What the boy's parents gave him, they in turn had received. His mother had been raised on the bayou by wise, intelligent, but barely educated farmers who believed in the power of hard work, self-discipline, and education to lift Negroes out of the poverty and misery of the Jim Crow South. Both his folks benefited from their civil rights struggle, an early fruit of which was a decent neighborhood for people like them to raise their families, just like everybody else.

The boy had been given a life unimaginably richer and freer than his forebears had known, all because of their own patient sacrifices, and the conviction they held in their hearts that, one day, the dark night of racism and violence would give way to a new dawn of justice and opportunity. He had been given a life by the people of Pontchartrain Park—by the civil rights activists whose early victories led to its founding, to the men and women who staked their claim on the American dream there, and who built a village in which to raise their children together. He had been given a life by the city of New Orleans, that singular urban gumbo of cultures—Native American, African, French, Spanish, American—that has been simmering in the Louisiana heat in that pot between the river and the lake for three hundred years, and whose distinct flavors have melted into each other to make a tradition all its own.

It was a grace, and it was a gift. All of it. It was a gift that came from faith—in God, in America, in family, in the future, and in the ability of each of us, and all of us together—to overcome any hardship, and not only survive, but triumph. It was a gift that came from home, and a gift that came from hope—hope that as hard as life is right now, our suffering means something, and it will lead to better days for those who come after us. It was a gift that came from love— a love of life so bright and true that it refused to let slavery, it refused to let segregation, it refused to let poverty and ignorance and injustice and terror and hatred knock it down, wash it away, and bury it in a sea of darkness forever.

If my ancestors and all those who struggled alongside them had endured and conquered all those challenges to give me and my generation the life we have today, how dare we give up in the face of this hurricane? As Vladimir, my character in *Godot*, says, "What's the point of losing heart now?" Given the impossible odds against them, those generations had all but walked on water to get where we are today. For me—for us—to lose heart, to let that precious patrimony of faith, hope, and love slip through our fingers, would be to sink beneath Katrina's floodwaters and drown.

No. These lines of Vladimir's from act 2 sounded in my heart like a prophet's incantation and a call to arms:

Let us do something, while we have the chance! . . . At this place, at this moment of time, all mankind is us, whether we like it or not. Let us make the most of it, before it is too late!

Yes. I must keep faith with my fathers and mothers, the ones of my blood and the ones of my spirit. I must keep faith with those ripped by slave traders from the arms of their mothers and fathers, with those who withstood the blows from white supremacists and earned the education that uplifted the race. I must keep faith with the Moses Generation, those who demanded their rights as Americans, who refused to accept that they were second-class citizens in a nation their ancestors helped to build, and who led our people to the Promised Land. I must keep faith with the mothers and fathers of Pontchartrain Park, also members of the Moses Generation, who carried on the everyday struggle to prepare the Joshua Generation to live and prosper in the land of milk and honey (or in our case, cold beer and Creole gumbo).

"Mr. Pierce, what did you do in New Orleans's darkest hour?" that kid in the future will ask. I will tell him that the catastrophe of Katrina revealed to me who and what I love. It revealed to me the boy I was, the man I am, and the man I want to become. It called me home to New Orleans, to honor my ancestors and the people of my hometown, the living and the dead, by giving whatever I could to restore and build anew the beloved community.

Let us do something, while we have the chance!

And so I did, by going home to New Orleans.

THIS IS THE STORY of my homecoming. This is the story of my part in the pilgrimage of my family and my people out of exile. It is a story of faith, hope, and love. And it is a story that begins with a slave child waving good-bye to his family on the banks of the river, as the boat carried him south into an abyss of suffering. That I am here to tell the tale at all means it is not a tragedy. It means that as long as we draw breath, tragedy—even a tragedy as overwhelming as a hurricane that nearly destroyed a city—does not have to have the last word. Like the poet W. H. Auden says, we "stagger onward rejoicing."

Those car lights I saw that night on the Claiborne Avenue bridge belonged to New Orleanians who were also part of the pilgrimage. I did not know it then, and they didn't either, but I am certain of it now: Those fellow pilgrims were headed into the Lower Ninth Ward to affirm by their presence that the power of art, the bonds of the beloved community, and the perseverance of the human spirit are all lights that the darkness cannot overcome.

In American culture, we have turned away from an awareness of the prophetic power of art, of its role as a means of revealing the hidden order beneath everydayness, and its power to transform us and the world.

Art tells us who we are, and it tells us who we must become. Art doesn't give us life's answers as much as it empowers us to live life's questions. Art, like religion, is how the eternal and the ideal enters time and becomes real. In turn, it is how we mortals experience, if only for a moment, immortality. Art is how we humans, individually and collectively, impress our seal on the wax; it's how we charge ordinary matter— wood, paint, stone, a word, a voice, a note, a gesture— with life and spirit and harmony.

Art is the most serious thing we can do, because when making it, we humans, forged in the image of God, are most like our Creator. We tend to forget that. This production of *Godot*, in that weary time and in that storm-battered place, helped me remember. And I was far from the only one.

Early in the play's first act, Vladimir hears a noise and thinks it might signal Godot's approach. "Pah!" snorts Estragon, dismissively. "The wind in the reeds." We would be wrong to dismiss that sound.

Man is only a reed, said the French philosopher Blaise Pascal, but he is a thinking reed. When the winds of adversity blow hard against him, the sound they make as they pass over his contours may be mere noise—or they may be something like the music a teenage Sidney Bechet, grandson of a slave, made when he blew across his clarinet's reed and, standing on the back of a New Orleans furniture truck next to a horn-playing juvenile delinquent named Louis Armstrong, helped create jazz.

I learned from the late Albert Murray, the great Harlem connoisseur of black music, that art is the way individuals and cultures react aesthetically to their experiences in life. Jazz and the blues, the most American of all musical forms, is the sound made by history's savage gales blowing hard on African people in the Diaspora. The storm-tossed reeds may be humble, but the reeds are thinking, the reeds are feeling—and the reeds are resilient.

The reeds sing a song of triumph. The harder the wind blows, the stronger our spirit, the purer our art, and the greater our victory.

TWO

DOWN THE BAYOU
AT THE SOURCE

We know who we are by the stories we tell about ourselves and the world. We know who we are through the family and community of whose stories we are a part.

We make our stories. And our stories make us.

I am not sure the stories of my family are art, exactly. After all, they came down to me not as objects to be admired for their beauty. Then again, they contain so much truth and goodness that they cannot help being beautiful as well. Their trials, their triumphs, the virtues that gave them the strength to overcome—all of these things live in the stories my family shares as an inheritance that grows as we invest in it each successive generation.

I draw creative strength from my roots buried deep in south Louisiana. Until the storm, I did not appreciate how much those roots were the veins connecting my heart to the body of historical experience that gave birth to the man I am today, and the man—and the artist—I am becoming every day.

Here are some of the stories that made me.

SOMETIME IN THE 1850S, nobody can say exactly when, on the banks of a Kentucky river, a boy named Aristile rested in the basket of his slave mother's arms as she said good-bye to their family and sailed away. One white man had sold mother and child to another white man, as the child's father, brothers, and sisters stood on the water's edge in tears. Five hundred miles downriver, the passage of the mother and her child ended on a sugarcane plantation near Bertrandville, in Assumption Parish, a moist and fertile patch of land between the Mississippi River and Bayou Lafourche. The master forced his name on the mother and child: Harris. That is how my family came to south Louisiana.

Years later, after emancipation in 1865, Aristile would tell his children that his earliest memories are of his mother teaching him to say his prayers at night, and telling him when freedom comes, as it surely would, to go on a quest. "You are not a Harris. You are a Christophe," she would say. "If you ever get free, go back to Kentucky and look for your family. The Christophes."

He never did.

The story of Aristile's descendants is a story of a parade through American history—sometimes a mournful dirge, sometimes a raucous stomp—from being symbolically owned by the bayou to owning a piece of it. That is, from being treated as no more important than the land they worked for the white man as enslaved exiles, to becoming masters of themselves and that land, which would become, in the fullest sense of the word, home.

Why am I telling you this? Because I would not be the man I am if my ancestors had not been the men and women that they were. In southern culture, family and land are everything—especially to African Americans, whose families were broken by slavery and, in liberty, left with little or nothing.

In my clan, the ancestors live on through the stories we tell our-selves and our children, and in the family farm on Bayou Lafourche. My cousin Nicole, the family historian, reminds us older folks that we have a responsibility to tell these family stories to the younger gen-eration. Family can easily fall apart. You can't take it for granted. My mother and father showed me the value of family and why it's worth fighting for. Whenever I wonder why I'm hanging on to these people who are becoming strangers to me, I take a step back and think about our shared history.

If we forget our stories, we will forget who we are, and we will forget who we must be to one another. The family is our strength. My personal triumphs are not mine alone; they represent the victory of all my forebears. You can trace a line from the Hollywood soundstages where I work to the sugarcane fields of Louisiana's River Parishes. These stories, stories of ancestors I never knew, are my story too, not only because they formed the moral imaginations of those who formed me, but also because these tales from my family's oral tradi-tion tell me who I am.

In the days before the Civil War, Louisiana plantations produced nearly one-quarter of the world's exportable sugar. To support the booming industry, New Orleans became North America's largest slave market, and Louisiana's sugar plantations were notorious for their unsurpassed cruelty to slaves. At the start of the Civil War, more than 330,000 slaves worked the fields in Louisiana. But according to family legend, my great-grandfather wasn't yet one of them. The boy was not yet a field slave, but enslaved nonetheless, his master grinding as much work out of the child Aristile as he could.

When Aristile was a young teenager, not quite old enough to be sent into the fields—this would have been in 1862 or 1863—he stood wearing nothing but a big shirt and watched Union soldiers riding along the banks of the bayou. Freedom came after the North's victory, but Aristile did not return to Kentucky to look for his kin, and no one in my family ever has. For better or for worse, our home was now in Louisiana.

Freedom from bondage did not mean freedom, though. After the Civil War, most former slaves expected to get some share of the land they had worked. The idea was that each freed slave was entitled to "40 acres and a mule" as compensation, and as a foundation on which to build a new life. It never happened.

Aristile's former master moved him to what was known as the Williams plantation as part of a plan to undermine land redistribution to freed slaves, or so the story came down through my family. The planter took Aristile to three brothers, former slaves who had been given the name Williams, and told them they were to consider Aristile their brother. They were older than Aristile and ordered the teenager around. When the Williams brothers received a little piece of property, they gave Aristile a quarter-acre lot off the main road. It was nothing, really.

But that's where Aristile founded his family. My grandmother Frances Harris and her nine brothers and sisters grew up on that tiny spit of ground in Assumption Parish. My uncle L.C., the last survivor of my mother's generation, heard from Frances that Aristile "was a lover who didn't do nothin' but make moonshine and sell it. That was his forte." Aristile told his children that he had seen and done enough fieldwork as a slave, and he was finished with that.

Frances, Aristile's daughter, grew up to marry Herbert Edwards, who came from the Southall family, from the other side of the bayou, in the early years of the twentieth century. The Southall clan descends from Collins and Causey Southall, who were born into slavery and had twelve children. The Southalls were all about education, believing that it was the key to overcoming racism, making material progress, and generally improving the family's position in the world. They lived in a black settlement on the flat green fields of south Louisiana's Cajun plantation country, an hour west of New Orleans. To be precise, they were on the banks of Bayou Lafourche, between Plattenville and Paincourtville, on College Point Lane—so called because the African American families who lived there became known for sending their children to college. Education has always been a sacred value passed down in my family—and we can trace it back to the first generation out of slavery.

Frances and Herbert Edwards were known to us all as "Mamo" and "Papo." They raised their seven children during the Great Depression, eking out a living on their portion of the forty-four-acre Assumption Parish farm that Papo shared with his brothers Johnny ("Parrain Johnny") and Ashley ("Nonc Ash"). Nonc Ash eventually left the farm and, like their brother George, became an educator, but Papo and Parrain Johnny stayed in Assumption Parish and worked the land.

Of the two Edwards men who stayed behind, Papo was the stolid, no-nonsense farmer, but Parrain Johnny (*parrain* is Creole French for "godfather") was a rascal. With his ever-present short stogie in his mouth, he chased women up and down the bayou.

One family story has it that Parrain Johnny was once working for a white man who was having an affair with a black woman and hid it from his wife. Whenever he needed to send his mistress something, he would use Parrain Johnny as a go-between. But in the middle of being a go-between, Parrain Johnny became an *in*-between. When the white boss found out Parrain Johnny was loving on his mistress, he and his friends beat Johnny to a pulp and threw him on a trash pile to die.

Another version of the story has it that Parrain Johnny was having an affair with a white woman in Paincourtville whose family nearly lynched him when they discovered their forbidden love. Whatever the truth, Johnny nearly died in a beating. Somebody found him and got him to the doctor. He recovered, though he suffered from epilepsy for the rest of his life.

Parrain Johnny died when I was five or six. They said he fell into his fireplace and burned up, but the family never believed it was an accident. Who falls into their fireplace and doesn't try to get out? He was supposedly running around with another man's wife, and the jealous husband, we think, pushed him into the flames. My cousin Louis says that Parrain Johnny's death was such a shock for the same reason you're surprised when a stray dog gets run over by a car. It's been so good at dodging traffic all these years that you can't quite believe it finally got popped.

From the 1920s through the 1940s, Papo was just about the only black farmer in Assumption Parish who owned his property and brought his own sugarcane to the mill. He put his entire family to work there. During the fall grinding season—that is to say, the harvest—the whole family helped bring in the crop, even Mamo and Papo's daughters.

AND DID THEY EVER HAVE DAUGHTERS! There was Inez, Evelyn, Yvonne, Gladys, and my mother, Althea, whom I grew up calling "Tee." Two boys—Louis Herbert (L.H.) and Lloyd Carroll (L.C.)— filled out the family. (An eighth child, a daughter, was stillborn; the old midwife named her Matilda, and Papo put her into a little coffin and buried her in the backyard, past the pecan trees from which hung the children's rope swing.)

Theirs was a religious household. Papo was a lifelong Methodist; Mamo, a Catholic. All the Edwards children were baptized into the Catholic faith, and Papo saw their upbringing as loyal sons and daughters of Rome as a sacred obligation. If one of the children didn't want to go to Sunday mass, Papo wouldn't let them play outside that afternoon. Every night, Papo would get on his knees and pray aloud, presenting all his family's needs to the Lord, while the children kneeled quietly beside him. He read the Bible to the children and explained it to them as best he could.

The way my mother and my aunts and uncles told it, everybody in College Point was as good as family, and you respected them as such. It takes a village to raise a child? That's how it was in College Point. Any adult could scold any kid for doing wrong. They knew how your mama and daddy would want you to behave, and they also knew that your mama and daddy would appreciate the reinforcement of the community's standards. In the Edwards family, as in most other black families in College Point, life's purpose was to serve God and get an education. If you did these things, and held tight to the family, you were going to make it.

Papo refused to accept from his children anything short of excellence. When one of his kids would say, "Daddy, I can't do it," Papo would respond, "*Can't* died three days before the creation of the world!" He believed in you, and he expected you to rise to the challenge. Education was one of the most precious gifts a man or a woman could have, Papo believed. "If you get an education," he told his children, "they can take away your job, they can take away your house, they can take away everything you have, but once you get something in your head, they can't take it away from you."

Another of Papo's sayings was: "There are those who do not have your best interests at heart." That is, be careful whom you trust. People are not always what they seem. If you leave yourself too open, those who do not have your best interests at heart will seize the opportunity to defeat you. Don't be afraid of them, but understand what you're dealing with and use your wits.

Papo was a firm man, and a fussy one—Uncle L.H. used to talk about how hard his daddy was—but we grandkids remember him as gentle. We used to go to his house in Assumption Parish and sprawl on the floor watching TV while Papo sat in his big green wingback chair, presiding over everything. One summer day, with a bunch of us grandkids there, I found that Mamo had a litter of kittens in a box. I thought it might be fun to climb up onto the roof of the carport and drop them off to see if it was true that cats would land on their feet.

I dropped them from that height onto the grass, and thought it was amusing.

When I observed that they had all survived the fall, being a young scientist, I decided to experiment with increasing the kittens' velocity. Back into the box they went, and up onto the roof I clambered with the kittens. I took the little fuzzballs into my hand and threw them down toward the ground. They didn't all make it. As they wobbled away, a few never came back. I got bored and wandered off, and that was that.

Later that night, we were watching television together when Papo said, "I found one of them cats dead. Who was playing with the cats?" I didn't say anything then, and I never did. I feel guilty to this day about holding out on Papo. The detail that stands out in my mind is that Papo probably knew it was me, but he wanted to give me the chance to admit what I had done and take responsibility. He must have understood the importance of letting my young conscience convict me, and letting the guilt I carried be my punishment.

Papo was gentler with his grandchildren than he was with his own kids. When I hear tales of the harshness of Papo's old-school discipline with my mother and her siblings, it sometimes sounds cruel. It's hard for people today to understand it, but for black folk back then, a strong will like Mamo's and Papo's, joined to a rock-hard sense of discipline, was a tool of survival. One false move could mean ruin. My aunt Evelyn Mae—we called her "Tee Mae"—told a story one day about how Mamo had thrown her out of the house, thinking she was pregnant.

"They had told us that they would give us every last thing they had, but the one thing we must not do was bring an illegitimate baby into the home," Tee Mae said. "If we did, they were going to put us out."

After her first menstrual period, Tee Mae didn't have another cycle for three months. When Mamo saw that she had missed two in a row, she accused Tee Mae of having been with a boy and gotten pregnant. Tee Mae protested that it wasn't true, but Mamo refused to believe her. She gave her teenage daughter a brown paper bag with her things in it and sent her on her way.

Tee Mae ended up at the home of family friends, wailing. By the time it all got sorted, Tee Mae had been to a physician, who verified that she was not pregnant, and was still a virgin. She was welcomed back home then. To us, this sounds intolerably harsh, and it was. But in those days, contraception was practically nonexistent, and having a child outside of wedlock left a woman and her baby extremely vulnerable. This unforgiving code of honor was a bulwark holding back disaster.

It worked, too. "We never strayed," my mother told me. "We were too scared of Papo, and had too much respect for him, to do anything else."

For all his strictness, Papo used physical violence against his children only once. Several of the children had stayed out in a far field longer than their curfew. When they came straggling home, Papo was waiting for them with a switch and lashed them on the backs of their legs as they ran crying into the house. Papo felt so ashamed of his violence that the kids overheard him telling Mamo he would never lift his hands against the children again.

That was Papo. Mamo was different, and then some.

One autumn day, when Tee Mae was a teenager, Mamo went to a

quilting bee, leaving baby L.C. in Tee Mae's care. Tee Mae became absorbed in playing jacks and forgot all about the baby. He shat all over himself. When Tee Mae discovered her baby brother covered in his own feces, she scrambled to get him cleaned up before Mamo came home, but it was too late. When Mamo walked in and saw little L.C. smeared with his own filth, Tee Mae had already run out the back door and was headed across the field like a shot.

An enraged Mamo grabbed Papo's shotgun, ran into the yard, and taking aim at her fleeing daughter, pulled the trigger. Tee Mae wasn't hit, but when she heard the shot, she fell facedown in the dirt all the same. Before she got to her feet, she heard Mamo keening in the distance. "Oh, Lord, I've done shot my baby! I've done killed my baby!"

Tee Mae knew that it was about time for Papo to come home from work, and she also knew that Papo had warned Mamo not to touch his guns. So she judged that the smartest thing for her to do was to lie there on the ground and wait for her father to arrive.

Minutes later, a cousin walked up on Tee Mae, thinking she was dead. He poked her in her ribs with his pointy boots, trying to turn her body over to see her wounds. Tee Mae let out a laugh and sprang to her feet. Just then, Papo arrived home. Tee Mae knew she was safe. She got back to the yard in time to hear Papo lecture Mamo about her unorthodox disciplinary methods.

"Oh, Mama, I done told you that's not how to chastise those children," he said. "Don't be messing with my gun. Use a switch on them kids."

Mamo was vexed. "You see that black wench there?" she yelled to everyone present. "I'm going to get you for this! You did this on purpose!"

But from that day on, Tee Mae never had any more trouble with her mother trying to discipline her with firearms. "That was the second time she'd shot at me!" Tee Mae said.

Though Mamo had her angry moments, her children remembered her as strong-willed and extraordinarily capable. Despite her fits, they liked to say that she could get along with both the Devil in hell and the Lord in heaven. "She drove us to love ourselves and to make something of our lives," says Uncle L.C. "She was another Mary McLeod Bethune."

The one thing Mamo did not know how to do was manage money. That was Papo's job. Papo did not trust banks, and he kept some of his money in a chest in the house. The rest he stored in his barn, in a sack hidden in a barrel. He was a frugal man, but not a miserly one. One Christmas, his children received a vivid illustration of the value of their father's prudence.

Mamo worked as a cook and a maid in a white family's house, and she spent the early part of Christmas Day there preparing their dinner. Back at the farm, Papo oversaw the preparation of the Edwards family's holiday meal, which they would celebrate as the evening meal so Mamo could be with them. Christmas dinner was always rich with country food, including chicken, turkey, and goose from their farm, rice, green peas, and potato salad. For dessert, the family ate candy and cake Papo made himself. There wasn't much money for Christmas gifts, but Papo and Mamo made sure their children feasted well on the Nativity.

One Christmas evening after supper, the Edwardses went to call on their College Point neighbors, to wish them a happy holiday. The kids were startled to go into one house and to see that all that family had eaten for their Christmas meal was potatoes and grits. When they returned home, Papo told the children, "This is what I mean when I tell you it's important to save for a rainy day. If you put your money aside now, you will have enough to eat well on Christmas."

Given the man Papo was, if the Edwardses had any food left, he probably took it to that poor family and didn't tell his own children for the sake of preserving their neighbors' dignity.

His children remembered Papo as a slow talker but a deep thinker. He never made a quick decision, but acted only after prayer, deliberation, and sleeping on it. Whatever the answer was, he arrived at it through careful reason, not passion. Acting on impulse was the sure way to lose your money, in Papo's view.

Papo worked for a time in a sugar factory and received his weekly wages in a brown packet. He had a firm rule with himself: Wait twenty-four hours before spending a penny of it. Uncle L.C. said that as a young working man, he thought his father's rule was silly. You have the money, he figured, so why not enjoy it?

But when he got married and started a family of his own, he understood Papo's good sense and followed the rule himself. Uncle L.C., who worked at the DuPont chemical plant, has done well through saving and investing over the years. To this day, he credits Papo for teaching him by word and example the importance of being careful with your money and not letting your passions guide your decisions.

If L.C. was the patient, deliberate brother, L.H. was the family firebrand. He was a veteran of the Vietnam War, and fiercely proud of his military service. He was a stalwart patriot but also a black nationalist equally outraged at the oppression the country he loved and fought for laid on the backs of black men and women. When she was old and gray, and L.H. had long since passed, my mother told me that her brother's volcanic temperament came from a place of great decency.

"If L.H. could give you his heart and still live, he would do it for you," Tee said. "The thing I liked most about L.H. is that he would tell you he did not mind dying if he was dying for what was right. L.H. loved justice, and he was not afraid of nobody, and he spoke his piece to anybody and everybody."

There was little doubt where the fighting spirit that animated L.H., Tee Mae, and my mother came from. Tee once told me about a time in the 1940s when, as the Edwards children were walking home from school, a troublemaking white boy threw rocks at them, hitting L.H. in the head. When the kids made it home and told their mother what had happened, Mamo rocketed out of the house, up College Point Lane, and walked all the way to Bertrandville to confront the white boy's mother.

When the white lady, a Mrs. Aucoin, answered the door, Mamo told her how it was going to be from here on out.

"I pay taxes just like you pay taxes," my grandmother said. "My child has a right to walk on this road like anybody else. I told all my children that if that one"—she pointed to the boy—"even *looks* at them, they all supposed to jump on him and beat him till he's dead. And if they don't kill him, I will."

"Did the white lady call the sheriff on Mamo?" I asked Tee. It was hard to imagine that, in a culture ruled by the ideology of white supremacy, a white woman would take that kind of dressing-down from a black woman.

"No!" she said. "That lady was trembling. She knew that boy of hers was bad. She told Mama it would never happen again. And it didn't."

L.H.'s rage against those who had done him wrong—racists and everybody else—sometimes worked to his disadvantage. Said my mother, "L.H.'s biggest enemy was himself."

L.H. had a good job working for the local sheriff, but rashly quit one day, out of pride; he thought the sheriff ought to take his advice more seriously.

L.H. didn't need the sheriff's department job. He owned a nice store in Bertrandville. Trouble was, he had gotten way behind on his commercial taxes. Our cousin in parish government told Mamo to get L.H. to pay his back taxes or there were some white people who were going to use his delinquency to harm him.

"But L.H. wouldn't listen," my uncle L.C. said. "He made a mistake. He left the sheriff's department. Two days after that, they put a lien on his store for twenty thousand dollars in back taxes. That's how he lost his business."

Papo had a saying: "Always keep a dollar in your pocket, because you never know when the world is going to be sold for a dollar." He meant that a wise man always held money in reserve to take advantage of unforeseen opportunities, and that a wise man always keeps a close watch on his financial matters. As brilliant as he was, Uncle L.H. didn't do as Papo taught, nor did he discipline his emotions to protect his exposed financial flank—and he suffered for it.

But he never gave up. Even after he lost the store, and his son Louis later had a similar setback, he was full of encouragement. "You know what, Lou?" he'd say. "Colonel Sanders didn't make it until he was in his seventies. So keep fighting." He always did, until his last breath. As he lay dying of cancer in 1999, his sisters thought L.H., a believer though estranged from the Catholic Church for parts of his life, would be willing to speak to a priest. But when Uncle L.H. saw a priest walk into the room, he all but rose up out of his deathbed and delivered a hellacious cussing to the poor man—and to his own sisters for summoning him. "Get him out of here!" he yelled. "Goddamnit, you niggers worship a white man like he's God! He don't look like you!" L.H. left his earth without last rites, but as master of his soul.

Here's what you need to know about Uncle L.H. and his anticlericalism: He had endured the Catholic Church's failing to stand up to racism on behalf of its black communicants, and he had seen a close family member drink himself to death, never able to recover from his childhood molestation by a Catholic priest. He never forgave it. In "Strong Men," a scathing poem rebuking hypocrisy in white Christians and passivity in their black brothers, the African American poet Sterling A. Brown spoke for Uncle L.H., a strong man whose spirit was never tamed. To honor my uncle L.H., I read that poem at his funeral as his body lay in St. Benedict the Moor Church, where he was baptized as a child.

It took incredible inner strength to survive Jim Crow, much less to thrive under it. Mamo and Papo raised their children in a time and place when whites held all the power and were not afraid to use it. No black man or woman could afford to make a false move. Black people were supposed to know their place, and God help them if they challenged the racist social order. To guard your heart by learning how to endure daily humiliations without fighting back was the only way to survive.

Papo was well respected within both the white and black communities, because everyone knew he was a righteous man. "He thought he was the equal of everybody," my aunt Tee Gladys told me once. "He never backed down." Except once, which was one of my aunt's most painful memories.

When my aunt Gladys returned home to the bayou from California after her first marriage broke up, she was dismayed to see that Papo was still selling his cane crops to a particular sugar-buying firm that paid Papo in credit at its grocery store. At the end of every growing season, the company would tell Papo that his cane crop was just enough to cover his family's grocery bill.

Tee Gladys told Papo that he was being ripped off by those people and he should quit buying groceries there. Mamo backed her up on this; she was tired of having to depend on that company and its store for the family's food needs when there were other stores in the area that offered better prices. Papo was afraid no brokers would buy his cane if he moved his grocery trade to a competitor.

"Daddy, it's like having your hand in the lion's mouth," Tee Gladys told him. But he wouldn't budge.

"The first and only time in my life I saw my daddy cry was after a bad year in the cane field," Tee Gladys said to me a few years before she died. "Cane didn't produce well. Me and my daddy, I'll never forget, it was a cold, rainy day in January. We went to that company store, shopping for all our groceries, and came to the cashier to check us out.

"One of the owners knew we were in the store, and he had not had the courtesy to send a letter to my father to tell him we didn't have any more credit there," she continued. "When we got up to the cashier, the man came and took Daddy to the office, and told him he couldn't have those groceries. They humiliated him."

When Papo and his daughter made it back home, he had to break the news to Mamo.

"He was crying, tears running down his face," Tee Gladys remembered. "But let me tell you, the white man didn't do him wrong. He set him free. He wasn't scared after that to shop other places. It hurt my father, but it got his hand out of the lion's mouth. In the end, he was victorious."

Mamo and Papo were well respected in the entire community. Most of the time, however, whites in Assumption Parish felt entitled to treat their black neighbors with utter disrespect. There was no grocery store in College Point when my mother was a child, so she and her siblings would have to walk to nearby Plattenville to buy food for the family. As they passed the houses of whites, children their own age would be playing in the yards and would call out to their own mothers inside, saying, "Hey, Mama, a little nigger is going to the store. You want anything?" If the white woman said yes, her child would call out, "Hey, little nigger, stop."

If you were a black child, you had no choice but to do as that white child told you. This is how it was.

My grandfather was a steadfast, quiet man, a poor country farmer of great dignity. That's why the rare occasions when that dignity slipped were so shocking to his children. Tee saw him lose his cool only once. It was during the Depression, when a white hobo came to their door, begging for food. Papo exploded with anger.

"Who are you to come here?!" he yelled, driving the beggar away.

Why would Papo treat someone like that? Tee wondered. She

saw him as the soul of justice and compassion. Then Papo said, indignantly, "He's a white man in America, and *he's* coming begging from *me*?!"

Papo saw the hungry hobo as privileged because of the color of his skin. Was that fair? No. Nor was it kind. But you have to understand his intemperate reaction in the context of the pervasive and overwhelming power the white man had over the black man, and how gratuitously cruel was its exercise.

WHEN TEE WAS A CHILD, a black family in College Point somehow scraped the money together to buy a new car. They were so proud of that automobile and showed it off to all their neighbors. It was like a gift to the community, because they could give people who walked everywhere a ride.

"I remember the night that the night riders came and burned that car," Tee told me. "They said, 'You niggers, don't you think about getting no cars. Let this be a lesson to you.'"

That infuriated my mother. What did that black family having a car have to do with those Klansmen? How did it hurt them? And the thing is, Tee told me, all the black folk knew exactly who the night riders were. The men may have worn white robes and hoods, but the people they terrorized knew them all. It didn't matter. They were the law. They burned the black man's car as a message to the entire black community: Don't think you can ever have nice things or get ahead in this life. You are made to be poor and beneath us, and the sooner you get that straight, the better off you'll be.

Right there, as a little girl, Tee resolved never to let anyone deny her anything—not the right to go anywhere she wanted to go, learn anything she wanted to learn, or be anything she wanted to be. But she also learned that you had to be smart about it, and she passed that childhood lesson on to my brothers and me.

"Know that those people who do not have your best interest at heart will always be there," Tee said. "Accept it. Don't be surprised when they show up. Know that you will have to face those folks and defeat them to achieve what you want to achieve. That's just part of life."

This was not just a lesson in race relations. Racism was how it manifested for us in south Louisiana, Tee said, but don't fool yourself: It will come in all forms, shapes, and sizes—and colors. It's human nature. So in any dispute, small or large, don't get mad when the bad guy lets his mask slip. Just know from that point on that he is the person who doesn't have your best interests at heart and act accordingly.

Was this a counsel of defeat? Not at all. It was, in fact, a canny strategy of winning a long-term victory against a more powerful enemy. You had to be willing to fight for justice, but you had to be smart enough to pick your battles carefully. Wiliness took all forms. In the 1940s, Mamo worked as a domestic servant in the house of the parish sheriff. Back then, when whites in the Cajun parishes didn't want black folks to understand what they were saying, they would speak French. What the white power elite didn't realize is that humble maid Frances Edwards secretly spoke French and would quietly report to her own people at College Point what the white men were planning. Her knowledge of French was the dollar in the pocket Mamo held to buy the black community advance warning to protect themselves from their enemies who held all the power in the parish and who did not hesitate to inflict terror on African Americans to keep them in line.

For all that, it would be untrue to give the impression that life on the bayou was about nothing but blood, sweat, terror, and tears for black folk. When I was growing up, my mother and my aunts talked about the joys of those days more than anything else. They lived a classic childhood in the rural South, tied to the land and to the rhythms of agrarian life. Today, it can be difficult to believe that a life as materially poor as theirs could be bearable, much less a source of deep happiness, but that's exactly what my mother and her siblings said.

Tee Gladys and my mother were too poor to have store-bought dolls, so they would take sticks from the yard and call them their babies. Sometimes they would pick corn from the field and pretend that the silk was their dolls' soft hair. They made dollhouses of pasteboard and dressed their humble dolls with dresses cut from the pages of a catalogue. "It was a beautiful life," Gladys once said to me, her eyes twinkling.

All the children of College Point gathered in the Edwards family's yard to play. The reason? Nearly every day, Mamo made treats for them. Tea cakes, gingerbread, muffins, and the like, and on hot summer days, a big waterbucket full of lemonade. The neighborhood children would come to Mamo and Papo with their problems, seeking advice. They were afraid to be open with their own parents, but they knew they could find a sympathetic ear and good counsel at the Edwards place.

In fact, Mamo and Papo were unusual in the respect they gave to youngsters, given the rigid hierarchy of age customary then. They involved their children in most decisions affecting the family and rarely hid anything from them. They talked everything out around the dinner table, which was a place of moral instruction. Mamo and Papo thought it important for their kids to know that family life meant sharing in both the blessings and the burdens of all its members. "They taught us that if one sister has two pieces of bread and the other has none, you must share," said Tee Mae.

Anything could be said at the table, but the sanctity of the family circle was inviolate.

"You better not breathe a word of it when you left the house," Tee said. "We never did."

Like many country people of that era, both black and white, the Edwardses had no running water indoors. They had to haul water from Bayou Lafourche for washing, and bathe in large, twelve-inch-deep buckets called "foot tubs." Uncle L.C., the baby of the family, remembers that when his oldest sister, Inez, would come visit from New Orleans, she would make it her business to bathe him. She would sit him in a no. 3 washtub full of water and scrub him hard all over with a bar of Octagon soap. It was a miserable experience, but Inez was diligent about cleanliness.

There were no indoor toilets either. If Mamo or Papo needed the bathroom at night, they had a slop jar in their room. The kids had to make do with a five-gallon can.

The Edwards children would be up early in the morning to work the land and the garden before going to school, and get out early to make it home to help with chores before sundown. They grew corn, beans, cabbage, mustard greens, and more, and raised hogs and fowl.

Nothing went to waste in their house. If the kids didn't like what they were served, Papo would say, "Eat it, and if it kills you, you won't have to eat it again."

"Our garden was out by the levee," Uncle L.C. recalls. "You stayed there and worked all day. After working, you would go back down the road, take a bath in a foot tub, and go to sleep. That was it. That was a joyous time."

It was an era of simple pleasures. "You enjoyed the company of the College Point people," L.C. continues. "You enjoyed the sound of the rain on the tin roof. The sound of that rain falling, and everyone coming out of the field.

"Nine months later, you saw an increase in everybody's family," he chuckled.

The cane harvest generally happened around October, which meant schoolchildren in Assumption Parish had the entire month off to help. Everyone in the black community had each other's backs, watching each other's kids, helping on each other's farms. They were poor black country folks in the Deep South, and knew that the only people in the world they had looking out for them was each other.

A *boucherie*—butchering a hog—was a big event in the life of the community. When I was a kid, we would go to these things in Assumption Parish, and aside from the scary thrill that came when Papo demanded all us boys touch the dying hog and hold the bucket into which blood from its punctured heart poured, I couldn't figure out what the big deal was. Later, I came to understand that every member of the community took home a piece of that hog and had something to eat, no matter how poor they were. In that sense, Papo's instruction to lay our hands on the animal as it struggled against death, and to collect the life pouring out of the hog's breast, was a ritual with deep meaning. As boys who would one day be men of the community, we had to lose our fear of doing something traumatic, because it was essential to the continuation of communal life. The hog was giving its life to sustain the community; the role of men was to take the life of that animal for the sake of all, even the least among us. We were not to fear the sacrifice.

As much as he loved his sons and grandsons, Papo was unusually progressive for his generation when it came to his daughters. Papo took a lot of criticism from his friends for educating all his daughters, especially during the Depression. Back then, it didn't make a lot of sense to country people to send girls for higher education. But Papo came from the Southalls, for whom reverence for education was a defining value. It took a great deal of courage and vision for Papo and Mamo to educate their daughters in the face of not only poverty and racism, but also the skepticism of their community.

Their tenacity emerged in part from their profound hope. Papo and Mamo really raised their children to believe that things were going to get better for black folk, but they also taught the kids that they had a part to play in making that happen for themselves. For Papo, having an education was important for the same reason keeping a dollar in your pocket was important: You never knew when opportunity was going to open up, so you had better be ready to take advantage of it.

Papo had only a third-grade education, while Mamo had been through seventh grade. But their wisdom and devotion to the transformative power of schooling could not be measured by academic transcripts. In fact, Mamo went back to school when she was sixty-five years old to earn her high school diploma, which she did in three years. To this day, it hangs on the wall at Uncle L.C.'s house, in a place of honor.

When my mother would become indignant at racial injustice, she knew that education would be the greatest weapon she would have with which to fight it. Her education would give her the tools to define her own destiny—and as a professional teacher, she knew it was the best hope her black students had for delivering themselves.

Yet she never forgot where she came from, or how she got where she was. After graduating from Southern University with a degree in education and home economics, Tee returned to the bayou to teach. Back then, the only middle-class professions open to African Americans were teacher, preacher, and undertaker. If you were one of those, you held elite status in the black community.

Though she was working at the black school in Paincourtville, Tee, a tomboy in her youth, helped out on the farm by driving the tractor as Papo, Tee Gladys, and the others gathered hay. One of the kinfolks chastised her for lowering herself in that way.

"You finished college," the relative chided. "You have a sheepskin. You're not supposed to be on this tractor."

"If I hadn't *been* on this tractor, I wouldn't *have* a sheepskin," Tee shot back. In her family, there was nothing undignified about hard work.

When my older aunts were children, there was no advanced education available to black children in Assumption Parish, nor any other kind of training for the trades. During World War II, Aunt Inez, the oldest daughter, moved to New Orleans to live with one of our cousins. She learned a trade and became a seamstress in the Tulane Shirt Factory, making shirts on U.S. government contract. All the Edwards girls—Evelyn Mae, Yvonne, Gladys, and my mother, Althea—went to New Orleans in their turn to complete their high school education. They lived with and helped each other.

INEZ EVENTUALLY MARRIED, but she died in childbirth. After her passing, Papo took Tee Mae aside and told her she was now the head of all her sisters and brothers. This was a heavy burden for my aunt to assume, especially given that she was living in Crown Heights, Brooklyn, far away from the bayou, and working as a nurse.

But family was family, and Tee Mae was not about to let them down. She had a special relationship with her little sister Althea, the fifth Edwards child. Earlier, when Inez was still alive, Mamo was down with malaria and feared death was near. She had six children at that point (L.C. wasn't yet born) and gathered the three older girls around her, assigning each of them one of the three younger siblings to care for when she passed. Mamo decreed that L.H. would go to Inez, Gladys would be Yvonne's responsibility, and little Althea would belong to Tee Mae. Though Mamo recovered, Tee Mae always considered my mother to be like a daughter to her.

In the 1940s, eighth grade was the end of the road for black students in Assumption Parish. When Tee—my mother—came of age,

Papo and Mamo sent her to New Orleans to complete her studies at Booker T. Washington High School. Tee enrolled in 1944, staying in a Carondelet Street apartment with Tee Mae and Tee Gladys.

"She was a mama figure for me," Tee recalled. "I cried all the time in those days. I wanted to go home to my mama. Mama told my sister, 'Just let her come, just let her come.' But she wouldn't do it. She told our mother that if she let me go home, I would never come back. That would be the end of my education, and education is the most important thing."

Tee Mae prevailed, as usual, and my mother, the granddaughter of a slave, went on to become the first in my immediate family to earn a college degree.

"She would say, 'You will always be my child, because Mama gave you to me when she was on her deathbed,'" my mother told me. "She would send me clothes and things when I was in college. But she would give you pure hell if you didn't do what she said to do. My sister was as good as gold, but Lord, she was a bearcat."

By the time my two uncles finished eighth grade, Assumption Parish black kids could complete a full high school education at a local public school, but they didn't attend it. They had been going to a one-room schoolhouse at St. Benedict the Moor, the local black parish, where all students studied under the same teacher, from first through eighth grades. The older kids helped the younger ones with their lessons. Priests from the Josephites, a Catholic religious order founded during Reconstruction to serve black Catholics, taught religious education classes.

The Catholic Church in America was a segregated institution back then. In Louisiana towns where African American Catholics did not have parishes of their own, blacks and whites shared the local church building. But Sunday mornings were a humiliation for black worshippers. Churches typically reserved the back two pews for African Americans; when the pews filled up, blacks had to stand, even if there were seats available in the white section. Mamo told us that when she was a child, the Church segregated catechism classes. All the kids in the parish would go into a church for their instruction. The white kids would go first, and the black kids after them. When the white boys were done, they would clamber up into the choir loft and pee on the black children below.

"And the only thing the priest would do is say, 'Stop that,' and go on with the lesson," Mamo said. That memory would fire my grandmother up—and I saw that same flame flash in my mother over the years. After all that time, Mamo was still mad at that priest. "All this talk about 'love your neighbor,'" she said, "and he barely lifted a finger to stop those white boys."

Racism like this was why my uncle L.H. left the Catholic Church as a young man and cursed a priest his sisters had summoned to his deathbed. The other Edwards siblings held on to their faith by force of will, recognizing the hard truth that there is a difference between the Catholic faith and the fallen humans who serve the Church.

And every so often, one of those fallen humans would shock your conscience by their courage and righteousness. Harry J. Maloney, a big, bluff New York Irishman sent in 1948 by the Archdiocese of New Orleans to care for the Negro missions along Bayou Lafourche, was just such a man. Nobody in Assumption Parish, white or black, had ever seen anybody like Father Maloney.

"He was a great man," Uncle L.C. said. "He opened the eyes of many people. Mamo and Papo always said there's something better coming by, and that something was Father Harry J. Maloney."

As soon as he hit the ground, Father Maloney started building the St. Augustine parish church and a new school at St. Benedict the Moor for black children. L.H. and L.C. stayed in the Catholic school system because Father Maloney organized a school bus service up to Donaldsonville, fifteen miles to the north, taking older black children to St. Catherine High School, where nine nuns, all black, taught them. Tuition was twenty-five cents per week, which was hard for Mamo and Papo to pay.

But they wouldn't dream of depriving their sons of a Catholic education if they could possibly afford it. After all, *can't* died three days before the creation of the world. Even some non-Catholic black parents sent their children to study with the black sisters, because they wanted their kids to benefit from a stricter disciplinary environment.

"When those nuns and those priests finished with your ass, they always instilled in you that you had to have something in your head," Uncle L.C. remembers affectionately. "When we had a class reunion, none of us had been in trouble in life, and all of us had done some good. What's the reason? It was the sisters' school. That's what I call Catholic school. Ain't no Catholic schools today. You got your lay teachers, and you call it Catholic school, but it ain't nothing like those goddamn nuns and priests, the sisters and the brothers."

Back in my aunts' and uncles' day, the black children of this part of the world had strong families, deep religion, and a burning desire to learn. All they lacked was opportunity—and that's where Father Maloney came in. He used his privilege as a white man and a Catholic priest to break down barriers of racial prejudice and systematic injustice.

He started a federal credit union to help black folk who couldn't get loans from local banks. He began a bus service to take black workers on the seventy-mile trip to the Avondale Shipyard near New Orleans, so industrial jobs that paid good wages could be theirs.

Through these measures and others, he dramatically undermined the control that landlords had over the black workers living and working on their plantations, home to two out of every three African Americans in the parish back then.

In those days, black folk lived in what they called "the quarters" on the various plantations' grounds. Plantation owners would lock the gates at five o'clock, and nobody was free to come or go. No vendors were allowed onto the plantation; tenants had to buy from the plantation store. Many of them were illiterate, so they had no idea what the store was charging them. All you knew was that every month you were going deeper into debt. If no vendors were allowed onto the property, the black folk living there would likely never learn what things were like on the outside, or what was available for them.

So Father Maloney founded a food bank. He would go by the local stores and collect canned goods and other donations and put them in the church hall. If you needed food, you bypassed the plantation store and went to see Father. Most amazing of all, when Father Maloney saw that black people made up 42 percent of the parish's population, but only three were allowed to vote (the undertaker and two Baptist preachers), he organized a voter registration drive for African

Americans—this in the early 1950s, a decade or more before the civil rights movement undertook them all over the South.

The white power structure in the parish did not like that at all. They went to New Orleans to see Archbishop Joseph Rummel several times to complain about the "nigger-loving" priest. Archbishop Rummel told them to leave Father Maloney alone, that he was doing the work of God.

He was with the African American people of Assumption Parish for only four years, but Father Maloney made a huge impression on the black Catholics there, who were accustomed to a church that defended the racist status quo. He demonstrated that faith could give you not only the strength to endure hardship and injustice, but also the courage to fight for a better world.

Father Maloney was rare among white people in the South in his day, but he was a harbinger of a better America to come. Mamo and Papo had faith that things were going to change, and they prepared their children to play their part in that change. They saw things many others could not, and because they taught their children to believe in God, in family, in education, and in themselves, they empowered the next generation to make their dreams real.

Today, many of the descendants of Herbert and Frances Edwards have gone far from the farm at College Point. Every one of us knows how much we owe them. My great-grandfather Aristile was an orphan and a slave. His daughter Frances was a farm wife and mother. Her daughter Althea was a schoolteacher. And I, her son, became an actor. In every generation, we've built on what we've been given. The gifts Mamo and Papo gave to me, both directly and through my mother, have been like greenbacks in my pocket with the world on sale for a dollar.

DURING MY CHILDHOOD, I would see my parents dealing with some difficult situations having to do with racism and protecting us kids, in particular teaching us how to navigate a hostile world. As hard as that was, I can barely imagine what it was like for Herbert and Frances, or for Aristile. *I know you're a slave, son, but if you ever get free, you have a father, and sisters and brothers. Go find them.* How do you endure the loss, the injustice, the cruelty, and the indignity of daily life without going crazy? How do you endure it at all? How did they maintain courage and dignity and pursuit of the humanity of their own existence, in the midst of the filthiest, cruelest, most degrading treatment anyone can endure, all because of the color of their skin? How did they do it every single day, knowing that one false move could cost them their lives? And to have faith that they would somehow pass on to their children a sense of security, of dignity, of vision and hope for a better life?

They did it for love of each other. They did it because they had faith in God—a God of justice, and a God that suffered with them. They did it because they had faith in the future, a future that they believed would be better, and would be so in part because they had the power, through education, to make it better. They did it through the power of ancestral memory, of practicing gratitude and taking strength from the sacrifices of past generations. And they did it through the love of family and community, which bequeathed resilience. Standing alone, any of us would have been crushed. Standing together, we could not be defeated, at least not for long. Because we knew who we were, and what we had to do. Our stories—the hand-me-down art incarnating the virtues that made our family strong—told us so.

I think about what those three generations carried through slavery, Jim Crow, the civil rights movement, all the way to the day that a black man was elected President of the United States, and I know in that humbling, awe-inspiring moment, I don't need to look outside my family for heroes.

Papo dropped dead in his fields in 1969. Mamo passed in a Napoleonville hospital twenty years later, with three of her children at her side. Nearly all of their children are gone now; the baby, Uncle L.C., who remains vigorous in his eighties, is the last of the family reserve. We still have the original farm in the family, but none of Herbert and Frances's descendants work it. The world of College Point has faded into history too, as the grandchildren and their children have scattered, carrying with them memories, and for the younger generation, memories of memories. They will never know the hardships that marked the lives and shaped the vision of Mamo and Papo, their children, and all the people of College Point. This is a blessing beyond all telling.

Yet I can look inside myself and see that the best parts of me come from that narrow lane cut through the sugarcane fields once worked by African slaves, including my great-grandfather Aristile. Those fields and that path were walked by my forebears, for whom it was a road to somewhere better than any generation of African Americans will know since they were brought to this land in chains. For me, the path to success began on that humble country lane, where my beloved mother grew up in the cradle of a close family and community whose love and strength prepared her for the crucibles through which she and all of black America would pass in the middle of the twentieth century.

Half a century after she left home for good to marry my father and settle in New Orleans, I sat with my mother in Mamo and Papo's old house, which was then occupied by Tee Mae, talking about the old days. I asked her what College Point meant to her. A light within her welled up, and her face bloomed.

"College Point means home to me," Tee said. "College Point means family to me. College Point means forever to me, because that's where my roots are."

THREE

THIS LAND IS OUR LAND

The childhoods of both Daddy and Tee taught them the big lesson that every African American parent must pass on to his or her children: that things are going to get better, and people are going to change, but never, ever forget that that ugly side of human nature is not going to go away. You have to buffer yourself against it even as you work to evolve yourself and the rest of society away from it.

My father, Amos Edward Pierce, Jr., came out of the projects, back when that was nothing people felt shame over.

His family was one of the first tenants in the newly built Calliope housing project, a Depression-era development built as a place for working-class black people and their families in New Orleans. But he did most of his growing up in Gert Town, a neighborhood near Xavier University.

Even in the midst of Jim Crow, New Orleans was a very spatially integrated city, more integrated than people know. When Daddy was growing up, the nearby Uptown district of New Orleans, long the neighborhood of the city's wealthiest whites, was more diverse than you might think, he said. He had all kinds of boyhood adventures roaming the streets of Uptown: playing on the levee, throwing rocks in the canal, jumping on and off the streetcar.

No matter how idyllic it sounds, and however far removed his urban childhood was from the harshness of black country life, you could never forget the reality of race. When I take him riding around town these days, Daddy will point out all the places he and his mother, Blanche, used to go.

"And there's Palmer Park," he once said. "We had to fight the white boys to go across it all the time."

"Whoa, what?"

"Oh, yeah, we'd have to fight the white boys to play in Palmer Park," he said. "We knew we would have to get that out of the way before we could play there that day."

I heard that, and I was thinking, *Oh my God, here beginneth the lesson.*

In 1930s New Orleans, my father had to fight in that park simply to be allowed to play the way any white boy could. Little did he know that forty years later, he would be sitting down with me, his third and youngest son, teaching me the same lessons he learned as a little scrapper in Palmer Park. Change comes to society, but it comes too slowly.

Daddy was an only child. As his mother raised her boy, his father, Amos Sr., was an inconstant presence. The man died before I was born, but he had never really been a part of his son's life. He was a chef on the railroads, and he chased women. Whenever my father would see his dad in the neighborhood, he was with another woman, parading her through Gert Town, indifferent to the pain and humiliation that must have caused Blanche.

Amos Sr. decided that he wanted to be part of his son's life when he married "up"—my mother was a schoolteacher, and for black people in those days, that was considered social advancement.

Amos Sr. died not long after his son married Tee. The pain of fatherlessness made my own dad pledge to himself and to God: *I will never, no matter what happens to my wife and me, abandon my kids.*

Daddy didn't have to talk about the responsibilities fathers have to their children, or about strong family values. He lived them. And he wasn't the only one, in the neighborhood where he and Tee raised their three boys.

The family values debate in our culture is more politicized than it ought to be. Everybody on both sides of the argument understands the value of the nuclear family. The fact is, when we had intact families, we had fewer problems. As the history of my own family demonstrates, when we African Americans held our families together, we drew from them the strength and solidarity we needed to combat the evils of racism, prejudice, and attack from the enemies of our community.

The French novelist Honoré de Balzac said, "Hope is a memory that desires." The hope I have now for the restoration of Pontchartrain Park, the single-family black neighborhood where I grew up, and which was destroyed by Katrina, comes from the memories I have of growing up in a time when every home there had a mother and a father in it. With all those moms and dads around, I felt protected. I knew if anything happened, there was an adult who would help and protect me. I want black children and their families to experience this. My memory of Pontchartrain Park, and my desire to bring it back to life, is the source of my hope.

Daddy went to elementary school at St. Joan of Arc, a Josephite-run Catholic school for black children on Burthe Street in the shadow of the Mississippi River levee. As Daddy tells it, he came home one day and told his mother he wanted to be a Catholic. She was a practicing Baptist, but she agreed. It was important to her that her son be able to make up his own mind. That was a simple act of parental generosity, but it had a ripple effect in the lives of Blanche's grandchildren. From her, my father learned the importance of letting your children make their own choices in life, even if you disagree with them. When I was in high school, Daddy did not understand why I wanted to be an actor, but he made it clear that if this was the road I chose to walk down, he would respect my decision and not try to stop me.

When he was seventeen, Daddy was living with Blanche in the Calliope project when he received his notice to report for the U.S. Army draft. He had not yet finished high school, but war was raging in the South Pacific and his country needed him. He and two buddies walked the mile from the projects down to Lee Circle for their induction. Young men were streaming in from all over the city.

After the physical, an officer summoned my father and his two friends back to the induction center. "Out of two hundred men, only sixteen of y'all passed," the officer said. "You men should be proud." He told them when to report back for basic training.

It was a long walk home. Just before Daddy and his buddies made it back, all three began to cry.

"What's the matter?" Blanche said when her son slumped in weeping.

"I got to leave home," Daddy said. Not once in his life had he been outside the city limits of New Orleans. It was an overwhelming prospect.

Daddy enlisted as an Army private on July 1, 1943, and was eventually assigned to the 24th Infantry Regiment. Not even in the ranks of the military of the nation he was willing to die for could my father and men like him escape prejudice. Until 1948, segregation was the rule. White commanders—and they were all white—typically assigned only menial tasks to black servicemen. In the South, the black MPs who sometimes guarded German POWs were forbidden to sit down in the same restaurants that, on occasion, served our Nazi enemies who were allowed excursions away from camps on the honor system.

But military segregation was not absolute. Before shipping out to the South Pacific, Daddy had a brief sojourn at Fort Lewis in Washington state, where the sight of snow-capped Mount Rainier dazzled a young man who grew up in a subtropical city that sits below sea level. Once, he and some army buddies went to a USO in Seattle and, as southerners, were shocked to see that, unlike USOs in other parts of the country, that club was integrated. When a white girl asked him to dance, he froze, declining out of fear he would get shot. You can take the man out of the segregated South, but you can't take the segregated South out of the man.

And to be fair, prejudice didn't stay in the South alone—but neither did human decency. In Seattle, my dad and his buddies wanted to get a beer, but the bar refused to let black servicemen through the door. A white street cop saw the soldiers turned away and got so angry, he went into the bar, bought beers for them all, and took the beers out to them. "If you can fight and die for this country," the cop said, "you can damn sure drink a beer."

AFTER TRAINING IN SEATTLE, Daddy's regiment lived in the hold of a troop transport docked in San Francisco Bay, awaiting orders to ship out. When the word came down that they were going to sea, everyone knew that they were finally going to war.

When the big ship got under way, every man went to stand on the deck, in total silence. The ship sailed under the Golden Gate Bridge, from which hung a giant American flag. The men remained on the deck for as long as they could, straining to see land receding behind them. They did not know if that would be the last time they would lay eyes on America, their home.

My father was in an Army division attached to the Marines. He participated in the 1944 invasion of the Japanese-held island of Saipan, part of the Mariana island chain in the middle of the Pacific Ocean, bringing supplies to the front lines. They were spared the barrage endured by Marines at the tip of the invasion spear, but the Japanese knew that Daddy's unit was keeping the front lines supplied with ammunition, so they targeted them with artillery. The fire raining down on them like a monsoon took a heavy toll on Daddy and his men, at least on their nerves. During the worst of it, all they could do was hunker down in foxholes and pray that a shell wouldn't find its way in.

The Battle of Saipan ended with the Americans killing nearly every Japanese soldier on the island. But it was costly, too, for the United States, which lost more than three thousand troops, including ten men from Daddy's supply regiment, and suffered another thirteen thousand casualties—the deadliest and most destructive encounter with the Japanese enemy to date.

Not long after the battle, my father got a Section 8 discharge after he was found to be mentally unfit for service. Incredibly, this was itself a story of racism, one that I didn't learn until I was in high school. As a child, I remember checks coming to him regularly from the government, but Tee didn't explain them to us until we were older.

It turns out that after Saipan, my father was granted a rest-and-relaxation break and he took a transport over to a nearby island to see his New Orleans cousin. He arrived just after his cousin had departed. Overcome by frustration and exhaustion, Daddy told his commanding officer that he was tired of this war and wasn't going back.

"The hell you're not going back," his shocked commander said.

"No, sir, I'm not going back," said my dad. "I want to go home to New Orleans right now."

"No, you're going back," the officer countered. And that was the end of that. Daddy had no choice.

But here's the interesting part of the story. After Daddy rejoined his unit, he wasn't cited for insubordination, as he could have been, but was instead given a Section 8 discharge for combat fatigue. Talking back to a white officer was considered so beyond the pale that the military concluded that this Negro soldier had to have lost his mind. Unexpectedly, the war ended early for him because of racial prejudice.

Back stateside, as Corporal Amos Pierce was being processed through Fort Hood, Texas, he informed the military WAC officer, a white woman overseeing things, that he had commendations from his Army unit from the Saipan invasion. Daddy's papers hadn't caught up with him yet, so the officer dismissed his claim.

"You don't believe me?" he said, nonplussed.

"Yeah, right. I don't believe you," she said. The message to Daddy was clear: Black men aren't capable of heroism in battle.

Later, when the Army wrote him about his unclaimed medals, the pain of being humiliated at discharge compelled him to ignore the letter. He didn't want the damn medals. It was part of the raw deal black veterans got when they returned from laying their lives on the line to defend the same country that continued to treat them like second-class citizens at home. Daddy could go to Saipan under artillery fire, but he couldn't go to the French Quarter for a drink.

It's interesting that Daddy didn't pass on his bitterness over this to my brothers and me. In fact, my older brother, Ron, is a West Point graduate and retired from the U.S. Army at the rank of major. Our father raised us to be proud of our country and to love her for what she will one day be, not for what she is today. This was the legacy of the "Double V" campaign, a World War II initiative that was huge for the black community.

In 1942, shortly after Pearl Harbor, as hundreds of thousands of black men were reporting to draft induction centers, an African American named James G. Thompson, from Wichita, Kansas, wrote a letter to the editor of *The Pittsburgh Courier*, the most popular black newspaper of the era:

Being an American of dark complexion and some 26 years,
these questions flash through my mind: "Should I sacrifice
my life to live half American?" "Will things be better for the
next generation in the peace to follow?" "Would it be demanding too much to demand full citizenship rights in exchange for the sacrificing of my life?" "Is the kind of America
I know worth defending?" . . . "Will colored Americans suffer still the indignities that have been heaped upon them in
the past?" These and other questions need answering.

Thompson proposed what he called the "Double V" campaign:
"The first V for victory over our enemies from without, the second V
for victory over our enemies within. For surely those who perpetuate
these ugly prejudices here are seeking to destroy our democratic form
of government just as surely as the Axis forces."

The letter electrified black America. Two weeks later, the paper
launched its Double V campaign in an editorial that said, in part:

Americans all, are involved in a gigantic war effort to assure
victory for the cause of freedom—the four freedoms that
have been so nobly expressed by President Roosevelt and
Prime Minister Churchill. We, as colored Americans, are determined to protect our country, our form of government and
the freedoms which we cherish for ourselves and for the rest
of the world, therefore we have adopted the Double "V" war
cry—victory over our enemies at home and victory over our
enemies on the battlefields abroad. Thus in our fight for free-

dom we wage a two-pronged attack against our enslavers at home and those abroad who would enslave us.

WE HAVE A STAKE IN THIS FIGHT. . . .
WE ARE AMERICANS TOO!

Black newspapers around the country took up the cause and carried its banner throughout the war years. Of course, the promise of the Double V campaign was only half fulfilled. America won the war for democracy abroad, but refused to embrace it and prosecute it at home. Yet African Americans did not give up hope. They still believed in America, and wanted white Americans to believe in her too. The same faith in this nation's promise would animate the civil rights movement. In 1957, the Reverend Dr. Martin Luther King, Jr., would give a Christmas sermon in which he paid respect to the Double V campaign, using the same rhetoric that would ultimately prevail in the war for the hearts and minds of America and its future. He spoke of turning the other cheek, of loving our enemies though they persecute us. No amount of white hatred, he said could make the Negro hate back.

But be assured that we'll wear you down by our capacity to suffer, and one day we will win our freedom. We will not only win freedom for ourselves; we will appeal to your heart and conscience that we will win you in the process, and our victory will be a double victory.

In Dr. King's soaring words, I can hear the testimony of my family. Burn our cars to teach us a lesson, nearly lynch our men for loving your women, piss on our children in church, steal our money and our right to vote, throw our broken bodies into an unmarked plantation grave, send us to a foreign land to fight and die for you, but deny us the medals we earned sacrificing for this nation—and we will not stop loving America. But we will win our freedom with a victory against the enemies—from within.

THIS WAS NOT SENTIMENTALITY for my father. This was reality. I'll never forget the lesson he taught me as a boy, the night he took me to a boxing match at the Municipal Auditorium. Daddy hates cigarette smoking, but he wanted to see the fights, so he sat miserably with my brother and me in the uppermost part of the bleachers, surrounded by a billowing cloud of smoke, waiting for the matches to begin. This was the late sixties or early seventies, when the Black Power movement was in full swing. That ethos demanded that when the national anthem was played, black people protested by refusing to stand in respect.

That night at the Municipal Auditorium, the national anthem began to sound over the PA system, signaling that the fights would soon start. Everyone stood, except some brothers sitting in the next row down from us. They looked up at my father and said, "Aw, Pops, sit down."

"Don't touch me, man," growled my dad.

"Sit down! Sit down!" they kept on.

"Don't touch me," he said. "I fought for that flag. You can sit down. I fought for you to have that right. But I fought for that flag too, and I'm going to stand."

Then one of the brothers leveled his eyes at Daddy and said, "No, you *need* to sit down." He started pulling on my father's pant leg.

That was it. "You touch me one more time," my father roared, "and I'm going to kick you in your fucking teeth."

The radical wiseass turned around and minded his own business. That was a demonstration of black power that the brother hadn't expected.

Like my father, my uncle L. H. Edwards fought for the American flag—his war was Vietnam—and came home to face discrimination as well. Uncle L.H. was a far angrier and a politically more extreme man than my father, but no matter how mad he was at what America had done to him and his people, his faith in America's ideals and his loyalty to that flag did not waver. Like his son Louis says, "My father might have put on a dashiki, but he was going to wear it while he waved that flag."

"You have to understand, my father was an officer," Louis says. "He was so proud of that. He believed that there was no military in this world greater than the U.S. military, and you had better speak to him with respect because of it. He might have sung the black national anthem, but he wasn't going to fly the flag of any African country, or any other nation but our own."

Those brave black soldiers, Amos Pierce and L. H. Edwards, taught me about true patriotism. This land was their land, too. It was made for them, same as everybody else. They never forgot it, and they weren't going to let their fellow Americans forget it. Their patriotism said, "America is a great country, but we're going to keep fighting to make it greater."

In 2009, I did my small part in this long struggle to make our country a more perfect union when I contacted WWL-TV reporter Bill Capo in New Orleans and asked him to help me get Daddy his medals. I couldn't let that injustice stand, not after all Amos Pierce had done for me and for his country. I explained what had happened and Bill started looking into it. He contacted U.S. senator Mary Landrieu, a fellow New Orleanian, who put her staff to work researching the issue.

What they found was that Corporal Pierce had not been awarded two medals, as he believed, but rather six of them. There was a Bronze Service Star, an Asiatic Pacific Campaign medal, a World War II Victory medal, a Presidential Unit Citation, a Meritorious Unit Commendation, and a Good Conduct medal, along with an honorable service lapel pin.

Working with the National World War II Museum in New Orleans, we arranged a special ceremony on Armed Forces Day, 2009, to present my father, then eighty-four, with his country's thanks and honors. True, they were half a century late, but it's never too late to do the right thing.

Major General Hunt Downer of the Louisiana National Guard spoke warmly of my father, telling the audience that we must never forget the debt of gratitude we owe to the Greatest Generation. Museum board president Gordon "Nick" Mueller added, "We would not have won World War Two without the African Americans, the Native Americans, the Hispanics, the Japanese Americans."

My brother Ron rose to speak, fighting back tears. He told the audience that our father "truly believed in the American dream, and he bought into it. And when he would tell us that we could do anything, he wasn't just spouting words, he meant it." (Ron said later that the event was surreal for him. "Here I was in the presence of a real-life American war hero, and it was my father—and I had no idea about it.")

When my turn came to speak, I was as emotional as Ron was. My heart was bursting with love and pride in Daddy and all his comrades-in-arms. "It's a great honor to stand here today," I said. "But it's not just for us. It is for all the men and women who couldn't live to see this honor, and receive the honors they received, but still had love and faith for this great nation."

Tee stood with us, at Daddy's side. I hoped that my oldest brother, Stacey, who had died of heart disease a decade earlier, could in some way share that moment of triumph with our family.

Then it was time to give Daddy his medals. His face beaming, Daddy made his way with his walker to the stage. I stood at his side, holding the six medals in my hand, while Ron pinned them on the left breast of Daddy's pin-striped suit. Tee looked on, cradling the box the medals came in.

Later on, his chest laden with colorful ribbons and bronze medals, Daddy told WWL-TV that he felt like General MacArthur. For us, it was enough that he was U.S. Army Corporal Amos Pierce, Jr., war hero. His family had always known it, but now the whole world did. America had finally lived up to the promises it made to a young black man who crossed the ocean and walked through fire and thunder for her. America had finally kept faith with an old black man who, despite everything, had taught his sons to believe in this great nation.

Whenever I hear people say, "So many people died for our freedom," I say yes, you're right—but I'm not thinking of battlefields alone. I'm also thinking of bayous and creeks and rivers where so many African Americans died, or endured the murders of their beloved husbands, sons, and fathers, at the hands of their fellow Americans who would never answer for their crimes in a court of law. And I'm thinking of the busy city streets and the lonesome country roads where so many black folk risked their lives—and in some cases, gave their lives—for the cause of liberty and justice for all Americans. There is blood on the ballot box, and it is the blood of black soldiers who fought for America—whether or not they ever wore the uniform.

They loved the country that persecuted them and treated them like the enemy. To me, that is a vision of supreme patriotism. It's like my father always said to my brothers and me, every time we would see a triumph of American ideals: "See, that's why I fought for that flag!"

Amos Pierce never stopped fighting for that flag, and never stopped loving it, either. On the day he finally received his medals, he said nothing at the formal ceremony, but at the gala afterward, he decided that he wanted to offer a few words to the crowd.

He hobbled over to the microphone and, despite his hearing loss, spoke with ringing clarity.

"I want you all to remember those who didn't come back, I want to dedicate this night to them," he said. "So many who fought didn't even have a chance to live their lives. I was given that chance, as difficult as my life has been."

Daddy thanked the audience for the honor, saying he was not bitter for having been denied the medals for so long. He was simply grateful to have them now.

"We've come so far as a country," he continued. "I've realized now a lot of what we were fighting for."

And then he paused. It took all of his strength to stand as erect as possible at the podium. He saluted crisply, and said, "God bless America."

That's when I lost it. For someone not to be debilitated by pain and anger and embarrassment after all he had been through; who fought for this country when this country didn't love him and wouldn't fight for him; to come back from war and still have to fight for the right to vote and the right to go into any establishment he wanted to—that made me think of the vow he made to me as a child: "No matter what, son, I will never abandon you."

I have never known a greater man than that old soldier on the night he received his due.

WHEN HE RETURNED FROM THE WAR, Daddy went back to high school, though his long semester in the South Pacific made him older than his classmates. He had been drafted before graduation, and now he wanted to earn his diploma. After that, he used the G.I. Bill to enter Southern University in Baton Rouge, the historically black college founded after Reconstruction.

One night, at a campus dance, Daddy saw "this little red girl," as he would always say, who caught his eye. That was Althea Lee Edwards, my mother. Daddy remembers that she was "just a little red thing"—he referred to the bright hue of her skin. After they became sweethearts, his pet name for her was "Black." He would say, affectionately, "You little red-skinned thing, you don't want to be black." That's where the name came from.

As a college man, Daddy always held his little Dobbs fedora on his forearm, which was the style at the time. There he was, drunk, trying to chat up the woman who would become my mother, and he kept dropping his Dobbs. Tee was not impressed with the fast-talking drunk boy from New Orleans who couldn't keep his hands on his hat.

But he was persistent, and he kept courting her. Finally, Tee invited him down the bayou to meet her parents. Daddy caught the bus to Assumption Parish for the weekend. All the old folks in my family loved to joke about how all it took was for Amos to get one taste of Mamo's good country cooking, and he was hooked. Seemed like he came down every weekend after that.

They were still an item when Daddy left for photography school in New York City. He moved in with Tee Mae in Brooklyn. At some point after Daddy's arrival, he began to date a woman from Baltimore. When Tee Mae found out about it, she blistered him good. "Oh hell no!" she said. "You're not going to live in my house and run around on my sister."

She called Tee back home in Louisiana to break the news. By then Tee had graduated from Southern and was living in New Orleans with her sisters and working. My mother asked Tee Mae to put Amos on the line. When she had his ear, Tee spat, "We're through. Stay up there with your little Baltimore girl."

"Oh no, no, no!" wailed my father. He wept inconsolably. Days later, he withdrew from photography school, packed his bags, caught the next train for New Orleans, and when he rolled into town, found my mother and asked her to marry him. She said yes. Daddy worked for a while as a studio portrait photographer, but when he left New York, he said good-bye to serious artistic ambitions.

Many years later, when I was studying at Juilliard, I finally learned why my father had been so adamant that I think hard before committing myself to an acting career. My brother Ron, who was more observant than I, said, "Did you ever see Daddy's photographs in his study?"

I had not. He had brought a sheaf of beautiful, artistically composed photographs home with him, which he kept in the bottom of a desk drawer. These images, photographs of New York and its people mostly, were aesthetically sophisticated. I was floored. There was one in particular, a self-portrait, that involved a double-exposure technique of startling technical accomplishment for a photography student.

"Daddy, you never told me you were an artistic photographer, not just a studio photographer," I said.

"Oh," he said. "I thought you knew that."

Daddy might have made it as an artist, but he chose to return home to marry the love of his life. He never expressed regret, but when my brother Ron showed me those images, I knew instantly that had our father stayed in New York and pursued his artistic dream, he had the talent to have become a first-rate photographer. Daddy understood what it felt like to put one's dream of becoming an artist away forever. He resisted my early acting ambitions because he had wanted to protect his boy from that pain.

All along I thought Daddy didn't respect my talent and my passion for acting—that his skepticism was a failure of paternal love. Once I knew what the real story was—that his gruff pushback came from an *excess* of paternal love—a tremendous burden lifted.

Daddy and Tee married in 1952 and moved into a rented house on Deslonde Street in the Lower Ninth Ward. Half a century later, the world would know the Lower Ninth Ward as the epicenter of Katrina's wrath. In the 1950s, though, it was a neighborhood where poor and working-class folks, mostly African American, lived and raised their families. Fronting the river only four miles east of the heart of the French Quarter, the swampy Lower Ninth has always been one of the poorest and most isolated parts of New Orleans. In the 1920s, dredging the Industrial Canal connecting the Mississippi with Lake Pontchartrain due north further separated the Lower Ninth, both geographically and psychologically. Historically, African Americans had to live in the lowest-lying, most mosquito-infested and flood-prone parts of the city. The Lower Ninth was the boondocks of the Crescent City, but black New Orleanians didn't have much choice.

Three years later, when Tee was home with their first child, my brother Stacey, Daddy came home from work with a surprise.

"Hey, Black, I bought us a house today."

"You *what*?!"

"Just ten dollars holds the contract."

Daddy packed his wife and baby son into their car and drove north toward Lake Pontchartrain, into the farthest edge of the Gentilly neighborhood, to show them where their new house would be. Coming to a bare two-hundred-acre tract of land hard up against the Industrial Canal, sandwiched between the lake and Chef Menteur

Highway, was a new housing development called Pontchartrain Park. When complete, it would be the first subdivision built exclusively for the city's rising African American middle class.

From a twenty-first-century perspective, you might see Pontchartrain Park as a Negro Levittown, a square mile of separate-but-equal, cookie-cutter suburbia built on a drained swamp that was some of the worst, lowest-lying land in the city. In a nation trying to shake off the burdens of segregation, you might think it was an insulting attempt by the white power structure to buy off a black community that they were increasingly powerless to intimidate.

You might see it that way. And you wouldn't be all wrong. But that's not how men and women like my father and mother saw it. For a generation of black New Orleanians, Pontchartrain Park was the closest they had ever been to the Promised Land of the opportunity to live like regular Americans. It was where the Moses generation in New Orleans planted its flag and laid claim to the middle-class American dream.

It was where they took something Jim Crow ugly—a cynical attempt to divert the rising tide of hope and change coming out of postwar mobility into the stagnant swamp of segregation—and made it blossom into something beautiful.

New Orleans neighborhoods were not always segregated. In fact, Tulane University geographer Richard Campanella calls New Orleans "America's first multicultural city." Founded in 1718 as the capital of the French territory of Louisiane, New Orleans spent four decades under Spanish colonial rule, until Napoleonic France briefly regained custody before selling it to the United States in 1803.

By now it's a cliché to call New Orleans a "gumbo," but the metaphor didn't come from nowhere. In all its local variations, the iconic southern Louisiana stew—which comes from European, African, and Native American influences—really does reflect the sociological and cultural reality of a city that's unique in North America. True story: When the Cuban-American architect Andrés Duany came to post-Katrina New Orleans to help plan the rebuilding, he struggled with the characteristic inefficiencies of the city's government. Then one day, as he walked in the Marigny neighborhood, a banana tree next to a brightly painted cottage made him think of his native Cuba. It hit him: New Orleans is not American, but Caribbean. By that cultural and geographical standard, New Orleans was a model of competent civic administration.

"This insight was fundamental because from that moment I understood New Orleans and began to truly sympathize," Duany wrote. "Like everyone, I found government in this city to be a bit random; but if New Orleans were to be governed as efficiently as, say, Minneapolis, it would be a different place—and not one that I could care for." I don't quite agree with him, but it's a window into the psyche of the Crescent City.

Because of its origin as a French colonial city in the subtropics, New Orleans always had the same raffish mestizo atmosphere characteristic of New World cities colonized by European Catholic powers. Alexis de Tocqueville was one of many travelers impressed by the diversity in the great port city. Visiting New Orleans in 1832 on his grand tour of the United States, Tocqueville wrote in his diary that in the Crescent City, he felt very far from America: "Faces with every shade of color," he observed. "Language French, English, Spanish, Creole."

To be sure, this was not because New Orleans was uniquely enlightened among American cities on race. It was a matter of practicality. Tocqueville speculated that it was because the French and the Spanish colonists had largely been single men looking for wealth, and forced slave women to be their sexual partners. The English-speaking colonists in the rest of America had mostly migrated in search of religious liberty, he said, and had come with their families.

Until colonial rule ended with the 1803 Louisiana Purchase, Creoles—French-speaking Catholics of mixed European and African ancestry—lived amid whites. Many of them were what were called "free people of color" and had a distinct legal and social standing, sandwiched between white colonials and enslaved Africans. Black slaves, of course, also lived near their masters, either in slave quarters next to their masters' houses, or in nearby back alley dwellings. These free people of color remained strictly segregated in social matters, though.

After Protestant Americans took control of the city from the French, they brought with them American laws and more rigid attitudes toward race. Yet New Orleans remained one of the most racially diverse cities in the nation. The 1820 census found that the number of ethnic groups making up at least 5 percent of the population was seven—the greatest diversity of any American city at the time—and that about half the city's population were either slaves or free persons of color.

Black Creoles who were not enslaved settled heavily in the Faubourg Marigny neighborhood, to the east and north of the French Quarter. After the Civil War, freedmen leaving Louisiana planta-

tions for opportunities and what they hoped would be a more toler-
ant New Orleans settled in the Back o' Town districts. These were
mosquito-infested slum areas on the undesirable swampy outskirts,
far from any city services, where desperately poor black residents
lived in ramshackle housing.

The extensive drainage system the city installed between 1893 and
1915 was a game-changer. Before the massive pumps went into operation, the city's boundaries were confined to the higher ground along
the natural levees snaking east to west along the Mississippi River,
and the parallel Metairie and Gentilly ridges to the north. Behind the
Gentilly Ridge was swampland, running roughly three miles out to
the lake.

The drainage works allowed huge areas between the old city core
and Lake Pontchartrain to the north to be drained, opening them for
suburban development. Though this land was below sea level, the
pumps, drainage canals, and new levees protected it from flooding.

In the first decades of the twentieth century, white New Orleanians
seeking a suburban lifestyle leapfrogged over the Back o' Town black
folk, taking advantage of Jim Crow covenants that kept black families
out of the new developments, migrating out to the Lakeview neighborhood, west of what today is City Park. Middle-class black families,
including descendants of black Creoles, pushed in the same direction
into Gentilly, a lakefront area of town sweeping from the eastern
border of City Park to the western edge of the Industrial Canal. The
1935 founding of Dillard University, an interracial but predominantly
African American private religious college, drew many black profes-
sionals to Gentilly's Sugar Hill neighborhood, where the school was

located. In the 1940s and 1950s, the city's African Americans were no different from other Americans in the immediate postwar era: They wanted to move to the suburbs, too.

The migration of people of color into New Orleans's northern reaches during and after World War II coincided with the rise of black political power in the city. In 1946, an Uptown lawyer named De-Lesseps "Chep" Morrison ran for mayor with a reform agenda and openly courted the black vote—something no white candidate had ever done. Influential black leaders—chief among them the prominent black Creole civil rights lawyer A. P. Tureaud—backed him.

MORRISON WAS MORE PROGRESSIVE on race than many other white politicians, but "progressive" in the Jim Crow South was relative. He was publicly a segregationist—it would have been impossible for any white Louisiana politician to succeed otherwise—and not-so-privately a racist who referred to Negroes as "jiggerboos" and worse. Tureaud, who was the most important black Louisiana leader of the civil rights era and the local legal representative for the NAACP, later conceded that Morrison had never done much for his black constituency, but the fact that he made a point of consulting and being seen with African American leaders made him, from a black point of view, the best of a bad lot.

As a dynamic pro-business modernizer, Morrison pushed hard for the city's economic development. He led the demolition of run-down neighborhoods in what is now the Central Business District, displacing thousands of African Americans. To help some of them relocate and to relieve pressure from the growing city's housing shortage, Morrison endorsed creating the nation's first black-only single-family subdivision, bankrolled by Jewish philanthropists and a housing grant from the U.S. government. It would be the far northeastern corner of Gentilly, on a 213-acre plot of privately owned land. The new neighborhood would be called Pontchartrain Park.

It was not an act of racial magnanimity on the white mayor's part. When Morrison took office, he inherited a long-standing conflict over the beach at Seabrook, a strip of the Gentilly lakefront that black New Orleanians had been using for decades as a recreational spot to cool off in the sweltering summers. In the 1940s, African Americans were forbidden access to the new Pontchartrain Beach resort built where Elysian Fields meets the lake, so they moved down the shore to a site called Seabrook, east of the white neighborhoods. The city thought designating Seabrook a "Negro beach" would solve the problem.

But real estate developers fought to keep that from happening, fearing that giving black folks a beachhead in what they expected to be a prime real estate market would harm future profits. City officials did not formally set aside Seabrook for African Americans, but they did prevent all but the most minimal facilities from being built there, hoping that hardship would discourage black use of the site.

Black New Orleanians came anyway, despite substantial inconveniences and even mortal danger. The lakefront levee and seawall that made settlement in Lakeview and Gentilly possible also caused erosion, including offshore sinkholes that could suck swimmers under. The fancy sand shoreline constructed for the benefit of white bathers at sinkhole-free Pontchartrain Beach made the erosion worse for black bathers at Seabrook—and there were no lifeguards there to protect them. Black people responded to the threat by organizing swimming lessons and lifeguard services for themselves, and Seabrook's summertime population grew. Like all New Orleanians, they learned to cope with the water that surrounded them.

In 1932, black leaders reportedly petitioned the city to provide police and lifeguard protection for the Seabrook bathers, and it appeared that the city was going to comply. But vehement protest from white homeowners in the area derailed that plan. White housing developments were moving closer to that far corner of Gentilly, and white homeowners wanted the lakefront ethnically cleansed, in part to protect their property values.

FINALLY, in the summer of 1940, the city effectively banned black people from the lakefront. Families who had been swimming there for ages found themselves forced out by police patrols driving black swimmers off the beach. In a 2012 article for *Louisiana Cultural Vistas* magazine, Louise Marion Bouise told historian Andrew W. Kahrl what happened to her family that summer, after the truck driver who taxied them to Seabrook from the city dropped them off.

"We weren't there very long when policemen came along and told us we couldn't swim on the lakefront, that we'd have to go. We couldn't even stay on the lakefront and wait for the truck driver to come back to pick us up," she said. "We walked from the lakefront home, which was on St. Bernard and Broad. And in the party was one of our friends, a teenager, or he was ten by that time. He had a deformed leg, but these policemen [said] you'll have to move. And this young man with his brace on his leg walked all that distance home."

As the city increased pressure on black people to stay away from Seabrook, it encouraged them to relocate miles to the east, to a hard-to-get-to site the Levee Board had acquired and dubbed Lincoln Beach. The waters there were snake-infested and contaminated with raw sewage from nearby fishing camps, but it had one advantage from the city's point of view: It made black folk invisible.

Black New Orleanians were not eager to use this beachfront Bantustan, but the city was not going to let them return to Seabrook. During World War II, the city used the proximity of military facilities as an excuse to ban Seabrook bathers (though white fishermen could be seen along its shore). After the war, city government under the new mayor, Chep Morrison, attempted to resolve the long-standing conflict. The city made another go at establishing Lincoln Beach as a separatist enclave, equal to the whites-only Pontchartrain Beach, dedicating half a million dollars to upgrade the facilities. It opened in 1954.

Black people still did not show up in the expected numbers, not only because Lincoln Beach remained much too far away for many people to travel to, especially for those without cars, but also because black ministers urged their congregations to boycott it in resistance to Jim Crow laws. Meanwhile, the national NAACP resolved to undertake a full frontal legal assault on Jim Crow, which had been sanctioned nationally by the landmark 1896 *Plessy v. Ferguson* decision declaring that separate but equal was constitutionally valid. Local

NAACP attorney A. P. Tureaud championed efforts in New Orleans, where Homer Plessy, a Creole (black under Louisiana law) first challenged Jim Crow in 1892.

The feeling was rising among the city's fast-growing African American population that change had to come. Besides, black folk were starting to return to Seabrook, leading one horrified white Gentilly resident to write to Mayor Morrison to complain that black people changing into bathing suits "look like a lot of naked savages out of Darkest Africa."

Morrison may have been a segregationist, but he was also a pragmatist. He knew that the only chance white New Orleanians had for maintaining segregation was with separate accommodations for black people that truly were equal. In 1949, Tureaud filed suit on behalf of the NAACP to desegregate New Orleans city parks and golf courses—including Audubon Park, in the heart of Uptown New Orleans—all of which had been off-limits to black people except, in some cases, on specially designated days. Faced with mounting political and legal challenges to segregation, Morrison concocted a plan to solve several problems at once—black housing, restricted black access to city parks, and black need for a decent beach on the lake. It was to be an all-black middle-class housing development in the Seabrook area that would coincide with black access to the lake nearby. That was how Pontchartrain Park—the neighborhood where I grew up—was born.

At the center of the planned community was a Negro-only public park, about two hundred acres of playgrounds, ball fields, and an eighteen-hole golf course laid out by Joseph Bartholomew, an African American New Orleanian who had designed the city's best golf courses, and others throughout the South. Though Bartholomew, a childhood caddy for white golfers in Audubon Park, had created the city's best golf courses, Pontchartrain Park would be the only one on which he was allowed to play. That's the logic of segregation.

Tureaud strongly opposed Pontchartrain Park, correctly seeing it as a residential version of Lincoln Beach: a concession to black demands that was intended to strengthen Jim Crow. Nevertheless, in 1954, Pontchartrain Park opened with a thousand modern ranch-style homes on sale. Our prefabricated house was standard for the neighborhood: twelve hundred square feet, three small bedrooms, a den, a living room, a galley kitchen—all of which seems impossibly cramped by today's standards. The price? Between $9,500 and $25,000.

AMOS AND ALTHEA PIERCE were among the early buyers. They bought their dream home at the sales office downtown and stood there on Debore Drive, with their baby son Stacey, watching workmen deliver its parts on a truck and put it together.

At that time, decent housing for black folk was a rarity, a luxury. When you had an entire neighborhood of nice homes for black families, it was seen in the community as a whole that those black people must be rich. My mother said to us kids, "Listen, we are not rich. In case you don't know it, we are poor." She was a schoolteacher, and Daddy worked at the time at a furniture store. But housing was so bad for so many African Americans that, to them, our little brick houses in Pontchartrain Park were a kind of paradise.

The neighborhood filled up with families based on word of mouth. Shortly after we moved in, Daddy told one of his army buddies about the development, and he bought a house there. This also happened with teachers from Mary D. Coghill elementary school, where Tee taught. Dave Bartholomew, the lyricist who wrote hit songs with Fats Domino, lived around the corner. Ernest "Dutch" Morial, who in 1978 became the city's first black mayor, lived there. His son Marc, who served as New Orleans mayor from 1994 till 2002, and who now leads the Urban League, is a son of Pontchartrain Park. Grammy-winning jazz trumpeter Terence Blanchard grew up there too, as did Lisa Jackson, tapped by President Barack Obama to run the Environmental Protection Agency.

Most residents, of course, were only local heroes, but heroes they were. Coach Macburnette "Mac" Knox was our Eddie Robinson, our Vince Lombardi. He was at the center of the universe to us kids because he ran the Pontchartrain Park playground and coached football, basketball, and baseball. Coach Mac made sure all his players got home safely after practice. There was Leonard Morris, the postman and horn player, who would later save neighbors in his boat during Katrina, even though he was sick with cancer at the time.

Pontchartrain Park proved to be a magnet for black middle-class families because it helped build stable, secure lives in material conditions that, however separate, truly were the equal of whites. The only real difference between the housing and streetscapes in Pontchartrain Park and its next-door twin, Gentilly Woods, was the color of the homeowners' skin. The content of their character—hardworking, family-oriented, respectable—was exactly the same.

In 1959, post office worker and NAACP mainstay Arthur Chapital opposed the creation of a New Orleans campus of Southern University in Pontchartrain Park. (This was contrary to the initial inclination of the NAACP and A. P. Tureaud, though by 1969, Chapital persuaded them to file a suit against the dual-race college system.) A black newspaper derided it as "a Jim Crow commuter college." But SUNO was built anyway, opening in September 1959, providing the neighborhood with a historically black state university.

In the end, thanks to the tireless efforts of Tureaud and civil rights lawyers across the country, neither the Jim Crow subdivision, nor the Jim Crow golf course, nor the Jim Crow university protected Jim Crow. Court decrees would integrate parks and universities, and housing by outlawing restrictive covenants preventing sale of white-owned housing to black families. In the 1960s and 1970s, with all legal vestiges of segregation swept away, white flight from the city (in part a response to integration), opened up more Gentilly housing to African Americans. There's a startling historical irony here: Though New Orleans has never been more socially integrated, its housing patterns today have never been more segregated.

I WONDER WHAT TUREAUD, who died in 1972, would say about this. I've thought about what I would say to him about Pontchartrain Park, which became an incubator of so much African American excellence and professional achievement.

To give Tureaud his due, his belief that ghettoization had to go was noble and justified. He was not a single-minded integrationist. Tureaud was a sophisticated student of politics. He understood that if black folk had no access to mainstream economic power—that is, if they satisfied themselves with running small businesses that catered only to a black clientele—government would never take them seriously. Full citizenship requires full access. Every time black people accepted separate-but-equal crumbs from the table of whites, Tureaud believed, they strengthened white supremacy. Black self-sufficiency was an important good, but embracing it threatened to vitiate an even more important good—full access to all that the nation offers.

If I could sit down with Tureaud today, I would tell him: You were, and you are, absolutely right. We don't want separate but equal. But Amos and Tee's generation could not let the perfect become the enemy of the good. They had to take what was available to them, while they continued to stand with you in pressing forward the fight against segregation.

When Daddy came back from World War II, there were parts of the city in which he was born and raised that were off-limits to him because of the color of his skin. Yes, Pontchartrain Park was an act of appeasement by a white power structure that wanted to maintain its supremacy. Yes, Pontchartrain Park contributed to housing segregation in New Orleans. All of this is true.

But you know what? Pontchartrain Park gave our people a beach-head on which to establish a base that would carry the fight for equality into the next generation. When folks like Daddy and Tee bought their houses, they could not have imagined that they would see fair housing laws in their lifetime. They could not have predicted that the city's parks and universities would one day be open to them and their children (for which we have you above all to thank, A.P.). What they saw was the chance to make a decent life for their families, same as every other American had.

These ordinary black folks were civil rights pioneers too. They had to drive through the all-white Gentilly Woods to get home every night. They endured whites throwing batteries at their cars. My father bought the first gun he ever owned after white thugs began knocking on doors in Pontchartrain Park and punching black housewives when they answered. Yet they endured, they stood their ground and built a strong neighborhood where nearly everybody owned their homes, where folks were modest in income but rich with pride, where every child had access to a decent education, and where there were two parents in every household. Anything I am able to accomplish on stage, on screen, or on any other platform, I owe to my upbringing in Pontchartrain Park, Mr. Tureaud—and I know that I am not the only son or daughter of our neighborhood who feels that way.

The phrase "comforts of home" calls to mind bourgeois coziness, but the term actually connotes something more powerful. "Comfort" comes from Latin words meaning "to strengthen." In that sense, the comfort my generation received through their love of the Pontchartrain Park community, for us a haven in a heartless world dominated by white supremacist ideology, strengthened all of us, Mr. Tureaud, to carry forward the crusade that civil rights lawyers fought in the courtroom, and that my father fought in the South Pacific, for an America that lived up to its promise.

All his life, Daddy talked about the day he and Tee saw their house delivered to their little patch of paradise. He said that black folks back then would say, "Man, you must be rich if you live in Pontchartrain Park." It wasn't true. That modest rancher cost thirteen thousand dollars, and it took Daddy and Tee thirty years to pay it off. After he paid the last note, he framed the "paid in full" notice and hung it on the wall of his home office. It became an informal symbol of Daddy's authority, invoked whenever one of his sons gave him any lip. "You can say whatever you want," he would thunder, "but you see that thing on the wall? It says this is *my* house."

No, we weren't rich, but we were rich in spirit, and rich in dignity, and rich in love—and that intangible wealth paid off handsomely in the next generation, with political and economic gains made by the children of Pontchartrain Park. Maybe you couldn't have foreseen that back in the fifties, Mr. Tureaud. If so, that's understandable. You were putting your life on the line, literally, to fight for our freedom. The compromise my mother and father's generation made by moving into Pontchartrain Park looked to you like a retreat, a surrender.

And yet, if you were with us today, I am confident that you would agree with the judgment of Herman Plunkett, a Dillard administrator who moved into Pontchartrain Park in 1961: "It came out of something ugly, but it turned out to be something beautiful."

I know this because I saw it. I lived it. I breathed it, felt it, loved it. I am it. My all-American childhood is a testimony to what goodness can emerge when black folks in this country achieve what nearly all of us had been denied since we were stolen from Africa: the ordinary comforts of home.

And that private triumph, Mr. Tureaud, along with the public battles you won in the courtroom, produced for our people a double victory.

FOUR

THE FAMILY RESERVE

They say it takes a village to raise a child. For me, Pontchartrain Park was that village. The child it brought up was the father to the man that I am today.

I was born on December 8, 1963—the Feast of the Immaculate Conception of the Blessed Virgin, as my deeply Catholic mother would tell you—at Sara Mayo, a Garden District hospital on Jackson Avenue, two and a half blocks from the Mississippi River. Tee and Daddy brought me, their third son, home to the little brick rancher on Debore Drive.

That's the thing about Pontchartrain Park. Its utterly ordinary, 1950s-style, cookie-cutter Americana appearance veiled what was in fact an extraordinary accomplishment for black Americans: middle-class normalcy. The grandeur of the Garden District, the glorious townhomes of the Vieux Carré wearing wrought-iron balconies like garlands, the charming Creole cottages of the French faubourgs—we have none of that in Pontchartrain Park. No tourists will make the long drive out to see our neighborhood, because they have seen ones just like it a thousand times before, all over America. Strangely enough, tourists did come in the 1950s, on coaches where tour guides would show off the exotic Negro housewives, hanging out their laundry like any other American women. Mercifully, the novelty of that faded with time.

You can make the drive around the curving streets of Pontchartrain Park in just a few minutes. The entire neighborhood is only one square mile. The park and golf course are at its geographic heart; otherwise, it's one plain brick ranch house after another. The real value of Pontchartrain Park, though, is not what can be seen from the street, but what the neighborhood built inside all of us who had the good fortune to grow up there.

Here's the key to understanding Pontchartrain Park, the secret of its success: It was a place in which nearly everybody owned their house, and each house had in it both a mother and a father. Our dads never had to talk about the responsibilities fathers had to kids; they demonstrated them by example. Our moms did not have to carry the burden of raising children by themselves. They did it with their husbands. That was the norm in Pontchartrain Park: single-family homes, each family headed by a mom and a dad, and everybody's mom and dad obliged to support the other in their common mission of raising up the next generation.

My brothers and I were loved, and because we were loved, we were disciplined—not just by our parents, but by the whole community we lived in. I felt protected, with all those mothers and fathers around. I knew that if anything happened, there was an adult who would help me. Every grown-up in our neighborhood spoke with the authority of our own mother and father. We knew they loved us and had our best interests at heart.

When I was a kid, all of Pontchartrain Park was like my own backyard. This is not "Leave It to Black Beaver" nostalgia. It was real.

Debore Drive runs down a narrow strip of land between the park and the massive levee standing between our neighborhood and the Industrial Canal to the east. The canal had to contain storm surges during hurricanes. Because our neighborhood sat in some of the lowest land in the entire city, that big-shouldered wall of earth, over two stories tall, protected us from Armageddon.

If you had asked my older brothers, Stacey and Ron, and me, we would have said that the big shoulders that kept the danger far away belonged to our burly, barrel-chested Daddy. He worked as a stockroom clerk and deliveryman at Kirschman's, a furniture store right up the road from us. Every workday, Tee would grab her car keys and say, "I'm going to get your father." For a long five minutes, we Pierce boys would revel in the anticipation of Daddy's arrival so we could share our day with him.

Suddenly, the door would open and through the portal the conquering hero would return to tell his boys tales of adventure. This was what my dad didn't have growing up, and he was determined to give it to us.

Every afternoon, we had our family ritual. He would sit down in his chair and tell one of us kids to get him a cold Budweiser. I would climb up onto him just to be close. I could smell his own musk clinging to his Dickey's workshirt, an aroma that said, *I have worked hard all day to provide for my family*—what a great comfort that was to me as a child. It was enveloping, and it planted a powerful sense memory. It conveyed a sense of safety, of protection, of strength—and all these things in an atmosphere suffused with love.

The Pierce family also had a Sunday-night ritual that brought every week to a close. Tee would lay out a cheese-and-cracker platter on the coffee table and bring in beer—a Bud for Daddy, a Miller pony for herself—and we would settle in to watch *60 Minutes* on CBS. When Mike Wallace and Morley Safer signed off, that was when our school week began. My mother would begin her lesson plan for the week, and we boys started our weekend homework.

Evenings like that—the family at home, at peace, learning about the world together—were golden. But Amos and Tee's boys didn't always make it easy for them. I was the mischievous one, always doing something to get into trouble. Some days Daddy would come home from work bone-tired, flop down in that chair, and tell me to go get the belt (on the short drive home, Tee would have briefed him on my misbehavior that day). I would hand him the belt, he would say, "Stand right there," to the side of his chair, at perfect arm's length, then *whap!* he would deliver a lick across my backside. And I would be thinking, *Damn, Daddy, you couldn't even stand up to whip my ass?*

Amos ran a tight ship. When I was sixteen, I went on my first car date and drove to the fair at St. Mary's High School. My brother Ron was at his girlfriend's house nearby. He wanted to borrow the car while I was at the fair with my date, so I let him.

When the fair closed down for the night, Ron was nowhere to be found. I had to call my girlfriend's dad to pick her up. It was humiliating. Finally, Ron comes barreling around the corner in the family car. I was furious with him for screwing up my date. When we got home, I told my parents, who said, "Ron, you shouldn't have done that."

I couldn't believe it.

"That's it?" I said. "That's all he gets?"

My folks and I had a huge argument that ended with me storming out, going over to my friend Cedric's house. I complained that my parents weren't paying attention to me, and I resolved that I was going to show them: I wasn't going to go home.

Cedric's mom wouldn't let me stay the night there—that Pontchartrain Park parental solidarity again—so when I went back to our house, I slept in the backyard, in the cold. The next morning, when I was tiptoeing around the backyard, trying to figure out how I was going to manage my entrance, the sliding glass door opened. Tee stuck her head out. She was not as happy to see me as I had hoped.

"Come in here," she said sharply. "Boy, your father's so angry, you'd better get in here right now. You think you can just hang around here? You're not going to school?"

I said no, I know the rules. In our house, the understanding Daddy and Tee had with their sons is that we were welcome to live at home as long as we were in school. But if we were not in school, we had to support ourselves.

"I have a job Uptown," I lied. "I'm going to get an apartment, and as a matter of fact, I'm going to stay in school, too."

"Okay," she said. "Now that we know, you'd better get your ass on out of here. You can't stay."

"Fine," I told her. "I'm going to my place now. I'm going to come get my stuff later."

Lacking any other plan, I went to school. When I came home that evening, it was already dark—it must have been winter, because the sun had gone down early—and I noticed that something was blocking the light that usually came through the living room window. I crept into the house with trepidation, not knowing what to expect.

"Wendell's here," said Daddy. He turned to me. "We're going to have dinner, and after dinner, you and me are gonna talk."

I walked straight to the table and sat down with the rest. As soon as my plate was clean, Daddy leveled his gaze at me and said, "You finished? Okay, let's talk."

I ducked into my room to put my books down and couldn't believe what I was looking at. Everything was gone! The closet was empty, all the books were gone from the shelves, the dresser drawers were open, and empty, all my football trophies had disappeared, as had the mattress. The only thing that remained was the box spring from my bed.

"I'm waiting on you in the living room," my father said.

When I stepped in, everything I owned was there in the living room, piled high against the window. It took my breath away.

"Sit down," Daddy said.

I sat down.

"So, you gonna run away from here, have us worried last night?"

"Yeah," I said. "You guys weren't fair to me. You didn't tell Ron that—"

"Okay, so here's the deal," Daddy said. "You got a choice. You either live in *my* house, and live by *my* rules and do what I say, or you take all of that shit that *I* bought for you—I'm going to give to you— and take it to that so-called apartment of yours tonight, and get the hell out of my house."

He was on a roll.

"I am *not* putting up with this shit," Daddy continued. "You don't so-called run away from home and don't call home, and have me and your mother all worried about you. Don't you ever do that, *ever.* So you have a choice: Live here by my rules or take your shit and get out. Now, Wendell, what's it going to be?"

"I guess I'll stay here and live by your rules," I muttered.

"Good," he said. "Now take all that shit back to your room."

I spent the whole night putting my room back together. As humiliating as that incident was, it was one of the best things my father ever did for me. It was all about a strong father showing discipline.

As fierce as Daddy was in maintaining moral order and respect in his own home, he was, if anything, more fierce in defending his sons against outside threats. He might blister our backsides if we acted up too much at home, but we never once doubted that on the other side of that threshold, Amos Pierce had our backs.

My brother Stacey was nine years older than I, and he endured traumas that I was too young to understand at the time. When I was just a toddler, Stacey, who was still just a child, was on the civil rights front lines. He was part of the Ruby Bridges generation, the first to integrate New Orleans public schools.

Bridges was one of the first children to integrate New Orleans schools after U.S. District Judge J. Skelly Wright ordered the city, after six years of delay, to obey the Supreme Court's *Brown v. Board of Education* decision. On the morning of November 14, 1960, federal marshals escorted the black first-grader into William Frantz Elementary, five blocks from the Bridges home in the Upper Ninth Ward. A white mob stood outside, waving signs and Confederate flags, and screaming racist epithets at the six-year-old girl. Bridges would later say that she at first thought the frenzied crowds and the police barricades must mean it was Carnival time.

Newsreel footage from later that day shows white mothers hustling their little children out the front door of Frantz as if rescuing them from a plague carrier. The next day, Judge Leander Perez, the cigar-chomping militant segregationist political don of St. Bernard and Plaquemines parishes, led a massive rally at which he urged white parents to withdraw their kids from the integrated schools.

"Don't wait for your daughter to be raped by these Congolese," he thundered. "Don't wait until the burr-heads are forced into your schools. Do something about it now."

That kind of hatred doesn't dissipate overnight. Five years after Ruby Bridges and a handful of black children first broke the wall of segregation, opening the door for more black children in New Orleans public schools, my brother Stacey learned what race hate meant in his first week at P. A. Capdau Junior High.

He came home from seventh grade one day in tears. The next day, Daddy took him back and walked into the principal's office with Stacey in tow.

"Stacey, tell the principal what's going on," he said.

"These kids are hitting me and calling me 'nigger' every time I come to school," my brother said.

The principal apologized and said he did not know it was happening. He promised Daddy to protect Stacey. Daddy told Stacey not to let it happen again, and if it did, to go to the principal and tell him.

"Now you know what's been going on, please take care of it," Daddy said.

"I will," said the principal.

"Because if you don't," Daddy said, "you'll have to deal with me."

The principal was shocked. "You don't have to get indignant, sir."

"Now, now, I'm not," said Daddy. "I'm just telling you. If you don't deal with this, if it happens again, you *will* have to deal with me."

When I found out years later how my father had handled it, I was astonished by his courage, daring to say something like that to a white man in authority during the early days of desegregation. You have to remember that the Selma-to-Montgomery marches were happening at the same time. On the television news at night, America saw images of black people being fire-hosed, tear-gassed, and savagely beaten for standing up to white authority. Black parents like Daddy and Tee had to teach their children how to navigate a world like that.

There were no cameras to record deeds like what my father did that day at Capdau. It was a minor detail in the scope of civil rights history. But it took countless small but significant acts of courage and dignity like that one by mothers and fathers and children, walking through history with heads unbowed, to make a revolution. A new day was dawning in America, and Amos Pierce wanted to make sure that his boy and the white man who had authority over him knew it.

Stacey was so smart. He was a scientist from boyhood. One Christmas, he got a chemistry set and a microscope. One day, he took a drop of water from our dog's bowl, put it on a slide, and invited me to take a look. It was crawling with amoebas. That knocked me flat.

"There's a whole world inside that drop of water, Wendell," Stacey said.

That scientific mentality defined my oldest brother to me. But Stacey graduated from high school in 1972, just as the draft ended. He joined the Army ROTC at West Texas State University (today, West

Texas A&M University), anticipating that the Vietnam War would be over by the time he graduated, and that he could enter the military as an officer. Military service was such a tradition in my family. My father was thrilled that his firstborn son was going to be an officer.

He got homesick at West Texas and transferred to Southeastern Louisiana University, in Hammond, not far away. It was there that Stacey got into serious trouble—and my parents taught me a valuable lesson about what family means.

In my family, my folks never talked down to their kids. They always shared information, often in family meetings. One night, they called Ron and me into the living room.

"Stacey got arrested tonight," Daddy said. He had been caught with marijuana.

"Lesson number one: You're not supposed to be dealing with drugs," Tee said. "See what happens? He might be kicked out of school because he was messing with drugs. That's why we tell you guys not to fool with drugs.

"Second," she continued, "whatever you do doesn't just affect you; it affects the whole family. Your daddy has to go up to Hammond and get your brother out of jail, and then he's got to go to work in the morning. He's not going to get any sleep. Everything you do affects the whole family."

She explained that they were going to have to take money out of my college fund to bail Stacey out and pay a lawyer to handle his case. Because I was younger than Ron, they would have more time to replace it, Tee said, and she promised that they would. But she wasn't going to let the teaching power of this crisis moment be lost.

"See how what you do affects your whole family?" she said, pounding home the lesson. "See how what you do ruins things for every-body?"

Maybe Tee thought this might all be too much for Ron and me to deal with, given how young we were. She quickly reassured us.

"Other families say you shouldn't talk to the kids about these things. That's not our way," Tee said. "We share things with you kids, so you will always feel free to share things with us. We're your family."

That taught me the strength of family, and the meaning of family. We all have each other's back. We will help each other when one of us gets in trouble, and we will fight for each other. But we will also hold each other accountable.

Stacey recovered and went on to finish his undergraduate work. Then he left for Howard University to get his Ph.D. in zoology. While he was there, Georgetown University across town in Washington, D.C., recruited him to attend its medical school. Though Stacey wanted to be a doctor, he couldn't handle the pressure of that grueling first year, trying to complete both of these complex degrees. He had a nervous breakdown.

He was renting a room in a woman's home in the District. Stacey's landlady phoned my parents one day to sound the alarm. "I'm really afraid your son is going to commit suicide," she said. "I think he has a gun. I hear this clicking."

Tee and Daddy got on a plane at once, and Uncle L.C. joined them. It turned out that Stacey didn't have a gun at all, that he had merely been clicking the light switch on and off. But it was clear that he was in serious mental trouble.

"Come home," my parents said to him. "Just come home and rest."

When Stacey returned to New Orleans to convalesce, we all entered family therapy together. This was a great thing about my parents. They didn't care that seeking out therapy was taboo in the black community back then. They just wanted to do whatever they needed to do to help their son get better.

After he recovered, Stacey started working in research at the Louisiana State University medical school on Tulane Avenue in New Orleans. My uncles L.C. and L.H. were thrilled to discover that Stacey was working with a famous researcher who experimented on pigs. At the end of a research project, the school had to find some way to dispose of the pigs.

"Y'all got hogs?" my uncles asked Stacey. Indeed they did. Off my uncles went to the LSU medical school to pick up free pork. We had a couple of *boucheries* with LSU's pigs. The folks up the bayou couldn't believe their good fortune. "Stacey, this is brilliant," they said. "You get to be a scientist, and we get free hogs."

Later, after I had started at Juilliard, Stacey told us that he had been thinking about going to dental school. Daddy pushed back, telling him that he had a good job as a researcher at LSU. Why give that up?

"Because I've always wanted to be a doctor," Stacey said. "Maybe I can be a dental doctor."

"Man, do it," I advised. By then, I had already been through the drama with my folks about convincing them that I should follow my dream and become an actor. Fortunately, I knew how to deal with that pushback. This was the first time for Stacey. I'm sure Tee said, "Good, son, whatever you want to be, you can be." Daddy, as usual, wanted him to consider all the pros and cons.

Stacey was older than most of his classmates at the LSU School of

Dentistry. Because of his med school background and extensive work on his Ph.D., he caught on so quickly that he was able to serve as a teaching assistant his first year. Yet he had trouble making models of teeth, which was a requirement for passing the course. Rather than give my brother a chance to work on his modeling over the summer, which was standard practice, the professor forced him to repeat his entire first year of dental school.

I had never liked LSU because, with the exception of a few graduate students, until federal courts ordered full integration of the university in 1964, black citizens of Louisiana could not attend the state's flagship school. When they humiliated my brother Stacey, it got personal. Since then, LSU has been dead to me.

Stacey was deeply discouraged, but my parents, true to form, told him not to give in. *You'll be a doctor for a long time,* they said. *Play the long game.*

And so he did. He graduated from dental school, married his beautiful wife, Debbie, and a short time later, in November 1994, was ready to celebrate his fortieth birthday. The family was throwing him a big party in New York. At the time, I was in London filming *Hackers,* and knowing what a tough journey Stacey had completed, I negotiated time off in advance to fly back for my brother's birthday party. Producers pressured me to cancel at the last minute because of scheduling problems, but I wasn't going to give in. My brother meant too much to me. The producers had to fly me to New York on the Concorde to get me there and back in time for shooting.

I wouldn't have missed Stacey's triumph for the world.

Soon thereafter, doctors found that Stacey had a serious congenital heart condition. They told him he would one day have to be on the transplant list. But that day seemed far off; he was as active and apparently as healthy as ever. He was living in Pomona, New York, teaching at New York University's College of Dentistry and giving dental care to migrant workers.

Then one day, when he was forty-five, his heart just stopped beating.

It was a beautiful Saturday morning in Los Angeles when my mother called.

"Wendell?"

"Yeah?"

"Your brother Stacey Pierce died at home this morning in his sleep." That's just how she phrased it: a clear, deliberate declaration. Though I could hear the grief and pain in her voice, she suppressed it out of concern for me.

After answering lots of my questions, she said, "Wendell, are you all right?" That was Tee: taking care of me even though she had gone through something even more devastating.

I'LL NEVER FORGET STANDING at my brother's wake, looking at my parents humbled by grief. I imagined them in that moment, staring with hollow, tear-soaked eyes at the body of their firstborn son in his coffin, as a young couple looking into the crib of their baby boy with eyes full of hope and wonder. The physical power of grief to work a transformation stunned me. They held on to each other, my father cradling my mother in his big arm.

They looked as if they had lost everything. And they had.

Ron didn't really know what to do at Stacey's funeral. He is the Pierce brother who is most like our mother in that he doesn't want to cry or to show emotion. Keep the fire concentrated within. Never did I hear my mother cry. Oh, you would see tears flow when she was upset, but she wept silently. Like our mother, Ron is fierce in the privacy of his emotions.

If STACEY was the scientist in the family, Ron was the athlete. He was good at sports and school, had lots of girlfriends, and never rocked the boat. Growing up, he was steady, gregarious, and loyal. Ron and I were born twenty-three months apart. My parents were honest with me, telling me, "Wendell, you were our surprise." They never said "mistake," only "surprise." My brother was a string bean, like our mother; I was like our father, stout and barrel-chested. But whatever Ron did, I was going to do next. It was a friendly competition.

Daddy put up a basketball goal in the backyard. Ron and I played basketball so much that we wore all the grass away and hardened the ground with our footfalls. Ron told me I played too much, but the truth is, I couldn't stop until I won a game. If Ron and I were wrestling or roughhousing, I wouldn't stop till I won a match.

We would compete all the time, as brothers will, but in our case it was undertaken with love, and the desire to make each other better. Within the family, we constantly tested ourselves against each other, but outside the family, we supported each other without fail. "I think you can beat that guy" was our mantra to each other.

I learned from Ron the value of staying focused and steadfast. He's unwavering when it comes to pursuing what he wants. He doesn't have to talk it to death and wonder what others will think of it; he just does it.

Like Stacey, Ron went through his baptism by fire when he helped integrate Holy Cross, a Catholic high school. He came home crying because his white classmates were calling him nigger, and my folks built him back up, telling him that he could not let them win by quitting.

My brother had strong principles, and he stuck to them. When his high school classmates said that they weren't planning to go to college, Ron said, "No, we're all going to college. We are meant for that."

When Ron finished high school and prepared to head off to further his education, he came to our father and said, "I'm leaving now. I don't want you to work two jobs anymore. It's just Wendell left at home, Daddy."

I had no idea what he was talking about. I knew my father did a little work at night, but it turned out that for years, Daddy had been working a night job as a janitor at the nearby University of New Orleans to provide for his family. He would come in from Kirschman's, the furniture store, in the evening, have supper, put us to bed, and then leave. It never occurred to me to wonder where he was going. All I knew was that he was there for breakfast in the morning. Now, because of Ron's disclosure, I learned that my father was sweeping and mopping floors while the rest of us slept, so his sons could have a better life than he had. I was just a teenager, but it was starting to dawn on me what a great man my father really was.

In high school, Ron resolved to apply to the United States Military Academy at West Point, a move that raised him in my father's eyes to the high heavens. Uncle L.H., a proud military veteran, was tickled too, and swore that if Ron got in, he would be at his graduation.

In the end, Ron did so well at Holy Cross that U.S. senator J. Bennett Johnston nominated him for West Point, even though our family had no political influence. Ron spent a year at West Point Prep preparing for the academy, and then completed his four years. Sure enough, Daddy and Tee were at his graduation, as were Uncle L.H. and Aunt Tee Mae, who still lived in Brooklyn and was the mother of all of us who came through New York. I can still see my father and L.H. right now, at graduation: When the graduates threw their hats up into the air, the two old veterans' eyes filled with tears of pride.

When Ron presented himself to them, Daddy and L.H. saluted him smartly, addressing him as "Lieutenant Pierce." And following the West Point tradition, our parents were the first to pin their son's lieutenant bars on his lapel. How poignant it was that almost twenty-five years later, Ron pinned Daddy's long-delayed medals onto his lapel.

Family, God, and country. That's what the Pierces are all about.

Lieutenant Pierce went on to work as a nuclear arms officer in the mid-1980s, in what turned out to be the final years of the Cold War. The Pentagon chose him for that critically important job because he had studied philosophy at West Point, and they trusted his steadiness. After he ended his military career, I asked Ron how he knew he had it within him to turn the key to launch nuclear missiles if the order came down.

"I knew that if that order was given, that you and the family had been attacked," he said.

In the early 1990s, at the height of the first Gulf War, Ron pointed out on television a news story about a family protesting their soldier son's death at his funeral. Ron said, "Wendell, if I'm ever killed in war, don't do that. I made a choice to be in the military. If something happens to me, bury me with honors and go on, but don't ever use that as an opportunity to protest. If you want to honor me, don't do that."

After leaving the military, Ron moved to San Francisco and went to work in telecommunications. He did well, but lost his job when his company downsized after the financial crash in 2008. His marriage ended. Ron was too proud to show emotion and reach out to any of us. We lost touch with him for months.

"I didn't want to be a burden on anyone," Ron says today. "Tee had raised me right, and I felt like a failure. I wanted to figure this out by myself."

Finally, our worried mother took me aside and gave me marching orders. "Wendell, that's your brother," she said. "Go find him and bring him home."

On the flight west, I wondered how in the world I was going to find my brother in a big city. I resolved that if I did locate Ron, I wasn't going to ask his permission to bring him home: He was coming, whether he wanted to or not.

Finding him wasn't as hard as I had expected. He was at home, but I could tell he wasn't staying there much. He was unkempt and visibly depressed. The conversation we had was simple.

"Ron," I said, leveling my gaze at my brother, "you are coming home. You are in trouble, and we aren't going to watch you fall. This is what family is for. You are coming home for as long as it takes to get back on your feet."

There was no protest left in him. He was exhausted.

"When are we leaving?" he murmured.

"Now!" I boomed. "We are family!"

Ron heard me. Soon, we were back on a plane to New Orleans, to our childhood home, in a place that welcomed him to heal in the care of those who knew and loved him.

Ron got back on his feet and went to work in Washington, D.C., for the Democratic National Committee, then on veterans' outreach for the Obama administration. Today, he is a PBS executive overseeing public television's Stories of Service initiative in support of veterans.

"I knew I could always go home," Ron tells me today, "but without you showing up in San Francisco, I would not have taken the initiative to go home myself. You can be tough and stubborn, but you're a very generous person who loves our family. That's what I love so much about you."

His time in self-imposed exile taught Ron how important it was to stay connected to family and never to let your pride prevent you from reaching out to your family for help.

"I've been able to share with my kids my whole story," he says. "One thing I want to instill in them: Life is a roller coaster, and everyone you pass on the street has had ups and downs. There is nothing you can tell me about yourself that would make me not support you. It's important to reach out to family, always."

That's a lesson we learned in Daddy and Tee's home. That's a lesson Tee learned around Mamo and Papo's table. And that's a lesson that my brother is passing on to his kids.

THERE WERE other important lessons to come from our childhood. Because Stacey was so much older than Ron and me, neither of us knew about the racist hazing he had been through at Capdau Junior High. When it came time for me to be bused to Mildred Osborne Elementary School to start the new gifted and talented program, the first time I would be in an integrated school, my parents sat me down and had The Talk—that sad but necessary ritual all black parents go through with their children, in which they pass on the hard-won wisdom of What to Do When Confronted by Racist White Folks.

"Wendell, you're going to be going out to the school with white boys, and they're going to come after you," Daddy said. "They're going to come after you in a group. There's always going to be a group, and you're going to get your ass kicked."

I didn't understand what he meant.

"You're going to get your ass kicked," he repeated. "But you look for the leader, or the biggest one, they're usually the same guy, and while you're getting your ass kicked, when they jump you, you make sure you grab him, and you kick *his* ass. You make sure you kick his ass, and he will always remember you. And they'll never mess with you again, because he'll come out of there, 'All right, we took care of that nigger,' and they'll never mess with you again."

"Dad, are you for real?"

"I'm telling you, that's how white boys operate."

I started school at Osborne hyped. I was in school with white kids for the first time in my life. I was on hair trigger. If a white kid had come up to me and said, "Hey, how you doin', I'm Johnny," I would have punched him in the mouth.

So I was waiting for the mob. And then, on the playground, it finally happened.

We were playing a game we made up called Kill the Man with the Ball. There was this one white boy, Chet. Crew cut, flannel shirt, sleeves rolled up. He looked like an extra in *Mississippi Burning*. He threw the ball up and screamed, "Niggers against the whites!"

There were only three black kids: me, Paul Jordan, and Alexander Brumfield. Alexander, who was also from Pontchartrain Park, was a gentle giant. He was so afraid. Paul, with his big Afro, looked like that era's version of Michael Jackson. All the girls loved him, but now he had to be not a lover, but a fighter. And there I was, as if giant screw pumps were pushing a flood of adrenaline through my veins.

This was just like my father told me. The white boys circled us. And I was like, "Oh, *yeah!* Bring it!"

I had gone through training, the ambush had come, and I had recognized it. Paul was like, "What's going on?"

"This is it, man! Get back-to-back! Get back-to-back!" I said, barking orders like a little general. The three of us got back-to-back, and I was like, "Come on, you bastards, this is it. Come on, Chet! I want you! Come on, Chet, I'm going to kill you! I can't wait! I can't wait!"

I was scared to death, but that's what it was all about: facing your fears. Paul and Alexander looked at me as if to say, *Wendell, what's going on?* and I was like, *No, I'm ready for these bastards.*

"Let's get these niggers!" Chet said.

The showdown started with twenty people surrounding us, but this crazy son of a bitch Wendell Pierce scared off about fifteen of them. They wanted no part of me. They were like, *Chet, this is on you.* Chet ran in and we had this big scrum. It ended up being just Chet and me going at it, and I whipped Chet's ass up and down the playground.

By the time it ended, Chet staggered off the playground in ignominious defeat, muttering, "Yeah, that's right, we got them niggers." Just like my dad said he would. And he never bothered me again.

I don't want to give the impression that our life was all about living under siege conditions. We had all the normal joys of an American childhood, just like my parents' generation. Despite all the racism and poverty they lived with, whenever my mother and her siblings got together, all they would talk about was the good times they had growing up on the bayou. In my case, Pontchartrain Park was like the Garden of Eden. I played football in the park, and basketball on the courts, and Little League baseball on the two diamonds. Walking across the golf course after school was a delight. Sometimes I would throw the golfers' balls into the lagoon, just to be mischievous. We went to concerts and festivals in the park. Life seemed so simple, so pure, and so beautiful.

"You and I didn't realize it, but we were growing up in Mayberry," Ron said to me once long after we were grown men. True.

The freedom we felt to play within the strict boundaries of the neighborhood was a great gift. The park at the center of our neighborhood was our wonderland, an enchanted landscape and a stage on which to act out our boyish adventures.

As much as we loved the park, not everything was idyllic. We kids were haunted by the Lady in White, a ghost who lived in the park's bathrooms. After dark, the single bulb illuminating the golfers' bathroom cast an eerie glow you could spot from far away. The echo of water running in the urinal made a sound we imagined as spectral.

If we gathered in the park at night, somebody would say, "I'll give you a dollar if you go in there."

"Nooooo!"

If the light flickered, that was our signal to run for our lives.

Right off the third fairway is a lagoon. In the middle of it sits a nub of land we boys dubbed "Nanny Goat Island." It might as well have been the Lost Island of Atlantis. We thought often about what happened on Nanny Goat Island, and how great it would be to cross the water and plant our flag on its shores. But there were no Columbuses in our gang. Could we build a raft? No, no; the lagoon was an uncrossable barrier. The mysteries of Nanny Goat Island would forever be out of our reach.

In 2013, when I went to play the golf course for the first time, I eyeballed Nanny Goat Island and realized the water in the lagoon was probably only thigh-high. We could have easily waded over. I'm glad we never tried. It was tantalizing to have a land at the heart of our neighborhood that we could never reach. It was a spur to our childhood imaginations.

One of the highlights of any Pontchartrain Park kid's year was the annual spring weekend fair at the Bethany United Methodist Church. I lived for it. It was like Christmas in springtime. It's astonishing to reflect on how something as simple as a church fair was all that it took to fill a child's heart back then.

My mother would give me ten dollars for the weekend and send me off to the fair. For fifty cents a round, I would toss rings on bottles and throw sandbags on checkerboard squares, all on a quest for a prize. There were all kinds of games to play with your friends, and when you got tired, you would go get a "church plate"—that is, a plate of food prepared by church ladies. You'd get stuffed peppers or stuffed crab, maybe some green beans and potato salad, served to you with a square of waxed paper on top. Somehow, the waxed paper made the food taste better, or so it seemed to me. You would pay for your cold drink, then have the privilege of sticking your hand deep into the ice in the cooler to fetch a can. It felt so cold, and so good. After the lunch break, it was right back to the games.

One year, dusk was falling late on a Sunday afternoon, and the fair was winding down. By then, my friend Carlton Watson and I were broke, but we had to squeeze just a few minutes more out of the fair weekend.

Though Tee had sternly instructed me not to borrow money from anybody, I devised a way around it. "Carlton," I said, "doesn't your sister have some money?" He asked her for five dollars, and she gave it to him. We spent every last cent of it.

The next day when I got home from school, my mother was on fire.

"Boy, what did I tell you yesterday?" Tee said. "Didn't I tell you not to beg anybody for money? I teach that Watson girl, and she told me today that you took all her money at the fair."

Now, here's where it gets interesting, and you see the particular way children of my time and place received discipline.

"Boy, you're out there embarrassing me," Tee fumed. We all heard that from our mothers and fathers back then. Parents drummed it into their children's heads that when they were out in the public square, they were representing the family. Southerners tend to judge the quality of one's parenting by the behavior of one's children. They raise their children to think of themselves as representatives of the family, and to behave accordingly.

My mother lived in the community where she taught. To everyone there, I was Mrs. Pierce's son. I had a responsibility to carry that name with pride, with purpose, and with honor and dignity. I didn't find this oppressive; in fact, I was proud to be Mrs. Pierce's son. It carried such weight.

I'll never forget that when I first went away to school in New York City, the local newspaper reported that Mrs. Pierce's son was headed to Juilliard. I came home on one break and saw Fat Albert (yes, we really had a Fat Albert in Pontchartrain Park). He had taken the wrong path. Fat Albert had not gone on to college and was still at home, hanging around, doing nothing with his life.

Fat Albert told me, "Man, you lucky."

"How's that?"

"You have Mrs. Pierce as your mother," he said. "She kept you on the straight and narrow, and look at you now, you doing good."

I felt pride, but I also felt such guilt. Albert didn't have what I had. I went home and told that to my mom, and thanked Tee for all she had done for me.

"If I didn't have you, I would have been like Albert," I said.

"Boy, don't listen to him," Tee said. "His mama is a principal. His mama did all the same things. Albert's been that way since he was a little boy. His mother's a good woman, and she did all the same things I did. He just didn't want to listen. You should feel sorry for his mother."

Next time I saw Albert out, I told him, "You ought to think about how you treat your mother."

Good parents provide all they can to prepare their children to succeed, but the children have to feel a reciprocal bond of obligation toward the parents. In turn, both parents and children feel a responsibility to the broader community to do their part to maintain the common good.

Everybody's parents looked out for everybody else's kids. I never knew the name of the man I passed by every day on the walk home from school. He would almost always be in his front yard, and when I passed, he would call out to me, saying things like, "Hey, Little Amos, you on your way home, huh?" A block later I would walk in our front door, and they were expecting me. The sentry of Mendez Street had phoned to say I would be there shortly.

There was one kid in the neighborhood, Brian, who had been pulling off some petty burglaries and putting the stolen loot under his bed. The way he got caught demonstrates the moral system of Pontchartrain Park. Brian's mother was cleaning his room and found the stolen property under his bed. Instead of making him give back what he had taken and apologize, she turned him in to the police. She had raised him better than that, and she wasn't going to have the family name smeared by his lawbreaking. There would be no excuses.

What happened to Brian would have happened to any of us had we done the same. The integrity and stability of the community that we all depended on required respect for the code, respect for the family, and respect for yourself. Community requires covenant. Growing up in that Pontchartrain Park cocoon helped us kids develop our inner strengths in an atmosphere of mutual trust and support. With the exception of the time white kids in a Volkswagen Beetle drove through our neighborhood taking potshots with a gun at kids (I don't know if it was a small rifle or a BB gun), the only time we had to confront racism on our turf was when we would cross The Ditch—a drainage ditch between Pontchartrain Park and Gentilly Woods that marked the no-man's-land between the black boys and the white boys. Every now and then, we would stage raids on the other side of The Ditch, for the sheer thrill of it. To see it now, it's just a puny groove in the soggy ground, but to us kids, it might as well have been the DMZ.

THE DITCH, and what it stood for, served to remind us that as good as we had it in Pontchartrain Park, there was a world beyond its borders in which we were seen as the enemy. But in our own little piece of paradise, we were free to let our guard down and just be kids.

Our father taught us the skills of combat with a world filled with people who did not have our best interests at heart, and our mother instructed us in the inner disciplines that would help us conquer that world. She had learned well from Papo and Mamo how to use her wits and her tenacity of character to overcome anything the world threw at her.

And it wasn't just her boys to whom she taught these things. She made sure her students at Coghill Elementary, the neighborhood black school where she taught, learned the same lessons her parents had taught her.

When the kids didn't have their homework and came to her with various excuses, she wouldn't accept them.

"You don't think I was poor?" she would say. "You don't think I had problems at home when I was your age? Two plus two still equals four, and you still have to know that."

"Yes, Mrs. Pierce, but my mama, she couldn't—"

"Okay, but what is two plus two? Isn't it four? Why didn't you write that down?"

"Well, I didn't get around to doing my homework."

Then she would let them have it. Tee's point was that the world is not going to cut you any slack, especially if you're black, and even more so if you're black and poor or working-class. You had better learn that lesson early, child, and commit yourself to working hard, getting an education, and never, ever giving up or giving in. There is no other way.

This was how she responded to the outrage of racism. The white-hot anger we had inside of us over the way we were treated is nothing to be ashamed of. The art is mastering it, so that it doesn't master us. Papo and Mamo trained their children never to give racists the satisfaction of victory. "Don't ever be the kind of person they think you are," they would say.

My mother never liked to show emotion, but she had a long memory. She never forgot the night riders burning the car on College Point Lane. She never forgot her father, a hardworking farmer, being taken advantage of by the white man at the plantation store. But she channeled all that indignation into a passion for education as the only path to victory over our oppressors.

Injustice was going to come, Tee taught, but turn that anger to your advantage, let it fuel your fire and inflame your knowledge. And always watch out for folks who are going to pretend that they have your best interest at heart, but who really might not want you to get ahead in life.

The temptation to leave the straight path could take many forms. It might even come from a well-meaning teacher who will tell you, "Don't worry, you're going through a lot right now, so you might not be able to understand these concepts." Tee always hated teachers like that, willing to demand less from students because the kids were hard-luck cases. She knew from her own life experience that those were precisely the kids who needed to be challenged so they could develop the strengths they needed to get out of the hole into which they were born.

When teachers would try to coddle me in that way, Tee wouldn't have it. "You don't have to patronize my son," she would say. "How much homework does he have? If he's supposed to do it, he's going to do it."

Tee stayed on my back about reading. Books opened up my young mind to worlds beyond Pontchartrain Park. In seventh grade, 1975–1976, I had a great teacher, a white South African woman named Mrs. Wagner. She introduced us to novels like *Things Fall Apart* by Chinua Achebe, about the spirit of revolution in West Africa, and Alan Paton's antiapartheid novel *Cry, the Beloved Country*. Mrs. Wagner opened my eyes to a lot of change going on in the world.

The way I was raised, reading was the norm. It got to the point in middle school where we would ask each other in the halls, "Man, what are you reading?" Our community drummed into our heads the imperative of education. And they all pulled together to help us succeed. When I was having trouble with trigonometry, I went to see Mr. Tanner, who lived on the other side of the park. That was the thing in our neighborhood: You're having trouble with math, go see Mr. Tanner, he'll help you. It was just part of life. First, I'll play a little basketball, then I'll run over to Mr. Tanner's to get help with my math. He helped me understand trig by showing me how to approach a problem with the same sense of creativity I brought to my high school acting classes. There was only one right answer, but there were often several ways to arrive at it.

My mother rode me hard on my lessons. If I was supposed to have two hours of homework at night and I finished it in one hour, she wouldn't let up: "Go on to the next chapter, then." That was because she knew education was key. She came from a time and a place where education really changed lives for the better. Tee's parents, undereducated country people who lived hard lives under oppression that black children of my generation could scarcely imagine, had taught her well how much education meant. She and her siblings were living proof that Papo and Mamo were right. They were living examples of what any child, no matter how poor and disadvantaged, can accomplish if he or she really believes that "*can't* died three days before the creation of the world."

As I said earlier, Tee instructed us kids not to let passion in the face of injustice overwhelm our reason, but she balanced that advice by exhorting us never, ever to forget our dignity as human beings or our right to be treated fairly. If we kids came back and complained about something we thought was an injustice, my mother's reaction was, "What did you decide to do? Did you just cower? What are you going to do about it?"

She delivered this lesson powerfully one day when I was in high school and competed in a Saturday morning race around the golf course. I came in second in my age group. But when it came time to award the honors, the officials said that I came in third, and awarded me the bronze medal.

My mother wasn't having it.

"Wait a minute," she said to me. "You *did* come in second."

"Yeah, but it's just a little fun run," I said. "Who cares?"

"Oh, no, you came in second, you go tell them."

"Let it go, Tee."

"No, don't you dare let it go."

She approached an official and made a big deal out of it. He admitted that there had been a mistake, but the medals had already been given out, so there was nothing he could do.

Tee stood her ground. "My son earned the silver, and you will give it to him." And so they did. I was so embarrassed—and told her so as we walked home. She wouldn't accept that from me, any more than she would accept the biased judgment from the officials.

"Don't be embarrassed when you're right," she said.

The lesson? Don't settle for injustice. You can't just sit back and accept it. You may be the only one, but you have being right, and fairness, on your side. And once you know something is right, and fair, even when others don't want to recognize it, you can take comfort in knowing that. You may be alone, you may be isolated, but it's right and it's fair, and once you've determined that, that's your shield and source of strength for all the attacks you'll face from standing alone. Even if you don't ultimately triumph, your enemies will still know in their hearts that they have done wrong, and they will also know that they could not conquer what is within you.

"Any man more right than his neighbors constitutes a majority of one," said Henry David Thoreau, who had nothing on Althea Lee Pierce.

It was hard for Tee to live at peace with the fact that you never really knew what people stood for. You could be getting along fine with everybody and think you had everything figured out, and then something ugly would erupt out of racism, or ignorance, or something like that. That upset my mother more than anything. *How can you see me one day and smile, try to hurt me the next day, then act like nothing happened?*

This deeply affected her relationship with the Catholic Church. My mother was devoutly Catholic her entire life. She was the church lady people would call on to recite the rosary at funerals. Nobody came between Tee and the Lord. But she didn't have a lot of use for the men who ran the Church—and she came by her distrust honestly.

St. Gabriel's was my mother and father's geographical parish when they moved to Pontchartrain Park. On their first visit, my mother sat down before mass. An usher approached and said to her that the Negro pews were in the back. She and Daddy rose, turned, and walked to the back of the church—and kept on going. They never returned. They started attending St. Paul's, an all-black Josephite parish a few miles away.

Some years later, a priest from St. Gabriel's came to the house while my mother was out. My father let him in and they sat together in the living room.

"We hear that you all are Catholics," the priest said. "Why don't we see you in the parish?"

"I'll be honest with you, Father," said Daddy. "When we first came here, we went to mass there, but we were told to go sit in the back of the church. That upset my wife and me. How could you have segregation in the house of God?"

The priest got his back up. "If you get sick or somebody dies," he huffed, "don't be coming to me."

My father rose and said, "Don't worry about that. Thank you." He showed the priest the door. When Tee got home, she wanted to blaze off to the rectory and blister that priest's ears, but Daddy calmed her down.

I suppose that it's the priests like Father Maloney in Assumption Parish who keep you in the Church, but priests like the one from St. Gabriel's make it hard to stick around. The Archdiocese of New Orleans had been an inconstant friend of black Catholics. Archbishop Joseph Rummel, a German-born prelate who served as the city's Catholic leader from 1935 until his death in 1964 at the age of eighty-eight, took stands against racism that were unusually strong for a white man in that era.

He was the first Catholic archbishop to break the color barrier at the city's Notre Dame Seminary, ordering it to admit black seminarians in 1948. When City Park refused to allow an integrated holy procession, he canceled it. In 1953, the same year he ordained the first black diocesan priest in New Orleans, Rummel issued a pastoral letter that ordered the end to segregation in all Catholic institutions of the archdiocese.

"Let there be no further discrimination or segregation in the pews, at the Communion rail, at the confessional and in parish meetings, just as there will be no segregation in the kingdom of heaven," he wrote, a year too late for Daddy and Tee at St. Gabriel's.

Rummel wasn't kidding. He closed one parish whose white members protested his assignment of a black priest to their community. But when time came to desegregate the city's parochial schools in the wake of the 1954 *Brown v. Board of Education* decision, the elderly archbishop's resolve faltered in the face of much stiffer white resistance than he faced in desegregating parishes.

The racial resentment of white New Orleans Catholics—including many priests—was so overwhelming that it defined them even more strongly than loyalty to Church authority and Catholic teaching.

The enfeebled Archbishop Rummel finally ordered the complete desegregation of New Orleans Catholic schools to begin in 1962. The outrage from white Catholics was so intense that several prominent lay Catholics tried to get the Louisiana legislature to pass a law forbidding Rummel's act. The archbishop excommunicated three of the militant segregationists, including the notorious Judge Leander Perez.

This is the Church that formed my mother. And yet, despite it all, she was unwaveringly faithful till the very end of her life. Tee always taught us the secret to staying strong in the faith despite the sins of the priests. She stressed that we have to separate the man-made from the divine, and that man is fallible. In our family, we never had that docile sense many Catholics cultivated toward clerics. You could always challenge a priest—and if you saw one behaving unjustly, you had better.

Years later, I visited Stacey one weekend when he was at Howard University. After Sunday mass, my brother asked the priest why, during the prayers of the people, he prayed for the peace of Jews and Christians in the Middle East, but not for Muslims. The priest looked at my brother strangely, as if being challenged by a parishioner was a bizarre new thing.

That was the Tee in him coming out.

Once, as an adult, I went to mass at St. Mary's, the church attached to the Ursuline Convent in the French Quarter. Inside the church, they display all the flags that have flown over New Orleans since its founding. One of them is a Confederate flag. After mass, I asked the priest if anyone had ever registered a complaint about that emblem as offensive to worshippers.

"Listen," the priest said to me, "you just need to relax."

"Whoa, hold it, Father!" I said. "Yes, I'm offended by it, but I asked if anybody else was. I know this is a tradition, but I would just like to add my name to all the other folks who have prayed here and who have a problem with the Confederate flag flying in the middle of church."

We got into it a little bit. That, too, was Tee.

This is all part of the experience of loving a Church or a nation that oppresses you, and does things that are offensive to you. Just as Daddy stayed faithful to America, though it had given him reason to break faith, so too did Tee stay faithful to the Church. Do not let your righteous anger, however justified it may be, cause you to break faith. Things are going to get better, but do not forget that the dark side of human nature will never go away. Keep your eyes on the prize. Hold on.

As an actor who has traveled the world practicing my craft, I can see now that everything my mother, my father, and our village of Pontchartrain Park did for me was, to paraphrase Papo, putting a dollar in my pocket anticipating the day that the world would go on sale. They were preparing me and all us children of Pontchartrain Park for the open road that we African Americans were finally going to have the right to take.

Daddy loved the open road. On the last day of school every year, he would sit down with us kids and say, "Where do you guys want to go this summer?" We took a family vacation every year, no question. This was what my dad didn't have growing up, and he was going to give it to us.

This was in the late 1960s and early 1970s, a scary time for many Americans. It was an era of war, protest, rage, drugs, radicalism, and violence. For Daddy, this was beside the point. The whole wide world, which had been tightly circumscribed for black folks, was now his to explore. He was going to make the most of it, and show his sons that this land was their land too.

On those road trips, we would stop at a roadside Stuckey's, one of those big cafeteria-style places. We would buy our food and sit down, and another black family would come in. The place might be empty, and that family could sit anywhere they wanted, but they would come and sit with us. My mother hated that. She'd say, "We don't have to be segregated anymore, but they're so goddamn scared!"

Amos and Althea Pierce weren't scared. They had come too far to give up now. This was what they had fought for all their lives: the freedom to leave their little brick house in their tranquil suburban neighborhood and get on the road to explore this land of dreams, like any American family. My mother, who once saw a neighbor's car incinerated by Klansmen as a lesson to black folk to stay put, lived long enough to drive across America with her own children in their family car, leaving their village and roaming as far as their desires would take them.

Daddy had a cheerful saying: "You can't get lost in America. Anywhere you go, it's still America." It is the land of the free and the home of the brave—and I never knew any two Americans freer or braver than my mother and father.

FIVE

MY TRUE NORTH

For part of my childhood, my school class would go three times a year to the New Orleans Symphony (which later became the Louisiana Philharmonic Orchestra). Sergey Prokofiev's *Peter and the Wolf* was an annual treat. I always looked forward to it and felt that I knew that world. The only way into the forest and into that magical realm was through the music and its performance. It was then that I began to intuit the power of art.

When I think about my journey to life as an artist, I think of Peter, I think of the Wolf, and I think of the gift my mother and father gave me by sending me to those performances. What if they had never done that? What if they had never opened their young son up to the life-changing possibilities in live performance? How would my life have been different, and poorer?

And I think about the time as a small child, riding with my parents out to the country and listening to a radio broadcast of Ossie Davis and Ruby Dee reading poetry. They created a world with words and performance that I found mesmerizing. While Daddy and Tee drove me to College Point, Ossie and Ruby transported me to a place I had never been.

There was a time when I was older and the actor Roscoe Lee Browne came to New Orleans to narrate some orchestral pieces at the Mahalia Jackson Theater with the Louisiana Philharmonic. When I saw and heard him read poetry between the passages of music, I was deeply moved by the beauty of his performance. I knew that I wanted to be able to handle words and language that way. He revealed to me the power of poetry and performance to take you outside yourself and your mundane world.

Later, as a drama student at the New Orleans Center for Creative Arts (NOCCA, pronounced "NOAK-uh"), a performing-arts conservatory for high schoolers, I was thinking about whether acting was the life for me. At sixteen, I went on a school trip to England, and in Stratford-upon-Avon, I saw a production of *As You Like It* by the Royal Shakespeare Company. It was the first time I really saw Shakespeare come to life.

By then I was in my junior year at NOCCA and had already been living in a world where people felt as strongly as I did about the connection between art and a meaningful life. There were young people and teachers telling me it's okay to think this way, and that there's a whole world of people out there who believe art is important. I felt that I wasn't alone. And to go from this to Stratford-upon-Avon to see the Royal Shakespeare Company, I thought, *You can do this with acting? Oh my God!*

That's when I knew what I was going to do with my life.

This vision, this hunger, this talent, and this potential—all of it was latent within me, and had been since I was a tiny boy. It took a classroom visit by an acting teacher to awaken a sleeping teenager to his calling.

ELLIOTT KEENER once told me that he knew from the first time he saw me that I was headed Uptown to study with him. But I had no idea. How could I have? I was just a ninth-grade boy then, a stranger to myself and to the world of possibility.

I was a freshman at Benjamin Franklin, a magnet high school in New Orleans across town from Pontchartrain Park, and planning to play on its football team. One day, I sat in the back of my English class, disengaged, hoping that this period would pass quickly. The teacher told us we had a special guest today, a Mr. Elliott Keener, the founder of the drama program at NOCCA. It was still in its early years and had yet to build its formidable reputation as an incubator of world-class talent.

"I saw you there in the back of the class, sitting up straight as I talked, getting interested," Elliott reminisced. "I knew that this wasn't the last I would see of that kid."

What captured my attention was that this man from NOCCA was taking a serious approach to the arts. This was the first time someone explained to me that being an artist wasn't just being an entertainer. Being an artist, he said, is about having a great impact on the world, and it's not something you can approach casually. It's something you achieve through study, through honing your technique and learning from those who have gone before you.

Really? I had never thought of it that way. Elliott had captured my imagination. I had to know more.

Then I went to an open house on the NOCCA campus, which was at the time located in a beautiful Italianate structure built in 1901 as a school. I had never been to this Uptown neighborhood. As I walked the leafy streets, amid its mansions and cottages, I first heard the birds, then the silence, and then out of that, music. Piano playing, solo trumpet or clarinet. Then I heard voices—hushed voices, then vivid voices—and they were speaking poetry.

THAT WAS NOCCA: an oasis of art and creativity in this quiet Uptown neighborhood. As I explored the conservatory, I saw kids in different parts of the old school building working on a piece of visual art, playing their scales, or dancing in the corner. There were young writers sitting outside, pens in hand, bent over their notebooks, composing. This was the first time I ever experienced a commune of artistry, of people who knew they were in a sanctuary where they could do what they had only dreamed of doing.

And they were my age.

At the open house, you could sit in on any class, so I drifted from session to session. In the basement, I saw a kid in a soundproof booth tackling a piece of music on his horn. I stuck my head into an art class where the teacher was describing how to define your object on the paper, and how to express that object. There were all these kids with total focus on their drawing, just like the young writers I had seen in class outside, enveloped in an intentional silence that was almost monastic.

A serious place, on serious earth, this was.

Then I went upstairs to the theater department and met Elliott Keener, once again, and his colleagues Bob Cronin and Nelson Camp. Bob, Elliott, and Nelson defined everything about the theater department at NOCCA. Nelson was the movement teacher. Bob was the text instructor and the theater historian. Elliott handled voice. All of them taught acting.

Elliott and I really clicked that day. He sparked in me a new and different appreciation for the lesson my folks had taught me from childhood: Anything I put my mind to, I could achieve. I knew that day I wanted to be at NOCCA. In the fall of 1978, I began my sophomore year of high school there.

On the first day, in orientation, the principal, Dr. Thomas Tews, told us that if we wanted to be professional artists, we needed to accept right now that we were probably going to have to leave Louisiana. That was a shock, but the truth is, Dr. Tews knew that traditional Creole culture of New Orleans all too well. He knew that old-school New Orleanians, no matter what their social class, believe that you shouldn't live farther than a hundred-mile radius of the city, if you should live outside the city at all.

In preparing nascent artists, Dr. Tews had been battling parents who said, "Why can't our baby just go on to Tulane? Why does she have to go to college so far from home?" After five years of this struggle as head of the new performing arts conservatory, he knew that he had better put it out there from the beginning.

"There are training programs, and museums, and theaters, and dance companies, and all kinds of things outside this state that we are training you for," he told us. "We don't want you to deny yourself those opportunities."

He went on to tell us newbies that if we found that we didn't like the long hours and intense training, and chose to withdraw from NOCCA, we shouldn't see that as a defeat.

"We would rather you learn now, at your age, the kind of commitment you have to have to your craft, and the difficulty of the challenges you'll face, if you choose this as your vocation," he said. "If you aren't ready for this kind of life, and prepared to make that commitment, then we will have taught you something important."

Later, we first-year drama students gathered in the classroom, wearing leotards, waiting for the first class of our NOCCA careers. Bob, Elliott, and Nelson walked in and said not a word. One of them wrote on the chalkboard: *The world is not fair. Theater is not fair. Bob, Elliott, and Nelson are not fair.*

Then they walked out of the room, leaving us students alone to stare at that board for fifteen minutes. It made me angry. Not fair? That's bullshit. *I'm going to* make *you fair,* I thought.

Then the trio returned to the room and asked us how we felt about what they had written. They explained that we students had chosen to embrace a craft and a profession in which it is very difficult to succeed. You have to decide how important acting is to you. This is not a hobby. This is not a job. This is not something you do for fun. This is a vocation, a calling. Part of your mission at NOCCA is to discover if that is true for you, or not.

We are going to work you hard, and ask more of you than you can imagine right now, they continued. *No matter what happens, you are going to change your life. With the education you receive here, you will be equipped to do anything you want to do.*

THAT FIRST DAY at NOCCA confirmed everything my mother and father had taught me about the value of hard work, education, tenacity, and vision. I had no doubt that as a member of the NOCCA Class of '81, I was standing exactly where I was supposed to be.

I took my teachers at their word. In my sophomore year, a kid in the music program who was two years ahead of me got into The Juilliard School at Lincoln Center in New York. He was a trumpet player named Wynton Marsalis. *Wow, somebody I know is going to Juilliard!* I thought. *Maybe I should start thinking about it.* Juilliard's acting school was one of the best in the nation, and one of the most difficult to get into. But why shouldn't I try? NOCCA gave me the confidence to believe that I had what it took to play in the performing-arts big leagues.

Then I had to confront what Dr. Tews had warned me about on my first day at NOCCA: the sense that, by leaving New Orleans, I would be turning my back on my family and friends.

Unlike most of the kids in the city, I couldn't wait to leave New Orleans. And I never had the sense that I would be far from my family in New York City. For one, my aunt Tee Mae, the matriarch of the Edwards clan, had been living in Brooklyn for four decades. For another, Stacey was already in grad school at Howard, so I wouldn't be the first in my immediate family to head East for college.

More important, I knew that if I was truly going to be a professional artist, I was going to have to seize opportunity in New York if it was offered. Even then, I could see how many artists I knew in New Orleans were restricted by the fear of testing themselves by leaving the safe confines of home. I didn't want to be safe. My father's mantra kept going through my head, strengthening my resolve: "You can't get lost in America." He was saying it from a navigational point of view, but there's a philosophical dimension to it as well. Daddy understood that it's fine to want to go to new places, explore new things. This is what it means to be an artist, and this is what it means to be an American.

Daddy was saying this at the dawn of integration, when he was put off by the fear he observed in other African Americans. They didn't want to jump into the pool of opportunity to which they had been given access. They just wanted to timidly stick their toes in the water. That wasn't Daddy's way. He wanted his sons to use the freedom that had been won for them to go, to explore, to create—and to do so in confidence, knowing that the door will always be open and the front porch light on at home. Our family's emotional bonds were so strong that geographical distance was almost an illusion.

It is impossible to explain how much that sensibility informed my work. When I was living in New York and going through culture shock, facing harsh challenges, or just feeling overwhelmed by the size of the place and the anonymity forced on me there, I drew courage from the assurance that back in New Orleans, my family loved me and would welcome me home. It was like being on the playground at Osborne squaring off against Chet and the white mob; I could feel my allies at my back, and could hear my father's voice urging me to keep fighting, to kick the big guy's ass even as he is kicking mine.

It's ironic that so many New Orleanians don't trust the fact that we have all these cultural tools that will sustain us when we are living far from home. Whenever you meet New Orleans expats, you have an immediate connection. They want to help you, and you want to help them, because even if you are perfect strangers, through this network of shared love for the city and its culture, you know each other.

If you have a shot to be an artist—if you have a chance to go to Juilliard—you've got to take it. If you wonder what you'll be giving up by leaving New Orleans, you're asking the wrong question. It's not about what you're going to lose; it's about what you are going to gain. You are going to add all that you will learn, see, hear, and accomplish to the legacy that New Orleans has already given you.

People who make young folks feel that it is wrong to leave what is safe, comfortable, and familiar in order to learn and to grow and to better themselves do not have the best interests of the youth at heart. When I was at Ben Franklin, I ran a student organization whose mission was to recruit more African Americans to the magnet school, one of the best in the country. My student colleagues and I ran into that mind-set all the time. Black students didn't believe that Ben Franklin was for kids like them. Black parents said, "My child will go to Ben Franklin and lose who they are. They won't have their identity anymore. They will start to act white." This is the excuse they use to keep their child from getting the best education possible, and gaining the prize that generations of African Americans struggled for.

That comes from a place of fear, insecurity, and ignorance. When my mother taught school, she had to deal with that all the time. Yes, the world is unfair. There is racial prejudice, and class prejudice, and all kinds of biases in our way. But that doesn't have a thing to do with whether you got your work done. Two plus two still equals four. Fight those challenges. My mother knew from a lifetime of experience that black kids who believed these lies were sabotaging themselves and their futures.

It's not a uniquely black problem. Everybody knows somebody whose friends or family have looked down on them for supposedly getting above themselves. Are some people snobs? Yes. Do some people forget where they came from? Absolutely. Shame on them all. But people who try to destroy an ambitious young person's confidence by making him think he is disloyal to the tribe are cowards and weaklings who can build themselves up only by tearing others down.

The fact is, success in any society often requires what linguists call "code-switching." Successful code-switchers are those who know how to speak the language of the group they're in at a given moment. I talk differently when I'm having a po'boy with friends in New Orleans than I do when I'm at a business lunch in New York. A white friend of mine from Louisiana who lived on the East Coast for many years noticed his accent thickening up when he came home to visit, the final *r*'s in his words dropping like leaves from trees in a gust of autumn wind.

This is not hypocrisy. This is code-switching. It's the linguistic equivalent of knowing how to dress appropriately for the occasion. This is normal. But that term can be problematic. It lends itself to the idea of a person being insincere. Being truthful to yourself is the goal. Being authentic.

As an actor, I deal with this when I'm teaching students, especially in New Orleans. In a session I taught at NOCCA a few years ago, I had a wonderful girl, one of the few black students in her class. She was a talented actress, but she had a very strong New Orleans dialect. And I knew that her teacher and her classmates were on her case about it.

A dialect is the sound created by your experience and region as you speak your native language. An accent is the same thing, but as you speak a language that is not native to you. I hate it when people don't know the difference. Dialect is so much more personal. When people try to get you to lose it, it can come off as an attack on your identity. She was a young lady of color, so I did not want her to hear that coming from me. That can be damaging, especially when you're dealing with an actor.

So I said to her, "You know something? I love the way you sound. You have probably been criticized for it over and over, but I love how thick your New Orleans dialect is."

I explained to her the difference between accent and dialect, and told her that people all over America have different dialects. In most New Orleans dialects, we drop consonants when we speak. We don't go to *school*; we go to *schoo'*. This is fine if the only people you ever talk to share your dialect. But if you want to communicate with those who don't share your dialect, you are going to hit a brick wall.

"Don't let anyone make you feel bad about having a dialect," I said. "But you have to know that not every character you can play as an actress comes from New Orleans. As one of my teachers told me, live in your dialect, but learn how to deliver a script in character. Learn your diphthongs and how to articulate them so you can play any character you want to. That way, you earn the right to keep your dialect, because you have the capability of doing it the other way."

She seemed to accept what I was telling her. I suspect that lesson opened up the world for that acting student, because it helped her see that she was not facing an either/or *problem*—either give up your identity, or give up your hope for an acting career—but a both/and *opportunity*: You can both keep your dialect identity and succeed as an actress. Gaining the facility to speak the language of the world in which you will move socially and professionally doesn't take away your core identity; it expands it.

If that young African American acting student believed the lie that learning how to communicate outside her dialect was a betrayal of her identity, she could not go far as an actress, because she could only play New Orleanians. If she learned how to speak in any dialect the role requires, she would be able to take the part of her that is true New Orleans and share it with the world.

Those who tell young people like her that the price of achievement is their identity are liars who do not have their best interest at heart.

It's hard for many to see this, though, and not necessarily because they are bad people who want to tear others down. When I first articulated to my parents my desire to be an actor, my father came down hard against the idea, not because he wanted to curtail my ambitions but because he wanted to protect his son from failure.

NOT LONG AGO, a New Orleans parent wrote to me for advice. She was afraid because her daughter was leaving the city for college in

New York. "Don't you think I was afraid, and my parents were afraid?" I replied. "Your daughter is so eager to conquer the world that she's not letting anything intimidate her into backing away from the chance to get a great education in New York. That's worth celebrating," I told that mother.

Conquering fear of the unknown gives meaning to the artist's journey. The creative artist gives form to chaos; part of that process is to bind and subdue the anxiety, even the terror, you have in the face of new challenges to your artistic growth—and then, through your art, show others how to face their fears of the unknown and overcome them. An artist who can draw deeply from the particulars of her upbringing and, through mastery of technique and form, can communicate that individual grace universally, has achieved something magnificent and enduring.

Together, we look for answers to the same big questions. That's why we go to the theater. That's why we go to the art museum. That's why we go to the club or the concert hall. Seeking that moment of connection and collective catharsis with our fellow human beings—that is the magic and the mystery that artists conjure. That is why we become artists.

When people come away from a performance talking not about the characters they've just seen, but about how the play told the story of people in their own lives, that's when you see the power of art to show you something deeper about life and how to live it, and to command you with the prophetic urgency to change your life.

My brother Ron and I once stood next to each other at an emotional ceremony—maybe it was a wedding or a funeral, I can't remember—and he was surprised at how moved he had been by it.

He leaned in to me and said, "So, acting, this is what it's like all the time?" I said no, it's not like that all the time, but we actors do it so you can have an understanding of what that moment you just had here was all about. And that is not trivial.

In American culture, we have turned away from an awareness of the prophetic power of art, of its role as a means of revealing the hidden order beneath everydayness, and its power to transform us and the world. In our schools, we've come to see art as mere decoration, as little more than entertainment. We deny its sacred character—and by sacred, I don't mean only what gets played and heard in church on Sunday morning, but the exalting sounds played and heard in the concert halls and nightclubs on Saturday night. You don't have to be boring and solemn to recognize that art is sacred, but you do have to understand that it's serious business. What thoughts are to the individual, art is to the community as a whole: the place where we reflect on who we are, who we hope to be, where we have failed, and where we have succeeded. It is the forum where we declare and define our values.

I gave the graduation speech to the first class coming out of NOCCA after Katrina. Remember the impact artists can have, I told the graduates, and remember that you have that power. Don't you remember the first time after Katrina that we all heard Louis Armstrong singing "Do You Know What It Means to Miss New Orleans"? I asked them. Those kids were born long after Ronald Reagan's presidency, but I told them about how the man had a gift for poetry in his political rhetoric that inspired and moved Americans in a difficult time for this country, even those who didn't share his politics. What did Woody Guthrie's music mean to people during the

Depression? It gave voice to people's suffering, and it lifted them up to hope for a better tomorrow. Think of how the majestic cadences of Dr. King's oratory galvanized a nation. It wasn't just the content; it was his delivery.

Great art speaks to all people at all times. It is why the imaginative journey a fourteenth-century Tuscan poet, Dante Alighieri, took through the afterlife still speaks powerfully to us today, even though we are seven hundred years and an ocean beyond the world he wrote about in his *Divine Comedy*. The American abolitionists read Dante's work for inspiration in fighting to liberate African Americans from slavery. Henrietta Cordelia Ray, a black poet and New England antislavery activist, even wrote a poem about Dante as a medieval abolitionist. We still perform the plays of the ancient Greeks, not because they are Greek, but because they are so profoundly human. Five hundred years from now, men and women will be listening to Satchmo's "West End Blues" for the same reason.

What did I, an ambitious kid from Pontchartrain Park, have to add to this legacy of humanity? If I became part of the eternal pilgrimage of artists through history, what would I take from my brief time on that journey, and what would I eventually be able to give to those who would come after me? I didn't know, but I had to find out.

I worked on my Juilliard audition pieces every evening with each of the three teachers at NOCCA, each taking another aspect of the work. Bob was literary and text teacher, Elliott was vocal and the emotional part, the emotional connection to the material. Nelson was the movement teacher who explored the physicality of the roles. We rigorously explored all three.

Oh, man, I thought, *I've got to go for a week with each one? This is going to go on forever, I'm going to be so tired.* But by the end of those three weeks, it seemed like they had just flown by. I learned early, then, that if you want to be a real actor, you can never stop analyzing your work and practicing to perfect your art.

I understood that my chances of getting into Juilliard were slim, so there was a lot of pressure on me as I approached the auditions. We arrived at the Tulane University theater department to meet with Juilliard representatives and try out. There were maybe ten other graduating seniors there, and I was the only one from NOCCA (all the drama students I started with had gone back to their home schools, one by one).

I performed a scene from the black playwright Ron Milner's drama *Who's Got His Own* and played Shakespeare's Clarence in his death scene from *Richard III*. I committed those lines so deeply to my memory that more than three decades later, I can still recite them. In fact, I didn't so much memorize them as live them.

All my hard work of preparation served me well, I thought after I finished, but it was a nerve-wracking experience. The next day, I had two auditions lined up for other schools. Before my time came, Buzz Podewell, then the head of Tulane's drama department, took me aside and said, "You got in." But he told me to go through with the remaining auditions as a learning experience.

In the end, I aced all my auditions. The letters from the schools started coming in. The University of Wisconsin–Milwaukee accepted me, as did the California Institute of the Arts. The University of Chicago accepted me, as did Brandeis. But I still had not heard from Juilliard.

Had Dr. Podewell been wrong? Or had Juilliard changed its mind?

I knew that out of the thousands of young actors who audition for Juilliard each year, only nineteen are selected for each class. If they tapped me, I had to go.

One afternoon, I was sitting on the bed in my room when Tee brought me the day's mail. In it was a letter from Juilliard. *Oh, man*, I thought, *here it is*. My mother shut the door so the experience could be mine alone. I opened the envelope, took out the letter, read it, then went into the kitchen to tell Tee.

"I did it! I got in! Yeah!" I whooped. We hugged and kissed. The good news thrilled Daddy when he came home from work. Dinner turned into a celebration that night, but my parents immediately began thinking of the practicalities. Juilliard doesn't have dorms, they said; maybe you can live with Tee Mae in Crown Heights, just like Daddy had done when he went to New York for photography school.

When I was a high schooler, Daddy had never discouraged me from pursuing acting, but he had never encouraged it, either. Now that I had been accepted to one of the most prestigious acting schools in the world, he was behind me all the way. The Juilliard letter confirmed the confidence I had in myself and my artistic future. Now I had it on paper that I wasn't crazy, that I wasn't an old Spaniard tilting at windmills. This young black kid from Pontchartrain Park who loved to play football but who thought he had it within him to become an artist—that kid was onto something. My heart had spoken to me, and it had not lied.

The weekend before I left New Orleans to start my Juilliard training, I went to a Saturday vigil mass with Tee. At the end of the service, the congregation was singing the recessional hymn, and I lost it. This was the last time I would be going to church with my mother as a boy who lived in her home. All the daily rituals of life in New Orleans, the family, the friends, the mothers and the fathers of the Church—all of that would change. They would always be there, of course, but I would not see them for a long time. Maybe I would never live here again. The weight of what I was about to do fell upon me, and I cried and cried.

Suddenly I saw that Tee and I were surrounded by people from the church. "Oh, Wendell's going off to school? Baby, we have your back, don't you worry." My church community, men and women who had seen me grow in that parish from a little boy, offered some version of this benediction over and over that heartbreaking afternoon. And it made everything right. I left mass that day swaddled by so much love and support that I had no doubt, no doubt at all, that if I fell, those good people would catch me. I had no fear of leaving home. All of that love and support went with me.

I left for New York City on August 19, 1981, age seventeen, thinking that I was about to conquer the world. I had no sense of limits whatsoever. I was completely free, knowing that every obstacle I would face would only make me stronger. My mother and father, my teachers at NOCCA, and my community at church and in Pontchartrain Park had given me all the skills I needed to overcome.

I expected Chet again, but I also knew that thanks to all that had been won for me and all that I had been given, Chet could no more beat me now than he could that day at Osborne. That was the legacy I brought with me to New York City. It's the legacy I still carry with me. Once you realize what a sacred trust it is, you would never dishonor it by letting it run through your fingers.

I moved in with Tee Mae in Brooklyn. She lived in a predominantly West Indian neighborhood. For the first time I heard soca, calypso, and hardcore reggae. People sat on their stoops on a summer night, just like in the movies. We had crawfish boils in New Orleans, but I had never seen people cooking on a street corner like they did in Crown Heights. It was a world of sound, color, smell, and delirious chaos. It felt like Mardi Gras every day.

Taking the subway into Manhattan was a new experience for a kid whose closest prior experience was the St. Charles Avenue streetcar. It was so hot and humid on those trains that summer and early fall. I would see young guys standing between the rushing subway cars to cool off, and despite the danger, I had to try it once. There I was, standing between cars with just a couple of chains between me and the tracks, barreling toward Lincoln Center at seventy miles per hour. It was exhilarating. I felt so free.

But there were some difficult cultural adjustments. In New Orleans, everybody says hello when you pass by, even if you don't know them. And if you do know them, even slightly, making conversation is just what you do. In New York, I had to unlearn the habits of what down South is considered to be civilized behavior. Don't look people in the eye. Don't engage strangers in conversation. A friend from Louisiana's chatty mother came to visit him in New York for the first time, and as they were exiting the subway, he leaned back into the car and told the puzzled Manhattanites, "She's not crazy, she's southern."

Like many New Orleanians, I would call both men and women "baby" as a term of endearment. It's common to hear one man say to another, "Hey, baby, how you doin', man?" And if someone uses it with a person of the opposite sex, that doesn't necessarily imply sexual interest. It simply means that the New Orleanian is trying to be nice.

That first semester, I frequently greeted both men and women at Juilliard as "baby." I didn't realize it, but in that first semester, I developed a reputation for being a ravenous bisexual—the "Hound of the Hallway" as one woman called me. A male student finally stopped me and said, "Wendell, I just want to tell you, I'm not a homosexual, I'd appreciate it if you would stop hitting on me."

My jaw dropped. I had no idea that's how my commonplace Crescent City charm was being received. I dropped the "baby" talk, and I learned how to be harder and more closed. I knew I was picking up a New York state of mind when Tee chastised me in a phone call for being snippy with her. "You are just so mean and cold," she said. "You need to be nicer to people."

At times, the sense of liberty I felt being alone in the big city turned into feelings of intense loneliness. I barely knew anyone my age in the city, and because I wasn't on a college campus, there was none of the regular sort of social opportunities a college student would traditionally expect. There were only eighteen others in my Juilliard class, and because most of them had gone there after earning a four-year college degree, they were significantly older than I was. Fortunately, I didn't have time to dwell on my isolation because acting school was so demanding, and the Juilliard experience was so awe-inspiring to seventeen-year-old me.

Out of the underground I would emerge into the dazzling light, clean lines, and open space of the Lincoln Center complex on Manhattan's West Side. There I was, a wide-eyed pilgrim making his way into these iconic temples of the arts. My mission: to study drama and technique at the highest level possible. In front of me stood the Metropolitan Opera. To the side, Alice Tully Hall, and just beyond that, the Juilliard School. *I have made it to the inner sanctum,* I thought. *If I can make it here, I will be initiated into the craft.*

This was the big time. The people teaching my classes in the day were often working on Broadway that night. They were coaching the world's best actors, they were being quoted in *The New York Times*. It made me aware of the stakes of the world this kid from Pontchartrain Park was now a part of. It gave me such clarity. There were no guarantees, of course; I could always fail. But the opportunity that had opened up before me was not an illusion, and the future as an artist that I had only dreamed about at NOCCA was much closer to reality.

It was all on me. It was time to get to work.

From the very beginning, Juilliard impressed upon me the importance of drive, of focusing on what's important and not letting go. New Orleans is a wonderful amalgam of culture and people and coming together in a community that lives its art, but when I got to New York, I realized that there were thousands of talented people who understand and appreciate what art is and who want to pursue it as a vocation. If I didn't step up my game, I was going to be left behind.

Part of that is simple professionalism, but there was more to it than that. I began to understand that I had entered into a covenant with the community of artists, living and dead, and that I was a novice who had a responsibility to learn all I could from them to uphold the values of the fellowship. The deep knowledge of and sacrifice for the art, the craft, the history, and the culture of drama would be necessary if I were to truly answer the calling I took as sacred and rise to the top.

In New Orleans, you tended to create from your own experience. In New York, I came to understand that there are so many people who have gone before me on this same journey and who have confronted the same challenges I will confront. I learned the importance of learning from them. The Juilliard experience taught me to discipline my individual passion according to the accumulated wisdom of the community. That's how I would discover and hone my own voice. This is not something they teach you in the classroom; it's in the ethos of a place like Juilliard.

It doesn't come instantly, though. When I first arrived, I thought NOCCA had given me so much training that there was nothing new to learn. That first semester at Juilliard, I discovered how wrong I was. We worked on the basics—on breath, on articulating vowel sounds, diphthongs, and consonants—but we also were introduced to new concepts. The late director John Stix taught us about the concept of sense memory, which is the idea that your body can have a physical reaction to the presence of powerful memories brought to mind. In class exercises, he asked each of us to make ourselves still and try to call to mind a smell, a touch, a sound, and to see what the memory would do to our bodies.

At first I couldn't even wrap my head around this. Then, as I watched the other students discover sense memory, I began to understand.

I'll never forget watching this happen to my classmate Ralph Zito. He closed his eyes and induced a sense memory experience. With his eyes still shut, he told the rest of us that he had put himself in the moment when he learned his father had died.

Stix asked Ralph more questions about the details of that moment and led Ralph through it. Ralph said that the phone rang.

"Hear that phone," said John. "What does it sound like?"

Suddenly, we saw the pain take over Ralph's body. "I wish I could get that sound out of my head," he keened. "I wish it could be gone." He began describing how painful the sound of the ringing phone was. Without knowing what he was doing, Ralph made the rest of us feel the existential agony of an ordinary telephone ring.

That's when I came to a new understanding of what acting was: the creation of an inner world so strong, of a conflict so powerfully delineated, that it induces behavior. You don't have to think, *How am I going to do this scene?* You create in your mind the reality of your character's situation, and you do it with such intensity and specificity that the acting flows naturally. It doesn't even seem like acting.

The sense memory class revealed to me something I had experienced in New Orleans but had not understood. When I was fourteen, I was in a play called *Sunshine*, in which my character, a black boy, fell in love with a white girl. I can't remember the name of the actress who played opposite me, but I recall that as we rehearsed our scenes over and over, the growing physical attraction between us was palpable.

But we seldom talked offstage. The scene culminated in a kiss, but out of respect for our young ages, the director said we could stop short of the actual kiss in rehearsal. In the first dress rehearsal, though, the director said that now we were going to have to kiss. There was a moment of silence. We were both professional, and we executed the scene flawlessly. That was one of the first times I really understood what a loving kiss was, and how it envelops the whole moment, is all encompassing. You could have heard a pin drop in that audience.

Thinking back on that experience from the perspective of Juilliard, I realized that I had not fallen in love with the girl. Rather, we had both worked so hard in rehearsal, and delved so deeply into our characters and immersed ourselves in such a profound emotional understanding of what these two characters were going through, that the truth of the moment simply flowed through us. That was the first experience I ever had with catharsis, when I realized that art can truly move people to tell the truth.

In text class, I learned how to study the language and text of a play to prepare my role. Shakespeare's iambic pentameter, for example, teaches the observant actor how to deliver his lines as the Bard wrote them. The rhythm inherent in each line of metered verse shows which words, or parts of words, Shakespeare believed to be most important to convey meaning and disclose the character's motivations. Actors who play Shakespeare have to know how iambic pentameter works so they can understand who their characters really are and convey that understanding to the audience. The meter of Shakespeare's lines is a coded set of instructions for the actors.

Juilliard also taught me the critical importance of historical research in creating a role. When I played the Reverend Hosea Williams, the civil rights leader in the film *Selma*, I immersed myself in the world of the 1960s struggle against segregation. I learned all I could about Williams and the experiences he carried with him to that fateful moment on Selma's Edmund Pettus Bridge at the film's climax.

Hosea Williams had fought under General George S. Patton in World War II and had been seriously injured in a Nazi bombing; he had to spend a year in the hospital recovering. But he earned a Purple Heart. After the war, back home in Georgia and still wearing his country's uniform, Williams dared to drink from a whites-only water fountain. A white mob beat him so severely that authorities called not an ambulance, but an undertaker. The hearse driver saw faint signs of life, and instead of taking Williams to the mortuary, took him to the hospital.

This was part of what was in Hosea Williams's mind as he marched across that bridge toward a white mob and a phalanx of armed Alabama state troopers and a local posse armed with tear gas, whips, clubs, and chains, poised to attack. When I walked over that same bridge in Williams's footsteps, portraying Williams for the cameras, I had those same thoughts in my mind. I drew on my Juilliard training to allow Hosea Williams to inhabit me physically: my voice, my breath, and everything about the way I moved in that scene.

If you have studied the script and its language, researched your character and the background of the story you're telling, and deployed sense memory techniques, and if you have integrated all of these approaches, then when the moment comes and you are walking across the Edmund Pettus Bridge in Selma, Alabama, as the cameras record, you don't have to think about what you're doing. You have created a world so vividly in your mind that all you do is live in the moment, and the truth of the character rolls through you like thunder.

These principles became foundational for my approach to acting. I have used them throughout my career. That's when I first became aware that acting isn't simply about performance, about reciting lines in a convincing way. It is much closer to psychology than I had considered, or even to religion. It is about cultivating the ability to open yourself to a powerful spirit, and at the right moment make that spirit incarnate in your character, and in turn make that spirit, and that character, come to life in the hearts and minds of your audience, in that moment of communion.

What the pagan did within a sacred circle, what the Catholic priest does at the altar during mass, and what the actor does onstage are all intimately connected. Each of us stops time with our liturgies and draw down the gods so that all present can commune with the sacred and live for a moment within the eternal.

I learned this and so many other things in my first semester at Juilliard. And I learned how small I was in the face of the task ahead. I had so much to learn, but I was alive in a way I had never been, and I was ravenous. I understood how easily you could work at acting from nine in the morning to eleven at night, six days a week, and still feel that there wasn't enough time.

No doubt about it, I was in the right place.

I wasn't entirely without friends in New York. When they weren't on the road playing music, Wynton and Branford Marsalis, my friends from NOCCA, would go out with me. One was a fellow Juilliard student, the other a recent graduate of Berklee College of Music. They invited me to hit the clubs with them. In the early 1980s, the Marsalis brothers were the new young lions in town. In their company, I went to Sweet Basil, the Village Vanguard, Lush Life, all iconic jazz clubs, and saw musicians like Art Blakey, Dizzy Gillespie, and others whose work I knew only from record albums. There they were, in the flesh, playing with a sense of freedom, individuality, and abandonment that was intoxicating to watch. Whatever sense of discipline and order Juilliard instilled in me by day, those nights in the jazz clubs gave me the experience of release—and this too was an important part of the making of me as an artist. Here I was, at the center of the world, working all day at one of the best acting schools in the country, hanging out with the Marsalis brothers at night and meeting legendary jazz musicians who shared their own journeys with me. I didn't have time to miss home.

I learned quickly that the total freedom those jazzmen celebrated onstage did not come naturally. They practiced all day, shedding (as in, go to the woodshed and work hard) so they would be ready at night to cut loose. Wynton and Branford introduced me to these musicians, who imparted their own lessons about what it meant to be a real artist. "Wendell, you have to shed, you have to shed," they would say.

Night after night of seeing and hearing this at clubs all over New York created a work ethic within me, and a way to approach my studies. I saw in the jazzmen how the greatest artists and the greatest art combine formality with improvisation. Once you have mastered the details of your craft/art and have absorbed them so deeply into your muscles and bones that you don't have to think about them, then you can release them and express your own individuality. You become the art you create.

Shedding, I discovered, was as important to me as an actor as it was to the jazz musicians. You shed and you shed and you shed until you can perform your lines with a sense of total abandon. If you've constructed your performance well and have shedded to the limit of your endurance, when you say that first line, the rest of the character falls into place, like pins in a lock that opens your best performance with just the right key, like a row of falling dominoes.

The best example from my career was in 1992, seven years after I graduated from Juilliard. I was playing Boy Willie in the Broadway production of August Wilson's *The Piano Lesson*. I was brought on as an understudy for the play's star, Charles S. Dutton. For some reason, the producers hid from me that Dutton was leaving the show and that this epic role would probably fall to me. I had two weeks to prepare.

My buddy Victor Mack and I holed up in an apartment and shedded day and night, working on the play. For two weeks I drilled myself on the script and watched every performance during that time. Then the night came when I took over the role. Everyone else in the cast had been performing it for almost two years. They knew how to breathe together. But it would all be new to me.

In the opening scene, Boy Willie bangs on a living room door off-stage. His first line, addressed to another character, is, "Doaker, I'm here!" The audience hears the pounding and the shouting before the lights come up. I was so nervous I could barely stand up, and certainly I couldn't bang on the door.

There was a wooden handle and a pallet on the side of the door so the actor could make as much racket as possible with the pounding. I turned to my costar Rocky Carroll, standing in the wings with me, and said, "Rocky, please knock for me. Take the hammer and knock."

He did. And with a tiny voice, I croaked, "Doaker, I'm here!" It was nothing. And I knew it.

That was when I told myself that, thanks to my shedding, I knew this play inside and out, and if I can just stand up and walk through this door and greet Doaker, I will be fine.

"Doaker, I'm here!" I said, this time shouting. "Doaker! Doaker!"

Doaker opened the door, and I ran onto the stage and lit right into the play. I was like a tornado that night in my Broadway debut in a lead role. It went magnificently well. When I returned to my dressing room, I sobbed. I knew that the intense two weeks of shedding had lifted me up over the forbidding mountain of anxiety and insecurity, and carried me sailing through the three-hour play. I wept tears of joy and thanksgiving that I had sent myself to the woodshed, and it had paid off.

I had learned to act like a jazzman plays, mastering the craft so profoundly that I didn't have to think about it. In other roles, I could improvise without losing the form and the sense of the tune. Jazz was teaching me how to act.

In fact, it was at the Village Vanguard that freshman fall that I cracked the code of how to play Shakespeare. I was taking a Shakespeare class and was having trouble mastering iambic pentameter. Then one night at the Vanguard I saw a musician named Arthur Blythe. There was one song he played—I don't recall the name of it, but I can hear it in my head even today. I was humming that song and looking around the club, when Blythe went into his solo. It was free jazz, and he took a long detour from the trail, clambering up and down chords like a fleet-footed mountaineer. Then he emerged back in the song, right in time with his band, which had never left the path. Suddenly, I realized that for the entire ten-minute solo, I had never stopped humming the melody, in time.

That's when I had my epiphany. Blythe wasn't just going out there and playing free jazz with no respect for the structure of the song. He was honoring the structure at all times, leading the audience on an exploration of the vaulting chords and side-chapel harmonies within the song's architecture. And when he finished his wild and crazy solo, he was right back at the top. He knew exactly where he was the entire time, but was able to do this astonishingly expressive feat.

Freedom within form.

Then it clicked for me: That's Shakespeare. Honor the form, honor the verse and order of the iambic pentameter—but find your freedom within it.

So I went back to school and suddenly I was able to deliver those lines from *Henry V* with real feeling for the first time: "O for a muse of fire that would ascend the brightest heaven of invention. A kingdom for a stage, princes to act and monarchs to behold the swelling scene!" I didn't fight the iambic pentameter, I used it as the form into which I could pour myself. I could be me! I could speak these lines, and I could be me.

That created my personal rule: *Freedom within form creates great art.* That was what studying acting in New York, both in the classroom and in the jazz clubs, taught me. It is what the first jazzmen playing on Congo Square in New Orleans knew as they fit wild African rhythms and exhilarating flights of melodic fantasy into the structure of European brass band music. When I lose my true north, I always think of that.

Wynton, who was both a friend and mentor, was two years ahead of me at Juilliard. He held the position of first chair in the Juilliard Orchestra, a high honor, while at the same time being one of the hottest young jazz musicians in New York City. Shortly before I arrived at Juilliard, the legendary jazz drummer Art Blakey invited Wynton to join his Jazz Messengers. He was nineteen years old.

When Juilliard heard that, the school gave him an ultimatum: It's us or Art Blakey and the Jazz Messengers. Wynton chose jazz and dropped out of Juilliard. He eventually returned and completed his degree after becoming one of the defining artists of our time. Today, over three decades later, Wynton is the leading jazz musician of his generation, was the founding artistic director of Jazz at Lincoln Center, and in the summer of 2014, took over as director of the jazz program at Juilliard—the same school that forced his hand. Nobody who knew him back in the day could possibly be surprised.

Many nights I would skip the train ride back to Brooklyn and crash instead at the apartment Wynton and Branford had in the Village. The Marsalis brothers were my primary connection to home. They gave me comfort. Once, I was at their place when Branford came in off the road. "Come here, I want you to smell something," he said, beckoning me to the fridge.

He handed me an old margarine container filled with something brown and icy. I scratched the ice and sniffed my fingernail.

"Gumbo!"

"Yeah, man, Mama just sent it up."

Art Blakey lived upstairs from the brothers, and the writer and jazz critic Stanley Crouch was a near-constant fixture there. The Marsalis apartment was a never-ending artistic salon, a New York jazz version of Gertrude Stein's famous gatherings at her Paris apartment in the 1920s. Through Wynton and Branford, I met jazz greats—artists like Elvin Jones and Sarah Vaughan—and got to spend time with them in intimate settings, talking about music and art. It's hard to overstate how much a young actor from New Orleans learned simply by being there among them.

I remember one occasion hanging out with Wynton and Stanley, when they pointed out that I was the one actor in their circle and put me through my paces. "Do you really know your theater history?" they asked. Yeah, I said, I know.

"Okay," said Stanley. "Tell me about the African Grove Company."

"That was the all-black theater company started in New York City in 1821," I said. "They staged a famous production of Shakespeare's *Richard III*, starring James Hewlett, who, by the way, was the first black actor in theater history to play Othello."

I hit my friend Stanley with more historical facts, concluding triumphantly, "So, yeah, that is the African Grove Company."

This sharp-edged discussion and debate was challenging, but it was the kind of intellectual camaraderie that fueled me. This was New York, and it was a kind of culture shock that jolted my heart and electrified my mind. I had had some of it at NOCCA, but by comparison, that experience was very insular. These conversations about art and its meaning and place in life didn't just happen in living rooms and cafés but were documented in newspapers and magazines. They were part of public life. And so was I. In just a few short years, I had gone from playing ball in Pontchartrain Park to rubbing shoulders and trading insights with performers and writers who were at the top of their craft, at the center of the artistic world.

It was exactly where I wanted to be.

I'll never forget the day in 1983 when Wynton got his first Grammy nomination for his solo instrumental performance on his second album, *Think of One*. When I stopped by the apartment to congratulate him, I found him listening to Miles Davis on the stereo. I was excited for Wynton's big news, but he didn't want to talk about that.

"Shhh, shhh," he said. "Listen to him, man, his use of space. If I could just play one note and capture what he captured in that single note . . ."

"Yeah, that's great," I said, "but congratulations on the Grammy nomination!"

"Man, I appreciate it. Thank you," he said. "But you know we don't do it for that."

That was a reminder: For a true artist, the awards are not the reward. The reward is being able to play a single, solitary note like Miles. That, not popular acclaim, is the moment of truth for an artist. That's what it's all about—and the only way to reach that summit is through study and shedding. Wynton helped me to see that.

Over the years, I watched Wynton's professional trajectory, and learned from how he worked to keep fame and fortune from compromising his artistic purity. Unlike most artists, he didn't have to compromise much. One time, CBS Records called him and said that Mick Jagger wanted to do an album with him. Wynton said he wasn't interested in that.

The people at CBS couldn't believe it. *Do you know who he is?* Yes, Wynton told them, I know exactly who Mick Jagger is. But I'm not interested in playing pop music. The record label told Wynton that he would get a big paycheck from this. That didn't move him either. Wynton could not bring himself to compromise his art.

When he told me about that conversation, I couldn't believe it. "Skain," I said, using his nickname, "are you crazy, man?"

No, he said, it's like this: As the artist, you have to make the decisions about your work. Don't let the businessman make decisions about your work.

Over the years I came to recognize the truth of this principle in my acting. There's the craft, and there's the business, and they rarely meet. You as an artist have to make that call. When I talk to my agents and my manager and tell them I want a particular job, I always know that I'm prepared to walk away from it if I come to believe that it will compromise my artistic integrity. No matter how big the paycheck or the promise of awards, you have to be able to turn your back on something if you believe it will compromise your art.

"You've worked hard at NOCCA and Juilliard," Wynton said to me once. "Why would you do that if all you want to do is something simple and easy?"

Wynton has long been criticized for being such a purist and so hard on pop music and rap. He and I were talking about this once, and how his critics call him an elitist. "But I know the level of artistry that so many people have created with jazz," he said. "The bar's been set high. I have the same expectations of myself. Pop music is fine, but that's not the same thing. I eat at McDonald's from time to time, but that's not the same thing as fine cuisine."

One of the best gifts Skain gave me was introducing me to Albert Murray, both the man and his work. Murray, who died in 2013 at the age of ninety-seven, was a great African American writer, jazz critic, and public intellectual once described by Duke Ellington as "the unsquarest man I know." Wynton first met Murray in 1982 and was captivated by his traditionalism, which seemed radical at the time. He made a habit of heading up to the apartment Murray and his wife, Mozelle, shared at 45 Lenox Terrace in Harlem, where she would cook southern comfort food and they would talk about art, music, and ideas late into the night.

Murray, who was in his mid-sixties when he took Wynton under his wing, tutored the young musician in the Western intellectual canon and taught him how the African American experience fit into the broader cultural and artistic history of the West. Murray cultivated in his eager pupil a reverence for tradition, and an insistence on the importance of knowing it and being committed to it. For Murray, "tradition" wasn't the same thing as "traditionalism." The historian Jaroslav Pelikan once said, "Tradition is the living faith of the dead; traditionalism is the dead faith of the living." Albert Murray couldn't have agreed more.

It was hard to characterize Murray, who managed to offend white and black people both with *The Omni-Americans*, the 1970 book that made his reputation. The title referred to African Americans—a term that Murray rejected, by the way, saying, "I am not African; I am American." In the book, Murray contended that the Negro experience was the quintessential American one. Ours is a pioneer nation, he argued, made by people who had to learn resilience in the face of hardship. Nobody had it harder than the African slaves, and the music that emerged from slavery—the blues, and later, jazz—was the purest expression of the American spirit.

"Frederick Douglass is a better illustration of the American story—the American as self-made man—than the founding fathers," he wrote. And: "The blues is not the creation of a crush-spirited people. It's the product of a forward-looking, upward-striving people. Jazz is only possible in a climate of freedom."

Murray had no patience for people he believed reduced African Americans to victims, either of the white man or of their own social pathologies. He denounced Daniel Patrick Moynihan's controversial report on the Negro family as "propaganda," and "part of the new folklore of white supremacy." But he also strongly criticized the writing of prominent Negro intellectuals like James Baldwin, who in

Murray's view did violence to the complexity of black lives and black history by representing it as nothing more than "oppression and repression."

"They are playing the other man's game rather than looking into the experience that he has lived, that his father and grandfather and great-grandfather have lived," Murray wrote. I suspect Mamo and Papo would have understood his point.

For Murray, though, whether or not the black man was socially invisible, as his great friend Ralph Ellison had it, he was also everywhere in the American imagination—hence "omni-Americans." In America, the national culture was "incontestably mulatto," he wrote, adding that "the so-called black and so-called white people of the United States resemble nobody else in the world so much as they resemble each other."

In the 1960s, Murray and Ellison both reacted strongly against an emerging separatist sensibility among African Americans. "Both men were militant integrationists," Henry Louis Gates, Jr., wrote in a 1996 *New Yorker* profile of Murray, "and they shared an almost messianic view of the importance of art." Gates astutely observed that for Ellison and Murray, integration was not "accommodation" to white-dominated culture, but rather "introjection" of the black sensibility into the broader culture.

As Murray would later put it in a public radio interview, American art reveals "how it feels to be an American, with American aspirations." Just as black folks are the most American of all Americans, the art they produce is the most American of American art. For me, discovering Albert Murray was like finding the intellectual version of Amos Pierce, war hero, who stood at the Municipal Auditorium singing the anthem of the nation that denied him his medals, affirming his Americanness in the face of his nation's determination to render him invisible. And it was like discovering the artistic iteration of Amos Pierce behind the wheel of the family sedan, taking to the wide-open road with joy and confidence, saying that you can't get lost in America.

I met Albert Murray only twice—once at Jazz at Lincoln Center, and on another occasion, back in the 1990s, at his Harlem apartment. Wynton kept telling me I had to meet the man, and at long last I made the pilgrimage uptown to sit down with the master.

We talked about jazz and about the music he heard as a young man. Born in Alabama in 1916, Murray had lived through virtually the entire history of jazz. The two of us spoke about how wonderful it was that Wynton was keeping up the tradition while at the same time exploring new avenues for jazz.

Murray told me about his long friendship with Ralph Ellison, which began when they were both undergraduates at Tuskegee in the 1930s. That made a deep impression on me. As a young man in your twenties, a lot of your pursuits are trivial. I plead guilty to that myself, but with me and the young black artists whose circle I was a part of, there was a lot more to our lives. We were trying to be serious about art and our calling as performers and creators. What a comfort to know that we were not strange in our dedication to high art, that black men as gifted and as accomplished as Ellison and Murray had walked this path before us, at our age.

On that visit, Murray showed me a sheaf of sketches by his friend Romare Bearden, the Harlem Renaissance painter. One of Bearden's most famous paintings, *The Block*, is a big, boisterous collage depicting Harlem street life. It now hangs in the Metropolitan Museum of Art, but it had its genesis on Albert and Mozelle's balcony. "Go take a look," Albert said. I stepped out onto the balcony where art history had been made. It was sublime.

TO HAVE THAT KIND of give-and-take with Albert Murray was one of those New York moments that I had only heard and read about. But it was my life back then: a big, boisterous collage of high and low and everything in between, all of it a gift, none of it lost, and every bit for the making of my own perspective.

Murray's way of thinking about art had a profound influence on my own aesthetic. In *The Omni-Americans*, Murray defined art as the stylization of life experiences. "More specifically," he wrote, "an art style is the assimilation in terms of which a given community, folk, or communion of faith embodies its basic attitudes toward experience.

"And this is not all," he continued. "Of its very nature, an art style is also the essence of experience itself, in both the historical and sensory implications of the word."

My own artistic style, then, if it was to be genuine, had to come out of my own experience, but also transcend it. Murray taught me to see myself and my future as an artist in both particular and universal terms. There is something that an African American man born in the middle of the twentieth century to a working-class New Orleans family can bring to the human dialogue. But if it is going to be a contribution that lasts, it must speak to the great conversation all humanity has been having with itself about life for millennia. You must recognize as an artist that you are one link in the invisible chain that connects us all, across civilizations and eras.

Murray impressed upon me that art is the tangible intersection of the consciousness of an individual and a people, and how they deal with the joys, the sorrows, the pleasures, and the pains presented to them by life in their own place and time. The artist dwells in that intersection and makes the ideas, the emotions, and the spirit of that crucible concrete, and accessible to all.

His point, ultimately, was that in exploring our diversity as artists and human beings, we must never lose sight of the fundamental unity of human experience and how that is expressed in art. I still think about that when I travel. Once I was at a funeral in Thailand and picked up a vivid sense of celebration coming from the mourners' parade. Then it hit me: This was the Thai version of a New Orleans jazz funeral.

Even though the music was different, how those Thai people dealt with death intersected in the way we in New Orleans deal with death. They had the dirge march toward the cemetery, with cymbals and drums. When they left the newly interred dead in the grave, the mourners returned to the world of the living with the whirling sound of wind instruments. They came back swinging hard.

Here I was in Thailand, in Phuket, in 1988, and I saw and heard the Thailand version of that old familiar cycle and realized that, six thousand miles from home, I had stood at a spiritual crossroads of humanity and known exactly what these strangers were saying with their sound and music and movement. The impulse was the same. This moment of recognition, of connection, brought clarity to Murray's teaching. The way you engage with life is your culture, and when you interact with other people in other cultures, if you have eyes to see and a heart that's open, you will recognize your common humanity. And when it reaches the highest degree of authenticity, this spirit will connect you across time to other human beings from centuries past and, if your own creation is pure and true, to peoples yet to be born.

Don't give up your identity as an artist speaking out of the Negro experience, Murray taught, but don't give up your identity as an American either—and if you would be an artist and a man in full, never forget that you are part of the human diaspora.

That's a powerful discovery to make as a young artist. Being with Albert Murray in his Harlem apartment was like going to the mountaintop to be with a guru. He instilled in everyone in our New York circle a craving for excellence and a fierce determination never to compromise in its pursuit. His was the Moses generation, the liberators who brought African Americans through the desert of Jim Crow after slavery. He handed responsibility to us, members of the Joshua generation, to lead our people into the Promised Land.

Skip Gates was right: Murray did have a near-messianic view of art. For Murray, art was the trait that made us human because it distinguishes us from animals that need care only about the bare elements of survival. The creation of art involves a constant struggle to raise what is beastly in ourselves out of the mud and to call ourselves to embrace and be transformed by what Abraham Lincoln called "the better angels of our nature."

If art is both a sign of our humanity and the means by which we embrace it, there could scarcely be a more serious undertaking than to become an artist. Murray's theories went hand in glove with the training I was receiving at Juilliard. As my instructors there taught me how to enter into the mind and historical circumstances of a character to find his *particular* humanity, so too did Murray teach me to dig deep into art to find our *common* humanity. Juilliard taught that this would help us actors understand the ground of character; Murray taught that this would help me understand the ground of human life.

My Juilliard teachers drew out and refined my talent. Before Juilliard, I thought my training was there to boost my natural talent and to give it an outlet. Juilliard taught me that there is actually a *developed* talent, through implementing technique. One can evolve as an artist and a performer at the same time, as the practice of technique and the understanding of theory perfects one's natural gifts.

My time in New York was teaching me that art and artistry don't just happen. It was teaching me that art is not a sideshow to the real business of life, it is at the heart of what it means to live as a human. At its best and highest, art changes people's hearts, minds, and even their lives. Art reveals truths of the human condition that, lost in our everydayness, we cannot see. It transfigures the ordinary. Because we must see a thing before we can love it, art clears our vision so that our hearts and minds can follow the right path out of chaos and hatred and hopelessness, toward order, love, and redemption.

A philosopher might do this for some. A theologian might, as well, and so too might a great orator. But no one can accomplish this as artists—poets, musicians, painters, filmmakers, and yes, actors—can. After our rigorous training perfects our natural gifts, we emerge with the near-miraculous power of alchemy, having the potential to take the plain stuff of life and transform it into gold.

This discovery was a visceral epiphany for me. I felt a sense of great optimism as a young actor in training. It opened my eyes to the ability of what an actor and an artist can do.

I started to see how much impact Shakespeare had on the world of his time and place. In a time of constant political positioning between factions, his insight burned like a lantern, illuminating his audiences about the workings of greed, of hubris, of the flaws of leadership, and the workings of power. Because Shakespeare spoke as no one writing in the English language ever had about the depth and the breadth of humanity's encounter with life itself, his art will live as long as men draw breath.

Artists, especially actors, are like priests and shamans in that they induce in their audience an experience, if only for a moment in time, of the transcendent, of the eternal. Alessandro, a character in Mark Helprin's novel *A Soldier of the Great War*, puts it movingly: "To see the beauty of the world is to put your hands on lines that run uninterrupted through life and through death. Touching them is an act of hope, for perhaps someone on the other side, if there is another side, is touching them, too." In a similar way, Fyodor Dostoevsky's Prince Myshkin, in the novel *The Idiot*, ponders the visions he has during epileptic seizures, which disclose to him an extraordinary "sense of life," of "a sort of sublime tranquility, filled with serene, harmonious joy, and hope, filled with reason and ultimate cause." Even if these rare and beautiful moments were caused only by his brain misfiring, Myshkin decides it doesn't really matter. The veil had been lifted, and he had glimpsed something so powerful that it gave his life meaning. This mystical awareness comes to us in moments of artistic communion, when nothing more than words, sounds, lines, pigments, or gestures become filled with the spark of divinity, and we feel, however briefly, that we are connected to eternity and that we are seeing the world, and ourselves in it, as it really is.

Here was the promise of Juilliard: If I mastered my craft, and absorbed its techniques into my marrow, then I could reach into the mystic, hold in my hands the threads that Albert Murray said connect us all, and draw the people gathered round the stage in the darkness, amid the chaos and confusion and pain of the human condition, together and into the light. Perhaps the revelation of beauty, and the truth, goodness, and harmony it embodied, would change their lives. Perhaps it would even save the world, or at least the world of some lost soul, desperate for a lifeline amid a raging flood.

I thought, *What a wonderful, powerful craft I've been called to.*

And I don't think I was the only one in my family who received the calling. I always thought Daddy didn't understand my desire to be an artist, but when I saw the sophistication of his photographs, I knew otherwise. Amos Pierce was born with the gift, but he never had the opportunity to develop it.

When I started talking to him about photography, it opened up a side of Daddy that I hadn't known. Listening to this furniture store stock employee by day turned maintenance man at night talking at a high level about aesthetics—I thought, *Who is this man?*

THAT MAN WAS MY FATHER, who by his example was reminding me that you can study your craft so intently that it won't ever leave you, no matter where you go in life. My conversations with Daddy taught me that art is not something that you do; it is something that you are. When I discovered the hidden side of him, Daddy was outwardly simply a stock clerk and a janitor in late middle age, taking care of his store and his buildings, and through that, providing for his family. But in his heart, he was an artist who in his early twenties roamed the streets of Manhattan with his camera, seeing the world through a lens and expressing his vision in photographs.

Now I knew that the artist that my father was had come down to me in my genes. I was the same age Daddy was when he left for New York to study art. That gave me great comfort. But I also carried the legacy of the artist that my father was never able to become. Life and love intervened, diverting him from his path. I owed my existence to this fact; how could I possibly regret it?

What he couldn't do with his photography, he did with his sense of manhood, with a sense of love and duty that allowed another artist to be born, to thrive, to grow, and to become the artist and man I am today. He sacrificed his artistry so that my artistry could bloom. But now the man who was once called Little Amos by a sentry in Pontchartrain Park was determined to fulfill the hopes his father held for himself as a young man.

I was going to be an actor.

But what kind of actor should I be? Juilliard exposed us to many different styles of drama. My teachers wanted us to understand Shakespeare and Chekhov, O'Neill and Odets, and even contemporary dramatists like John Patrick Shanley. I knew from this experience that the key to my success as an actor would have to be diversity. That is, I would have to train to do theater, television, and film. I would have to be adept in both classical and contemporary drama. And I would have to be as good at comedy as I was at tragedy. To be sure, this would help me professionally, but it was also what I wanted to do. The professional road was opening up before me, and Albert Murray had expanded my horizons further than I ever could have imagined. By the time graduation day arrived in 1985, my Juilliard education had empowered me to journey as far and as wide as my heart desired.

SIX

ART & LIFE:
"A MAN MUST HAVE
A CODE": BUNK

If you want to be a professional actor, it helps tremendously to attend Juilliard, Yale, New York University, or one of the country's other top acting schools. But you still have to pass your Leagues.

The League auditions—so called because they were once sponsored by the League of Professional Theater Training Programs—are the trial by fire that fresh theater grads must pass to launch their careers. All the major agents, casting directors, and theater movers and shakers come to New York for a weekend to see what new talent has to offer. It's not the only way to get a job in stage, film, or television, but there are no opportunities like the Leagues to show your stuff to the show business elites who can make your career.

The weekend of my League auditions, held at Juilliard that year, graduating seniors from the twelve top acting schools assembled to perform two short scenes each for the most intimidating audience imaginable. The unwritten rule at the Leagues was that you shouldn't do scenes from classical drama. At Juilliard, we had been studying classical drama intensely, but we warned ourselves that this training could be for a theater that didn't exist anymore. Tragic though that might be, lamentations for the golden age of theater do not pay the bills. Young actors need to work. Like all my colleagues, I chose to present something commercial.

I teamed with Thomas Gibson, who would later find television success on *Dharma & Greg*, *Chicago Hope*, and *Criminal Minds*, for a scene from the 1958 film *The Defiant Ones*, in which Tony Curtis and Sidney Poitier play escaped convicts chained to each other. They have to overcome their mutual racial hatred and cooperate for their own survival. That was a relatively easy scene.

The other one I chose was from *Caligula*, a 1944 drama by the French existentialist novelist and philosopher Albert Camus. Sidney Lumet brought the drama to Broadway in 1960. It's a dark and difficult play that portrays the sadistic Roman emperor as embracing violence, destruction, and excess as a way to give meaning to his life. The scene I chose, from act 2, is a dialogue with Scipio, a young poet and admirer of the emperor's, despite the fact that Caligula has murdered his father. When Scipio recites his verse to Caligula, the emperor belittles him about the power of poetry. Caligula taunts him about his "anemic" lines, destroying Scipio's artistic confidence and tempting him to join a conspiracy of assassins.

Maybe it was not the most appropriate material for a two-minute audition, but it turned out to have been one of the most effective auditions I've ever done.

Why? Because it left the professional audience curious about why I had made such a risky choice for a League audition. They thought it said something about my courage as an actor. Most actors will walk into an audition room and do what's expected. I learned from that experience at the start of my career that I should always be willing to do the unexpected. I hadn't studied for four long years in one of the world's best acting conservatories to hide my ability to handle verse, prose, and classical material. I wanted those producers and casting directors in the room to know that Wendell Pierce was a classically trained actor prepared for anything.

THE LEAGUE AUDIENCE'S positive reaction solidified my belief that if I was going to have a vital career as an actor, I was going to have to know how to perform classical theatrical texts as well as more accessible material. I would need to be equally facile on stage and screen, both big and small. I was going to have to be as good with Spielberg as I was with Shakespeare.

I came out of the League auditions with an agent, and I spent the first year of my professional life suffering from a bad case of "impostor syndrome." *Nobody knows that I'm not that good,* I kept thinking, hoping that I would complete each job before I was found out. My psychological safety net that rookie year was the assurance that if this acting thing didn't work out, I could always go back to New Orleans and get into local media.

At sixteen, I had produced my own community television show for WDSU, the city's NBC affiliate. It was a current affairs broadcast called *Think About It.* I also put together a black history radio documentary series, trying to sell it to WYLD-FM, the New Orleans R&B powerhouse. The station executives there said it was good, but it needed higher production values. Brute Bailey, the station's program director, brought me in on Saturdays to teach me the basics of radio: playing music, mastering announcing, doing commercials, and so forth. I was picking up how to be a talent both on the air and in the production process.

Brute eventually let me take over from him the weekly jazz show *Extensions from Congo Square*. I created my tag line, which I delivered in a slow, sensual, Barry White–like purr: "Extensions from Congo Square: the merger of technical proficiency and expressive thought . . . jazz."

During summers when I was home from Juilliard, Brute let me go on air. I learned so much from him about developing a work ethic. He loves radio, and was so meticulous about doing it right. He was listening to the station at all times, and if he heard a mistake, he would call you in the booth. He was aggressive, he was ambitious, he was a perfectionist—and he had a great influence on me.

If acting didn't work out, I knew that I had friends at WYLD who would find a slot for me. Besides, Joyce Eves, a Pontchartrain Park neighbor and community affairs director at WDSU, told me that on the basis of my work on *Think About It*, I could have a job at the TV station if I wanted it. A media career in New Orleans wouldn't have been a bad life at all.

And then I was cast in a movie—a small part in a scene with Tom Hanks in *The Money Pit*. After that, I landed a role in a revival of the Kurt Weill–Maxwell Anderson musical *Lost in the Stars*, a stage adaptation of Alan Paton's 1948 antiapartheid novel *Cry, the Beloved Country*. And then a producer cast me in a musical, a touring production of *Queenie Pie*, the unfinished (and rarely performed) jazz opera that Duke Ellington was writing when he died in 1974. With a

libretto by George C. Wolfe and the Duke's musical fragments knit-
ted together by his son, Mercer, *Queenie Pie* put me on the road to
Philadelphia, where the opera had its world premiere, and then to
Washington, D.C., Ellington's hometown, where the opera played
at the Kennedy Center.

I SPENT EVEN MORE TIME in Washington back then, doing a play
at the Folger Theater and an episode of the television crime drama
A Man Called Hawk, starring Avery Brooks. I was in D.C. working
when I learned a powerful lesson about acting, auditioning, and self-
confidence.

Actors often get tangled up psychologically in the audition process.
Some feel that they are compromising their integrity by having to
audition. They believe it is a form of groveling, of begging for work.
This is silly. An audition is a business presentation, nothing more. If
you don't get the role, it is not a judgment on your worth as a human
being. It only means that the people hiring actors for this project
didn't think you were right for that particular job.

My greatest audition experience was for a role I did not get. In fact,
that failed audition became one of the highlights of my career. As a
young actor, I walked into a rehearsal hall determined to make an
impact. I was auditioning for a new Broadway musical called *Big
Deal*, directed by the legendary director and choreographer Bob
Fosse. Fosse was one of the theatrical world's all-time greats. His
credits include the choreography for both the stage and film versions
of *Damn Yankees*, and direction and choreography for the Broadway

and silver-screen versions of *Sweet Charity*, *Chicago*, and *Cabaret*, for which Fosse won a Best Director Oscar, beating out Francis Ford Coppola's turn in *The Godfather*.

Bob Fosse was a giant, and his reputation and skill were expected to make *Big Deal* a very big deal. Writing about the show in *The New York Times*, critic Frank Rich said that Fosse was "the last active theater choreographer who knows how to assemble an old-fashioned, roof-raising showstopper in which every step bears the unmistakable signature of its creator."

I was determined to make my audition for Fosse memorable. When my moment came, I burst into the rehearsal hall and snarled that I was taking over this joint. It was from the scene in the play I was auditioning for. I entered in character, throwing everyone into confusion. Fosse sensed what was going on, and played along. He came around the other side of the table to do the scene with me, directed the stage manager to put some music behind us, and off we went, Pierce and Fosse, onstage together, snorting and pawing and ready to smash our horned skulls together like two raging bulls.

The scene as written was shot through with masculine ferocity, and for me, a young actor squaring off against this demigod of the American theater, I felt like Jacob wrestling with the angel. At the end of the scene, Fosse approached me in character and growled, "Let me tell you something."

"What are you going to tell me?" I snarled back.

Fosse broke character and said, "You're good, Wendell. I think you're a little young, but we've got to use you in something."

Relief!

Later that day my agent said, "What did you do today?" I told her about my daring showdown with Bob Fosse.

"Yeah, that's it," she said. "He called and said you're too young for this role, but he promised that he's going to work with you this year."

Could it be any more perfect?

A year later, I was back in D.C. on another project when I turned on the evening news and heard Bob Fosse was dead. He had been in rehearsals for a *Sweet Charity* revival in Washington that day when he dropped dead of a heart attack. I was crushed, first of all for Fosse himself, second for the loss to American theater, and finally, for myself: I would never be able to work with the great man.

Then it hit me: *Wendell, you did work with him.*

True, we had an audience of maybe two or three, but I truly worked onstage with Bob Fosse. That was precious. I had been given the opportunity to do something thousands of actors dreamed of doing. It changed my way of thinking about auditions. After that, I never took another one for granted.

After a year of supporting myself with film and stage roles, I had to admit a difficult truth to myself: *I'm an actor.* Why was it difficult? Because I am often afraid that I am an impostor on the verge of being found out. Every job I got my rookie year was a shock. *Really? They want me?* I found it hard to trust my success.

That's the hardest admission for a lot of artists to make—to accept they are, in fact, an artist, and need to stop withholding that psychological commitment to their vocation. The fear of failure is so very strong. It occurred to me at that early stage in my career that I was focusing on the wrong things. I would do ten auditions and not get a callback, and I thought those failures defined me, instead of the one callback I did get.

Not only was I wrong to give failure greater credence than success, but I was also wrong to see those unsuccessful auditions as failures at all. The audition process, I came to see, is your opening and closing night, all in one. When I took the stage at an audition, I was going to enter into that brief communion with another film or theater artist, and show them who I was and what I could do with the role. *Here it is, thank you very much, I hope you enjoyed it.* Keep moving on. Nothing is lost. Everything is gained.

I made my Broadway debut in 1988, in the American production of *Serious Money*, Caryl Churchill's financial-world satire. My parents flew to New York for the opening. It was especially gratifying to show my father, who had been skeptical of my love of the stage, that I was making it as an actor.

My big Broadway break came in 1991, when I took over the lead role in *The Piano Lesson*, playwright August Wilson's Pulitzer Prize–winning drama about the past, the future, and black identity. Then again, all of Wilson's plays are about the past, the future, and black identity. In discovering August Wilson's art, I not only found the embodiment of Albert Murray's vision of what the African American artist can be, but also gained insights that would define my own approach to my art and my life.

We had never had an African American playwright with a body of work that existed on the level of Tennessee Williams, Eugene O'Neill, Edward Albee, and Arthur Miller. And to have someone of that caliber give voice to the African American experience—*my* experience, and the experience of my family—was a great discovery for me.

Personally, Wilson revealed to me that Mamo and Papo's story, which I had always held dear, was the material of the highest art. In Wilson's plays, I see and hear the tales of my own family, their struggles, their victories, and their defeats. He shows how African Americans dealt with challenges and how, to steal a line from Faulkner, they not only endured, but triumphed.

August Wilson understood these people. My people. Our people. And with his gifts, he enshrined them in the artistic pantheon.

Professionally, I knew that I would be able to go further in my work as an artist and wouldn't be limited in my roles. Wilson was providing for generations to come a multitude of characters, a multitude of stories, a multitude of opportunities to enlighten the human experience through theater. As *The New Yorker*'s theater critic John Lahr wrote in a 2001 appraisal of Wilson's work, "His audience appeal almost single-handedly broke down the wall for other black artists, many of whom would not otherwise be working in the mainstream."

August eventually became a familiar and friendly associate after the few times I worked with him, as an actor in his plays and a producer of them, and he remained so until his death from cancer in 2005. Our relationship was professional. He knew me as one of many who were part of his repertory group. I loved playing Wilson's characters. As a writer, he gives you so much to work with and so much to discover in your research and preparation for the role. For an African American actor, digging deep into the history, the folkways, and the spirituality of African people in the American Diaspora will take you into parts of yourself you never knew.

Wilson was born in 1945 and was raised in the Hill District of Pittsburgh by his devoutly Catholic mother, Daisy, and her second husband. Daisy used to pray the rosary with August and his siblings, but August remembered the Church treating his family as second-class Christians, just as my mother and her brothers and sisters were. August was a brilliant young man who suffered from and raged against the injustice of racism. He confronted his own personal Chets at Central Catholic High School, but was also wounded by a black English teacher who accused August of cheating when he couldn't believe an unusually accomplished essay about Napoléon Bonaparte could have been written by someone as young as he.

In time, August managed to turn his pain into great art. He became one of the most celebrated playwrights of his era and created some of the most dazzling American drama of the twentieth century. He is best known for the ten plays of his *Pittsburgh Cycle*, nearly all of which are set in the Hill District. Each play features ordinary black characters in a different decade of the twentieth century. His examination of the African American experience over the past century exemplifies the black contribution to the universal human experience while telling the particularly black, particularly American story of triumph in the face of racism, violence, terror, murder, and abuse. August was not a religious man, but the spirituality in his plays speaks to the concrete connection we have to our ancestors, and the transformative power they can bring to bear on our lives in the present.

For August Wilson, as with Albert Murray, the experience of African people in America is one of a "blues people" marked by resilience in the face of unspeakable odds—and a resilience that produced a culture that ultimately changed, and continues to change, all of America. August's drama centers around the tension African Americans have in being true to themselves while assuming their rightful place as Americans in full. In August's work, you cannot go forward into the future without first reestablishing a connection to the past and to the wider black community.

Though critics, including my old friend Stanley Crouch, at times accused him of being too separatist, August contended that his Afrocentric vision was justified morally, historically, and artistically.

"As Africans prior to coming over here, [our ancestors] existed, and they were the center. Everything revolved around them in their worldview. Over here, all of that has been taken and stripped away," he noted in an interview with Carol Rosen in 1996. "So I say, 'Let's look at it. The world is right here in this backyard.' There is no idea that cannot be contained by black life. We have the entire world here."

Yet he would not give an inch on his stance that African American uniqueness fit harmoniously within the broader tradition. "All of human life is universal, and it is theater that illuminates and confers upon the universal the ability to speak for all men," August told Rosen. As he saw it, Western civilization had absorbed the African Diaspora, in the sense that the stories of Africans in America were now an inextricable part of the story the modern West told about itself. But the West must not dilute and dissolve the African contribution, the integrity of which is irreducible.

To fight revisionist history that doesn't give African Americans our due, we black folk have to celebrate the triumphs of our own culture. Yet we must resist those who claim that African Americans aren't part of the broader American artistic and cultural tradition. This requires a self-conscious vigilance that balances participating in the mainstream with guarding and nurturing the tradition that is our own and nobody else's.

The American storytelling tradition generally focuses on the individual discovering his true self apart from the crowd. August consciously rejected that idea in favor of a communal ideal he considered more representative of the black experience. Though he was deeply influenced by the Black Power movement of the 1960s, August's plays were not protest dramas and were only implicitly political. For him, the intractability of white racism was a given, but he did not want to preoccupy himself with it, because to do so would have meant granting more power to the oppressors than they deserved. (This echoes the advice Mamo and Papo gave to their children on how to handle white hatred with grace and dignity: "Don't be the person they think you are.")

Strengthening communal bonds, sustaining black life amid severe trials, and bearing witness to the tragedies and triumphs of African American life are the central concerns of August Wilson's dramas. As August told John Lahr, he wanted to show that black culture "was capable of sustaining you, so that when you left your father's or your mother's house you didn't go into the world naked. You were fully clothed in manners and a way of life."

In the theater of August Wilson, as in the criticism of Albert Murray, I found validation of all the teaching I had absorbed from my ancestors back home, and solid ground on which to take my stand as an actor and as a man. I also found my first opportunity to show Broadway what I could do.

The Piano Lesson begins with Boy Willie, a brash, reckless young southerner, showing up at his Uncle Doaker Charles's house in Pittsburgh, in the midst of the Great Depression. Boy Willie is fresh out of prison in Mississippi and has come North to persuade his sister Berniece, a widow who lives with Doaker and her eleven-year-old daughter, Maretha, to sell a family heirloom: a piano that has been in their family for generations.

The piano is unique in that it has images of their family members carved in its wood during slave days. Originally owned by the Sutters, the white family that also owned the Charles family, the piano became a totem of the Charleses, charged with spiritual power. Boy Willie sees the piano as his ticket to a new life. He wants to take the money he earns from selling it and return to the South to buy a portion of the land the Charles family once worked as the Sutter family's slaves. Prideful Boy Willie is preoccupied with proving his equality to the white man and holds fast to a characteristically southern idea that owning land is the measure of a man's worth.

Berniece won't have it. She is the custodian of the piano and cherishes it as a symbol of their ancestral legacy. But she is also afraid of what it represents. Even though slavery was long past, the siblings' father, Boy Charles, became convinced that their family would always remain bound to the Sutters as long as they owned the piano, into which his family's history had been carved. The Sutters killed him for his role in stealing the piano, which his two brothers, Doaker and Wining Boy, carried to the North.

Mama Ola, Berniece and Boy Willie's mother, poured her grief over her husband's death into that piano, which Berniece played as a young woman. After Mama Ola's death, Berniece quit playing the piano; she has hidden its legacy from her daughter, fearing that the sorrow and the suffering it holds will be too great a burden for Maretha to bear.

The conflict in the play comes from Boy Willie and Berniece fighting over the piano's fate. The piano cannot be divided in two without destroying its value. Berniece accuses her brother of selling his soul.

In Berniece, I see a reflection of those within African American society, and in my hometown, whose love of place, community, and tradition is so fierce that it manifests as fear and loathing of the unfamiliar. People will often hold so tightly to what they know that they harshly criticize, even reject, those within the family and community who deviate from it.

Ultimately, if you really understand your identity, and love tradition and authenticity, leaving its origin will never dilute it; it will only make it stronger.

In New Orleans today, whenever I say something controversial, there is always somebody who accuses me of being a fake and a turncoat to the city. This is a self-serving lie, and deep down, these critics have got to know that. The truth is that the New Orleans culture that you're born into and raised up in will be with you no matter where you go. You take it with you and add to it, and give back, renewing the tradition by making your own contribution to it.

Yet Berniece is not entirely wrong in her conservatism. Boy Willie maintains that the piano is nothing more than a piece of wood that can be used to stake him in a better future. In his egotism and pride, he has no reverence for the past and its legacy of blood and tears. To him, it is something he can relate to only as a thing to be manipulated. It has nothing to teach him and no hold on him. I think of Boy

Willie when I see the apathy and sense of entitlement so many of our young people have today. As the old Albert King blues song puts it, "Everybody wants to laugh, but nobody wants to cry / Everybody wants to go to heaven, but nobody wants to die."

Wynton Marsalis is perhaps the preeminent exemplar of the lesson August Wilson taught in so many of his plays. Wynton is a prophetic artist who stood up to the prevailing jazz culture of his day and said we cannot achieve greatness if we disrespect our ancestors and the tradition they have handed to us. The road to the future goes through the past. "If I have seen further," said Isaac Newton, "it is because I am standing on the shoulders of giants." Wynton couldn't have put it better himself.

When Wynton came along, jazz had become all about emulating pop music and rock and roll. Wynton rejected that and set out to reclaim the legacy of the jazz past as the platform from which to launch jazz into the future. When guys were going to clubs playing music in T-shirts and jeans, Wynton said, no, I want to be clean, I want to look good in the clubs. Pops and Thelonious Monk and those guys, they wanted to look good in the clubs. How can my music be taken seriously if I don't take myself seriously?

Wynton's critics have called him sanctimonious, but they don't understand the difference between reverence and sanctimony. The road to artistic greatness is narrow and few travel down it—but Wynton and his brother Branford inspired a whole generation of jazzmen to follow them along that difficult path.

They may even go pop; Branford played with Sting, after all; and Trombone Shorty, the young New Orleans horn phenom, has become a pop star now. But there's a depth of musicianship that Shorty can delve into because he has mastered the classics. He can play the most difficult intro in jazz, "West End Blues" by Louis Armstrong, and that is an education that nobody can take from him, ever. Shorty can blaze meaningful new trails into pop and jazz's future because he is deeply in touch with its past.

As with the Marsalis family's horns, so with the Charles family's piano. In *The Piano Lesson*, the deeper meaning of Boy Willie's struggle with Berniece has to do with what these siblings should do with their past. Is it something that is valuable only insofar as it can be converted into a profitable future, as Boy Willie thinks? If it should be conserved and revered, as Berniece believes, how can we keep the past from holding us hostage and preventing us from opening ourselves to new life? This is a question that all Americans must face, but it has particular emotional and philosophical resonance for African Americans.

When I read *The Piano Lesson* and decided to audition for the Boy Willie role, I felt in my bones that this was the story of my slave ancestor Aristile. The slave owner Sutter traded "a nigger and a half"—a mother and her little son, the Charles family's ancestors—for the piano, as a present for his wife. To me, this was Aristile and his mother, whose name is lost to history, sold away from their Kentucky family and sent down the river, never to see them again. My family did not have a piano, but we had the same pain. Every black family in America does. When I auditioned for the Boy Willie role, I turned upstage and said a silent prayer to Mamo, asking for her help in getting me the chance to tell the story of her father, my ancestor, our patriarch.

In the play, what exorcises the tormenting spirit of slavery and white oppression, and heals the rift between the two Charles siblings, is art—specifically, music that Berniece draws out of the piano in a moment of intense crisis. She invokes the ancestors in an incantatory prayer set to music, one she creates in that crucible of fear and suffering. The music breaks the curse that haunts her brother and keeps the family broken.

The Piano Lesson shows the power of African American art to bridge the past and the future, to bind the wounds of slavery and oppression, and to heal the generational violence we commit against each other as the legacy of the violence done to us. As August used to say, discovering Bessie Smith and the blues at the age of twenty was a turning point in his life, because it taught him that he had a history, and that the material of everyday African American life—his life and the life of his people—was the stuff of tremendous dignity and the highest art. He subsequently revered the act of artistic creation so highly that before he would sit down to write, he would wash his hands as an act of ritual cleansing.

Boy Willie's attitude toward the power of art and culture is unfortunately common today. He saw the piano's worth only in materialistic terms. He tells Berniece he wouldn't begrudge her keeping the piano if she would use it to make money somehow. This is how far too many of us see art: as something that's nice to look at or listen to, maybe, but separate from the real business of life, which is practicality.

This is tragically shortsighted. It assumes that decisions are made strictly from bloodless cost-benefit analysis, as if human beings were creatures of the mind alone and not also of the heart. It's not to say that engaging the heart is irrational, but rather that art and culture can provide a complementary way of understanding the truth of things.

In the *Divine Comedy*, when the pilgrim Dante climbs the seven-story mountain of Purgatory, he learns about the virtues by first encountering them depicted in art created by the hand of God. The lesson is that the initial encounter with beauty prepares the individual's imagination to accept moral truth.

Consider the impact that Harriet Beecher Stowe's 1852 antislavery novel *Uncle Tom's Cabin* had on American history. The book became a national and international sensation because it put a human face on slavery in America and galvanized the determination to put an end to it. During the Civil War, when the author met Abraham Lincoln, the president is believed to have said, "So you're the little woman who wrote the book that started this great war."

Uncle Tom's Cabin provides an unusual example of a work of art having a direct and consequential effect on how the wider society understands and deals with a political issue of utmost importance. Rarely can cause and effect in these matters be drawn so clearly. But to believe that one has to be able to measure and quantify the impact of art on the wider culture before that impact can be said to exist is absurd.

The second August Wilson play I appeared in was a 1992 Philadelphia production of the drama *Joe Turner's Come and Gone*. The 1984 play is about the dislocation of African Americans emerging from slavery, having to discover who they are in a condition of freedom. Wandering into Pittsburgh from the South in the first decade of the twentieth century, these "dazed and stunned" sons and daughters of freed slaves are, in August's words, "isolated, cut off from memory, having forgotten the names of the gods and only guessing at their faces."

Though in the industrialized North, the migrants are what the playwright calls "foreigners in a strange land," they arrive knowing that they must shape "the malleable parts of themselves into a new identity as free men of definite and sincere worth."

I portrayed Herald Loomis, a man who had been kidnapped and pressed into a chain gang by Joe Turner, a legendary white villain from blues songs. The real-life Joe Turner was Joe Turney, a politically connected Tennessean who in the 1890s rounded up black men on petty criminal charges and forced them to do years of hard labor on his plantation. In Memphis, when black men would disappear, their women would lament, "Joe Turner's come and gone." Turney entered blues mythology in W. C. Handy's song "Joe Turner's Blues."

In the play, Herald Loomis and his eleven-year-old daughter arrive in a Pittsburgh black boardinghouse, renting a room while they search for Martha, the wife who left Herald during his seven years of captivity. Herald meets fellow tenant Bynum, an elderly former slave who is a "root man"—a healer and visionary who keeps alive the African folk religious traditions. He is said to have the mystical gift of binding lost people together.

After Sunday dinner, Bynum leads the tenants in a "juba," a traditional African call-and-response ritual, calling on the Holy Ghost. An angry Herald, a church deacon who has lost his Christian faith, utters a blasphemy. Suddenly, Herald is possessed by a spirit and thrashes on the floor, speaking in tongues. Old Bynum understands that the terrified Herald is having a vision. Bynum asks him what he's seen.

"I come to this place . . . to this water that was bigger than the whole world," says Herald. "And I looked out . . . and I seen these bones rise up out the water. Rise up and begin to walk on top of it."

The bones sink back into the ocean, Herald says, causing a huge wave, washing them all ashore.

"Only they ain't bones no more," says Bynum.

"They got flesh on them!" says Herald. "Just like you and me!"

Bynum, we learn, once traveled supernaturally to the "City of Bones," a realm in the ocean where the bodies of enslaved Africans who perished in the Middle Passage and were thrown overboard now reside. August once described Herald's vision as a kind of baptism.

"He is privileged to witness this because he needs most to know who he is," August wrote. "It is telling him, 'this is who you are. You are these bones. You are the sons and daughters of these people. They are walking around here now, and they look like you because you are these very same people. This is who you are.'"

The City of Bones myth August created for his plays (it appears again in *Gem of the Ocean*, from 2003) is based in part on an 1803 report of a cargo of Igbo tribesmen (sometimes called Ibo) who, arriving in Georgia, had a premonition that they were about to enter slavery. It is impossible to be certain which parts of the tale are factual and which parts have been added over the years as the story took root in the African American folk consciousness, but it appears that the slaves revolted and drowned the crew, causing the ship to run aground in Dunbar Creek, south of Savannah. The slaves then leapt off the deck of the slave ship in chains, supposedly expecting to walk back to Africa. In truth, they chose to commit mass suicide rather than submit to forced servitude.

That moment was our Masada. Their death by drowning was a kind of baptism through which new life—a spirit of resistance—was born for African Americans who unite themselves to its power. Similarly, the City of Bones is not a graveyard but a source of spiritual renewal. It represents the collective memory of African Americans. Bynum tells Herald that he suffers because he has "lost his song." Herald does not find his song—that is, his purpose in life—until he connects in a deep and life-changing way to ancestral history and makes it his own.

Like Albert Murray's own aesthetic, August Wilson's art encompasses what W. E. B. Du Bois, in his 1903 book *The Souls of Black Folk*, called the "double consciousness" of the American Negro:

> One ever feels his two-ness, an American, a Negro; two souls, two thoughts, two unreconciled strivings; two warring ideals in one dark body, whose dogged strength alone keeps it from being torn asunder.
>
> The history of the American Negro is the history of this strife—this longing to attain self-conscious manhood, to merge his double self into a better and truer self. In this merging he wishes neither of the older selves to be lost. He would not Africanize America, for America has too much to teach the world and Africa. He would not bleach his Negro soul in a flood of white Americanism, for he knows that Negro blood has a message for the world. He simply wishes to make it pos-

sible for a man to be both a Negro and an American, without being cursed and spit upon by his fellows, without having the doors of Opportunity closed roughly in his face.

The moral grandeur, spiritual greatness, and artistic fecundity of the African American tradition emerge from the creative tension of his double consciousness. It is both the thorn in our side and the wind beneath our wings. Through inhabiting the roles of Boy Willie and Herald Loomis, I communed with the spirits of my ancestors and gained wisdom that would carry me far down the road on my personal pilgrimage toward finding my own song.

MY PROFESSIONAL MILESTONES didn't always come wrapped in such noble mantles. There was the time I acted a fool and humiliated myself in public and spent the night in jail for my troubles—and it led to the role of a lifetime.

In 2001, shortly after the September 11 attacks, my agent passed to me the pilot script for an upcoming HBO series called *The Wire*. It was the creation of David Simon, a former *Baltimore Sun* police reporter who had made his professional reputation with his nonfiction book *Homicide: A Year on the Killing Streets*, which became a crime drama on NBC in the 1990s. With *The Wire*, Simon wanted to do something more ambitious. It wasn't going to be simply an exceptional Baltimore cop show; Simon had already done that for NBC. He was going to attempt to create a visual novel, in which the storytelling arc would be much longer than a standard television drama, and the plotting would be far more complex. Simon felt that audiences were smart enough to stick with it for the payoff.

David—we would become close friends—hit his mark. The show ended its five-season run in 2008 as one of the most critically acclaimed dramas in television history. As the journalist Jacob Weisberg said after three seasons, *The Wire* "is surely the best show ever broadcast in America. . . . No other program has ever done anything remotely like what this one does, namely to portray the social, political, and economic life of an American city with the scope, observational precision, and moral vision of great literature."

All that was in the future. I could sense something big coming when I first laid eyes on that pilot script. It was like nothing I had ever read. The character for which I was auditioning, Bunk Moreland, a brilliant homicide detective known for his hard drinking, caustic wit, and natty taste in clothes, struck me as startlingly genuine. In fact, the realism of the entire program blew me away. *The Wire* was really an investigation of human nature. That was the key to my approach to acting. Plus, as in August Wilson's plays, *The Wire* would go deep into the heart of an African American character rarely if ever seen in drama: a black cop.

I was born to play Bunk, I thought. *This is one role I cannot miss.*

Days before my *Wire* audition, I got into a New York taxi in Midtown, headed to a screening at a hotel in SoHo. The cabdriver didn't want to take the route I asked him to follow. Instead, he went right through Times Square during rush hour. Traffic was at a standstill, and I was running out of time.

"Listen, I'll just get another cab," I said, then opened my door to exit.

"You're going to pay me for this," he said, and jumped out.

"Hell, no," I shot back. "I told you not to come this way, but you wouldn't listen."

We stood there in the middle of a Times Square traffic jam, arguing. Next thing I know, the cabbie takes a swing at me.

I couldn't believe this guy! I was furious. My glasses were askew. I put my glasses in my breast pocket and pulled an old schoolboy trick.

"Motherfucker, look," I said, and pointed to the ground. When he looked down, I clocked him.

There we were, two grown men, too old to be doing this shit, fighting like two schoolboys, with a rush-hour audience of thousands watching.

The cabbie swung at me again. "Look, motherfucker," I said a second time. Incredibly, he looked. I cold-cocked him.

Out of the corner of my eye, I saw what was obviously an undercover police van crawling through traffic. An officer sitting in the van had a clipboard and was hiding his face, trying to pretend not to see these two clowns fighting in the street. You could tell they were on a major manhunt of some kind—I found out later they were looking for suspects in a notorious multiple murder over the Carnegie Deli—and they didn't have time to waste on a stupid fistfight. But when the van stopped right in front of us brawlers, they had to act.

The cops jumped out, cuffed both of us, and grabbed a witness to get his story before questioning the cabbie and me. I heard the witness tell them that I had started the fight. When he turned to leave, I said, "Oh, so you're just going to walk away now?" And I took one step toward him. At that point, the cops jumped me and arrested me as the perpetrator.

I learned a valuable lesson that day: When cops don't know who started a fight, they wait for a sign of some sort to plausibly blame the incident on one of the parties. Without knowing what I was doing, I gave them what they needed.

Now I was in deep. "What happens now?" I asked one of the officers. "I've never been arrested before."

"We'll process you, you'll go home, and we'll be in touch," he said, in a business-as-usual tone.

Then the officer saw my driver's license. "Wait, we can't let you go," he said. "You live in California."

So I spent the night in a Manhattan lockup.

A couple of days later, I showed up for my *Wire* audition still mad as hell. Before the reading, I boiled over with anger telling the people in the audition about my arrest. Here I was in a major audition, and all I could think about and talk about was what had happened to me in Times Square. After the reading, I had a callback to read with Dominic West, who was to play Bunk's partner Jimmy McNulty, and then another call to say I had the job.

"You know what got you the role?" David Simon told me later. "That story. You *were* Bunk. You took us through every possible thing we could write about a character. We knew you were probably our Bunk before you read a single line."

That taught me something important about the human element in storytelling. It goes all the way back to the invention of language, to prehistoric people sitting around a fire, telling about hunting, running in the fields, and painting tableaux of their world on the cave walls.

Telling stories is at the core of human nature. It's how we connect with each other. That's what happened with me that day with David

Simon. I was simply telling a tale of what had happened to me in my run-in with the police, but the way I did it revealed my humanity. It showed David that I had within me all the elements he would be able to use to create Bunk Moreland's character.

This is what the art of acting—and indeed all true art—is about: to recognize the truly human, to authenticate it, to express it, and to document it in a way that makes it accessible to other human beings. What every artist will tell you is that we're all searching for the truth about humanity, to help ourselves and each other become more authentically human.

After taking the Bunk Moreland role, I went to Baltimore and began doing ride-alongs with police officers of the city's western division. David knew the people of Baltimore and the culture of police officers intimately. I wanted to get to know them too, especially because I had had two bad experiences with the police—one of them in Baltimore—that made me anxious about cops.

In 1986, fresh out of Juilliard, I was on the road tour of *Queenie Pie* and stopped in Baltimore to see a friend who was in a play at Center Stage. After we parted, I took a cab back to the downtown train station. When I tried to pay the cabbie, he attempted to cheat me. We got into an argument on the sidewalk. It ended with him putting his cab into reverse and running over one of my bags on the curb.

"Call the police!" I yelled. When an officer showed up, he talked to the cabbie and then spoke privately with me on the sidewalk. Both the officer and the cabbie were white.

"What do you want to do?" the cop said to me.

"I want to press charges," I said. "That guy tried to run me over with his cab, and he ran over one of my bags."

"What do you want to do?" the cop repeated.

We went back and forth like this, over and over. Finally he gets right in my face, puts his hand on his holstered pistol, and screams, *"What do you want to do?!"*

I got it.

"I guess I'm going to get my bags and get on the train and go to New York," I muttered.

"Yeah," he smirked, "that's what I thought you were going to do."

The second incident happened in 1999, when I was in south Louisiana for Uncle L.H.'s funeral. I picked up my cousin Kim and her two small children at the airport in New Orleans and was driving them to the church for the funeral mass. A Louisiana state trooper put his lights on behind us. I pulled over.

It was 100 degrees that day, so I kept the windows up and the air conditioner on, waiting for the trooper to come to the window. I immediately put my wallet on the dashboard; if a cop pulls me over for a traffic violation, I do that so he won't think that I'm reaching for a gun. There I sat, waiting for the trooper to approach the window. The radio was on, and I couldn't hear a thing outside the car.

I checked my rearview mirror to see what was taking him so long. There he was behind the car, his face scarlet, spittle flying from his mouth, gun slightly drawn.

"Goddamnit, get out of the car!" he screamed.

I lowered the driver's-side window, put my hand out, and opened the door from the outside. I wasn't about to give him any reason to shoot. I began walking toward him.

"Back up!" he yelled. "I'm going to blow your fucking head off!"

I stopped in my tracks.

"Why didn't you get out of the car?"

"I didn't hear you, officer. Why didn't you use your PA?"

"Don't tell me how to do my job! Where you going?"

I told him and handed him my driver's license.

"Oh, you're from California. You're a flight risk. I can't just write you a ticket."

He arrested me and said he was going to take me downtown to pay the ticket. He said my cousin Kim would have to drive my car behind him to the police station.

"If I'm under arrest, that's fine," I said to him. "But you see those two little kids in the back of the car? They're never going to see a police station in their life, and it's not going to start today."

The trooper walked to the car to speak with Kim outside of my earshot. In that moment, for the first time in my life, I understood what it meant to be in a blind rage. I was engulfed by wrath, but could not let it slip. My rage was so intense I could not pick out his badge number. All I recalled was that he was young, white, and had red hair.

Somehow, we got out of the situation, but my tears at L.H.'s funeral were from anger, not grief. If I had jumped out of the car and done something rash, my family would have had another funeral to deal with. The trooper, whose name I never learned, was on the verge of firing his gun.

I would not impugn all police officers because of the conduct of a few. In fact, the bad cops I've dealt with heightened my respect for the men and women of the badge who don't dishonor it by abusing their power. Still, I came to *The Wire* with some emotional baggage that was not easy to drop.

What a relief, then, to be welcomed so warmly by the Baltimore police officers who invited me to go with them on their rounds to see how it all works. The first detail that struck me was to see the effect the police car had on the people of the streets we cruised. Even though the police and I were in an unmarked car and the detectives weren't in uniform, everybody knew they were cops, and everybody was watching them.

People talk about how the presence of police can be a deterrent. I saw it firsthand. When we were spotted, there was an immediate effect. Everyone in the neighborhood is aware of your presence. When I watched police interview witnesses and suspects on the street, I saw people's behavior change. The power of the police to affect behavior in others was palpable.

I also saw how dealing day in and day out with criminality, the worst part of human nature, took its toll on police officers. They developed harsh black humor to cope with the bleakness of the world they had to live in. You saw that on *The Wire*, and believe me, it was not exaggerated for dramatic effect. Cops are always messing with each other. It's the boys' locker room times a thousand. Observing this helped me develop Bunk.

And there was this: As part of the coping mechanism for the cops I saw of the western division, every Thursday when they got off duty, they'd get a bottle of Bushmills and kill it. Every single Thursday. They drank a lot. Bunk's alcoholism in the series is based on real-life observations of the personal lives of police detectives. *The Wire* is set in West Baltimore, the historic heart of the city's African American culture but now overrun by drugs, crime, blight, and chronic poverty. The cops who work in the western division have a hard life there, and they don't always soften the psychic pummeling their work deals them in the best ways.

On one of the ride-alongs, I followed the two male detectives I was paired with to meet with a family. They introduced me as Detective Pierce. Back at the station, I went into the interrogation room, still in character, so to speak. I listened as the real detectives questioned a burglary suspect. At one point, the interrogator turned to me and said, "Detective, do you have any questions?"

Oh, God. What do I say?

I asked something very simple. "So, you are saying you were there that day. That you knew the man, but you didn't do it. But if you were there, then you saw it. Describe the man who did it."

The suspect didn't know what to say. Busted! After it was over, the real detective said to me, "Hey, man, that was a good question." That felt great.

One of the officers I shadowed, a veteran of decades on the force whom I will call Jimmy, told me back then that it's so difficult to become a homicide detective that those who do take pride in wearing fine suits. "You a homicide detective, man, you got to let them know it," said Jimmy, who favored a dapper hat and beautiful overcoats.

I built that style into Bunk. One of my classic lines from *The Wire* is: "The Bunk is strictly a suit-and-tie-wearing motherfucker." That really came from the pride these homicide detectives had in themselves and their appearance.

Jimmy also taught me the power of interrogation. He was so good at it that by the end of *The Wire*'s five-year run, I thought that if I could become a homicide detective, I would. The experiences that the detectives I observed had, and that I sometimes had with them, dazzled me as a student of human behavior.

"Wendell, if you're ever arrested, never fall asleep," Jimmy said. "We bring in a suspect, we put him in the box, and we just watch him for a while. If he goes to sleep, we know we've got the right one."

I told him I didn't understand.

"Think about it," Jimmy said. "You've just killed a guy. You've been on the run for two weeks. You can't sleep. You're running. Once we finally catch you, you've been up for two weeks trying to figure out how to get out of this, and running from us. When they go to sleep, we know we've got the right one.

"It's not scientific, and it won't hold up in court, but goddamnit, it's the right place to start."

In the same way, Jimmy said, innocent people tend not to fall asleep in the interrogation room. They're scared and agitated. Sleeplessness is no guarantee of innocence, the detective told me, but interrogators have learned from experience that it's a pretty good sign.

In researching my character, I found out that police officers can say just about anything in interrogations. Jimmy told me a story about two suspects in a shooting death. Cops were trying to get a confession out of one of them. They took one of the suspects aside and said, "Please tell us that you had the .45, because we just got the ballistics back and it was the nine-millimeter that killed him."

The relieved suspect said, "Yeah, yeah, I had the .45. I shot him."

"Good, good," said the interrogator. "You write that down." And so he did.

Then the detectives brought the second suspect in and flipped the strategy around. He too signed a confession.

"Wait, Jimmy," I said, "which bullet killed the guy?"

"Wendell, it doesn't matter which bullet killed him. They both confessed to shooting a guy who died. We just got two confessions."

A common ploy is the good cop/bad cop routine. Jimmy told a story about how he once had a murder suspect in the interrogation room. He told the suspect that he knew he was guilty, but hey, he could see why the guy did it.

"Here's the thing," Jimmy told him. "You're not saying anything, and you don't have to say anything. But the DA is going to come up with all of this shit to say why you killed him, and they're going to put you away. Now, they can tell their story, and you can tell the truth. If you tell me the truth about how you killed him, and why you killed him, I will talk to the DA for you."

"You'd do that?" the suspect said.

"Yeah, I'd do that," Jimmy said.

The suspect wrote out his confession and signed it.

"The next morning I talked to the DA," Jimmy continued. "I said, 'Good morning.'"

"Oh man, Jimmy, that was a trick!" I said. "How can you do that?"

He said, "Listen, man, you work for the family."

That principle came to the fore when a different detective took me to court to see a sentencing in a murder conviction. It was one of the most depressing, devastating events I've ever witnessed. The convicted killer was a young man, no more than twenty-five, a huge, strapping guy. The victim's family gave testimony at the sentencing hearing.

"You're a nothing, you killed my son, he was a thousand times better than you," said the mother. Then the next family member took the stand. "If I could right now, I would kill you and take my punishment and spend the rest of my life in jail." Then the next one. On and on like this.

Then the judge said it was time for the convicted man's family to speak. Would anyone care to testify?

No one stood. No one was there for him. No one.

And I thought: *No wonder.*

This kid rose and faced the judge. He was sentenced to life in prison. He did not blink. He did not waver. He turned and walked through the door. His life was over.

I was heartbroken. All the loss, all the pain. I turned to the detective and said, "Man, doesn't it just tear you up inside? How can you do this?"

Everyone involved in this case—the judge, the victim, the perpetrator—all of them were black.

"All of them are from our community," I said. "Doesn't that break your heart?"

"Wendell, stop. This is not our community. This is *affecting* our community," the detective answered. "Our community is hard-working people who are going out every day doing the best they can, trying to raise their kids. But it's a small percentage that's destroying it. That criminal is not our community."

"Don't you understand?" I said. "He had nobody here to speak for him."

"Yeah, I saw that. But did you see the family? Did you see all those people whose lives were destroyed? They got a lifetime sentence too, and they didn't do anything. Their son is dead and gone, and they didn't do anything. When you are a detective, you work for them."

Right then and there, I said if I didn't have to go through the boot camp experience, I would become a homicide detective. I would be one of the African American men who stood against those criminals who were destroying our community and defining it in the public eye. Ninety-nine percent of the people are decent, good, hardworking folks who are being hurt and even destroyed by that 1 percent.

Then I met the real Bunk Moreland. Oscar "Rick" Requer is his name. What a larger-than-life character he is. Rick was a pioneering black police detective who joined the Baltimore force in 1964, when black faces were scarce there—and unwelcome. I never was able to observe him work a homicide case. By the time *The Wire* started, Rick was in the courthouse, coasting toward retirement. But I could tell simply by being in his presence that he had the gift of being able to coax suspects into confession, like an exceptionally talented therapist.

Rick could be a good cop, and he could be a bad cop. He smoked a cigar like I did in the show. He loved to drink. There was a story—I was scared to ask him if it was true—that he had gone out and been on a bender, driving home, smoking a cigar, and flipped his car. When the police came, he rolled down his window—or rather, rolled up his window—and said, "Can I help you guys?"

His nickname was "the Bunk" because that's what he called people he liked. It came from his time in the military: Your "bunk" was your bunkmate. For Rick Requer, there was no more endearing term.

I never talked with him once we got into the series. The first day we were shooting, I saw Rick in the distance, driving by in his Caddy, smoking a cigar. He pulled over, got out, and had a quizzical look on his face. Watching him, I got the sense that he was thinking, *What the hell is that boy doing, portraying me? He doesn't know a damn thing.*

I was so intimidated by that moment that I never reached out to him again for the five years we shot the series.

One day, I was sitting in a Baltimore barbershop and someone said, "Hey, man, aren't you that actor that plays Bunk? I know the real Bunk. He's retiring. You better be there."

It was almost like a threat. I thought, *Oh God, that's the same look Bunk gave me five years ago.* I figured that he was going to take his retirement party as an opportunity to dress me down for how badly I had made him look for the past five years.

So I screwed up my courage and showed up at the party to get what I had coming. I knew Bunk was going to dress me down in front of all his colleagues and tell me what a dishonor I had done to him, to his family, and to the black men of the Baltimore police department who had worked so hard to be detectives.

I walked into the hall and saw him across the room. There he was, the real Bunk, looking at me with that quizzical look again. It took a lifetime to make my way across the crowded room to say hello. When I stood in front of him, he gave me a hard look, then melted.

"Bunk!" he said. "You came! Everybody, look, Bunk is here!"

He hugged me hard and held me tight. "Oh, you made me famous, boy! I can't believe you here!"

I felt like the Prodigal Son come home. I had to speak to the crowd, of course. I turned to him and said, "Bunk, how did I do?"

"Oh, boy, you did good. You made me famous," he said. Receiving his blessing was like hearing from my own father. To have that from the real Bunk was one of the greatest gifts you could give me.

I knew how hard it was for Rick Requer to work through the ranks of the Baltimore Police Department. I was proud of how *The Wire* depicted how black men chose to join the force. Almost all the black detectives and beat cops I met told me that they entered police work to defend their own communities.

They knew that what was happening in their neighborhoods wasn't right. They knew the Miss Annes and Mr. Joes, the law-abiding, hardworking folk, especially the working poor, who were trying to hold their families together against impossible odds. It was that 1 or 2 percent of hoodlums who made life miserable for everybody else. These black men became police officers because they wanted to get those criminals out of their neighborhoods. They didn't reflect the majority of the decent people just trying to get by.

As I heard those stories, I realized: Wow, that's Pontchartrain Park. I didn't grow up like that—Pontchartrain Park was crime-free—but I knew that all these officers came from wonderful neighborhoods that had once been like my own, but that were being ruined by such a small number of folks there.

Here's an inside story of how the storytelling genius of David Simon and his writing staff bore witness to some complicated truths about black police officers and the criminals they fight—and ultimately, to searing truths about human nature rarely seen on television, either in drama or on the news.

The Wire's writers kept everything close to the vest. They never wanted the actors to know what was coming. They would never tell us, which could be incredibly frustrating. We felt sometimes like they didn't trust us not to reveal spoilers. But David held the line because he wanted us as actors to be in the moment, to experience as authentically as possible what our characters faced as the arc of their stories took startling turns.

I look back on it and find that strategy, and the discipline with which David and his team followed it, very impressive. We would knock heads often over it, but I'm glad David didn't budge. As an actor, I'd literally not know what was coming in the next script. But that's how life is, too.

In the third season, Bunk is searching for a gun used in a crime. I was so frustrated dealing with this story line because it didn't seem to be going anywhere. I was bitching on set one day to another cast member and really getting on my high horse about it.

"I don't know where this gun is going, and all these great story lines are playing out around me, but Bunk is going nowhere," I griped. "I know all these black men who became cops because it's their neighborhood, and they know the criminals, they know their neighbors.

"It reminds me of my girlfriend's father," I continued. "He's a doctor who came out of Oklahoma. He knew he had to keep it together because there was so much threat from outside of his community. During segregation, there was a sense of unity to survive. Even back then, in the thirties, the thugs would say, 'Hey, schoolboy, you're not supposed to be here. You're going to make it out. You're going to college.' Even the thugs had a sense of community. And that's why, to this day, black men become police officers: that sense of community."

George Pelecanos, one of the writers, was sitting back listening to my sour social-justice soliloquy and took me aside.

"Wendell," he said, "the gun is going to lead you to Omar."

"*What?!*" I said. Omar Little (Michael K. Williams) was the show's seminal villain, the one person that people feared in the hood.

"The gun is going to lead you to Omar," he repeated. "I heard what you were saying just now. Do you mind if we develop some of that?"

And this was the genesis for what stands as one of the most powerful scenes in the entire series.

After a botched robbery and deadly firefight that has all the marks of an Omar operation, Bunk loses his cool when he sees little kids on the street pretending to be the criminal kingpin. When Bunk tracks down Omar, he reminds the coldhearted killer that they come from the same neighborhood—even the same school. Bunk says that he tried to be hard too, back in the day, but the real thugs knew he wasn't one of them.

"Shit, they knew I wasn't one of them," says Bunk, puffing his cigar. "Them hard cases would come up to me and say, 'Go home, schoolboy, you don't belong here.' Didn't realize at the time what they were doing for me."

Then his barely suppressed rage catches fire.

"As rough as that neighborhood could be, we had us a community," Bunk growls. "And now all we got is bodies, and predatory mother-fuckers like you. And out where that girl fell, I saw kids acting like Omar, calling you by name, glorifying your ass. Makes me sick, motherfucker, how far we done fell."

That scene is brought up to me more than any other—by police officers, by guys who meet me and say, "Hey, man, I'm in the game. I remember that scene you had with Omar."

Every time that happens, I'm reminded all over again about the impact *The Wire* made on everyone who saw it. I especially love it when black police officers tell me that that scene, and this series, finally told the truth about what police work means to them. This is why *The Wire* is taught in universities. It was—it is—art that reveals the human condition with unflinching honesty. This was a show about cops and drug dealers and politics and journalism in one American city. But in their worlds is the entire world. In their time and place are eternity and the universe.

This is what art can do.

What made *The Wire* real art, not mere entertainment, was that David kept pushing his writers and actors through layers and layers of moral ambiguity, searching for a truth that would never be entirely graspable, because human nature is ultimately a mystery. The series is about how individuals lose themselves within institutions, whether it's a police officer within the division, a neighborhood kid joining a drug gang, or an idealistic politician succumbing to corruption and becoming cynical. Audiences who loved *The Wire* thought it was speaking to them, even if they knew nothing about the bureaucracies and social hierarchies dissected by the show. Those viewers may not have known any cops, crooks, politicians, teachers, or newspapermen, but everybody knows what it's like to have your idealism sucked out of you by life.

Not long ago, I received a message from a Baltimore teacher who chose to teach in the city because of *The Wire*, and who teaches the show to students. Season four, which brought the Baltimore public school system into the series, is in my opinion the best social examination of adolescence in the inner city ever depicted on television.

There are some moments that season that are so true and heartbreaking, they leave you wondering what you're doing with your life. There's a scene in which one kid is sent to the principal's office and sees a bunch of computers that have been sitting in boxes, unopened, because nobody within the institution cares about those kids, their education, or their future.

In another plotline, Sergeant Ellis Carver (Seth Gilliam) persuades an eighth-grader, Randy (Maestro Harrell), to come forward and be an informant, promising him police protection. When criminals fire-bomb Randy's row house and put his foster mother in the hospital with second- and third-degree burns, the boy bitterly reproaches the detective: "You gonna look out for me? You promise? You got my back, huh?"

There is nothing Carver can say.

In that season, Zenobia Dawson is one of the most foulmouthed, violent students in the school. I had nothing to do with that character, so I never spoke with Taylor King, the young actress who played Zenobia. I met her at the season-four wrap party. A beautiful young woman came up to me and said, "Mr. Pierce, I'm a big admirer of your work. I'm graduating this year and going to Brown on a scholarship."

This girl was so impressive, but I didn't recognize her. I asked her what character she played. She told me Zenobia.

"No, no, baby," I said, "Zenobia is the girl who can barely read. She's the girl who slices another girl's face open for sitting in the wrong seat. You can't be the one who plays Zenobia."

"Mr. Pierce," she said, "that really was me."

I thought, *This is part of the problem. We should be telling Taylor King's story.* She is the image of a young black girl in Baltimore we never see. I went home angry and discouraged, determined to leave this fucking show. *We're part of the problem, not the solution.* I meditated on all the professionally accomplished black folk who had stopped me over the years on the streets of Baltimore and asked me why we showed only the worst part of life in the city.

The insight that allowed me to come back for the final season is that I realized that none of this was meaningless, none of it was gratuitous. The heartbreak and anger season four left me with came out of the humanity it revealed in those street corner kids from West Baltimore whose coming-of-age struggle was a major theme of that year's show. If you watched that season of *The Wire*, you would never be able to pass a corner kid again, in the toughest of neighborhoods anywhere in the country, and not see in him a spark of humanity.

It's not that *The Wire* sentimentalized these kids. You hold them accountable for their bullshit, but you have empathy for them in spite of it. That season revealed how fragile the lives of inner-city kids are, amid a level of poverty, violence, and chaos scarcely imaginable to most Americans. You see how only one element added or removed from their existence could make all the difference in their ultimate fate in life.

It's not by chance that black American men between eighteen and twenty-four are both the main perpetrators and the main victims of violent crime in our cities. Black and white, liberal and conservative, rich and poor—we all drive by those corner kids and reject them without ever really seeing them. These kids, they're ours. How do we know that one of them might not be the next Louis Armstrong, who was once a juvenile delinquent until he was given a chance? How do we know that one of these street kids might not cure cancer, if given the chance?

I hope that when they see the ongoing tragedy of inner-city Chicago, of New Orleans, of Newark, people will think back to *The Wire* and wonder: How did Michael (Tristan Wilds) succumb to it, and how did Namond (Julito McCullum) get out? All these stories are playing out every day in the inner cities of America. And they are all in the fourth year of *The Wire*.

This is life. This is art. This is *The Wire*. And it is forever.

Because David Simon gave me the chance to be part of something great and enduring, I will always consider him family. An actress said to me once, shortly after the series ended, "Wendell, I hope you realize that *The Wire* was your *Godfather*."

I asked her what she meant by that.

"Al Pacino, Robert De Niro, Robert Duvall, Diane Keaton—we'll always remember the characters they played," she explained. "No matter what else they've ever done, we will remember those roles. In *The Wire*, you found your *Godfather*."

I realized that she was right. *The Wire* will be in the first line of my obituary. Years from now, you may see me out on the street wearing a chicken suit, and some smart-ass kid might come up to me and say, "Look at this fool in the chicken suit!" But I'll be able to take my chicken head off and look that boy in the eye and say, with a heart full of gratitude and pride, "Hey, kid, I played Bunk."

SEVEN

IT'S RAINING SO HARD

When I first heard about a storm called Katrina, late in August 2005, I was in Los Angeles getting ready to fly back to Baltimore to start shooting season four of *The Wire*. From watching the news, I was vaguely aware that a minor hurricane had hit Florida that week, but that was about it. Sunny Southern California was a world away from the Gulf of Mexico.

I planned to stop in New Orleans for a short family get-together on my way back to the East Coast. Daddy had broken his leg in an automobile accident and was confined to a wheelchair. I was anxious to see him and to enjoy the last few days of summer before starting work. What I didn't realize as I boarded the plane at LAX on Saturday, August 27, was that Hurricane Katrina had crossed South Florida intact, and upon reaching the warm Gulf waters, was rapidly monstering into a hellstorm headed straight for my hometown.

As I stepped off the plane into the New Orleans airport, all was chaos. Crowds were everywhere and the air crackled with fear.

"What's going on?" I asked another traveler.

"The hurricane is coming!"

"The one in Florida?" I asked, nonplussed.

"It was in Florida, but it's headed this way."

As I walked to the counter to arrange for my rental car, the storm was growing so large so fast that it filled the entire Gulf of Mexico. Officials in several coastal parishes ordered all their people out. At five p.m. that Saturday, New Orleans Mayor Ray Nagin went on television to declare a state of emergency, asked city residents to leave voluntarily, and said he would open the Superdome as a shelter for those who couldn't get out. By then Katrina was about four hundred miles south of the mouth of the Mississippi River.

I checked into the W Hotel downtown, as I usually did when coming home to visit my folks, then drove out to Pontchartrain Park. I found Daddy and Tee anxious about the storm, mulling over whether to leave the city while they still could.

"Listen," I said, "let's not overreact. Let's just see what happens before we decide to hit the road." We had all come through hurricanes before, hadn't we?

My sister-in-law and her daughters arrived that night from New York. Late in the evening, I hit the town—and there was hardly a soul to be found in the clubs in this, one of the most defiant party cities in the world. Still, I managed to stay out pretty late anyway, expecting that the next morning would bring good news on the storm. How many times had the city been threatened by hurricanes, only to have them pass us by?

When the sun came up, my head was pounding from a fierce hangover. Somehow I pulled it together to drive out to Daddy and Tee's.

THE WIND IN THE REEDS

When I arrived, my folks, my sister-in-law, and my nieces had gathered in the living room and were discussing whether to evacuate. Nobody argued and nobody was afraid. It all seemed like a routine conversation for people used to living on the Gulf Coast. We figured we would be gone for three days, maximum, and be back in time for my nieces to have fun in New Orleans before heading back to California at week's end. I even reserved a suite at the W Hotel for us all so we wouldn't have to leave town.

Tee wasn't having it. She insisted that this storm was not going to be like previous ones. She had a feeling. We had to get out while we could, she said. The children wanted to be with their grandmother, so wherever she was headed, they were as well. So there it was: In a call that probably saved our lives, Tee decided we were going to head north.

But first, she said, we're going to mass.

Church wasn't as crowded as usual. The priest encouraged us all to get out of the city, or at least take shelter with friends. Pontchartrain Park, remember, sits in one of the lowest parts of the low-lying city, hard against the Industrial Canal and fronting Lake Pontchartrain.

"Be careful," the priest warned. "This hurricane is serious."

After mass, we spoke to the Bahams, an elderly couple who had been sitting near us during the service. Daddy had grown up with both of them, and they lived around the corner from us in Pontchartrain Park. The Bahams told us that they planned to ride out the storm at home.

It was the last time we would see them alive.

While we were in church praying that morning, the National Weather Service issued this public bulletin:

> Hurricane Katrina . . . a most powerful hurricane with unprecedented strength . . . Most of the area will be uninhabitable for weeks . . . perhaps longer. . . . At least one half of well-constructed homes will have roof and wall failure. All gabled roofs will fail. . . . All wood-framed low-rising apartment buildings will be destroyed. . . . Power outages will last for weeks. . . . Water shortages will make human suffering incredible by modern standards. . . . Few crops will remain. Livestock left exposed to the winds will be killed. . . . Once tropical storm and hurricane force winds onset . . . do not venture outside!

When my family returned home to Debore Drive from mass, we turned on the television for the latest and heard that Mayor Nagin had ordered a mandatory evacuation. "We're facing the storm most of us had feared," he said.

This shocked us deeply. This had never before happened. Every New Orleanian knew exactly what the mayor was talking about.

For generations, we had grown up knowing how vulnerable the Crescent City was to a bull's-eye from a powerful hurricane. People in Los Angeles fear the Big One—an apocalyptic earthquake that scientists say is an inevitability. For New Orleans, the Big One has always been a direct hit by a storm like Katrina, whose winds that Sunday morning had already reached 175 miles per hour.

Katrina was now a Category Five storm, making it one of the most potent Atlantic hurricanes in recorded history. And it was predicted to make landfall that night and roll over the city Monday morning.

Everyone in New Orleans knew this day would come eventually, but like everybody else, we hoped against hope that it wouldn't be in our lifetimes.

We began loading two cars with everything we could jam into them, while leaving room for four adults and two children. My head was still throbbing from the night before, and I was irritated by all the fuss the family was making. *Why are they taking so long to pack these cars? We're only going to Uncle L.C.'s place up the river for a couple of days,* I thought.

Frustrated and hurting, I said, "You guys go, I'm going to stay." Then I went back inside and went to sleep. The good Lord takes care of drunks and babies, and I ain't no baby: When I woke up after my catnap, my family was still piling things into the cars. *Okay, hell,* I thought, *I might as well go with them.* I resolved to drive Tee and Daddy in my rental, and let Debbie drive her daughters in Tee's car.

The last thing we did before shutting the door was to put the most precious framed pictures we had on top of the cabinets, to keep them safe in case a little water made it into the house. I locked the front door, climbed behind the wheel of one of the cars, and off we drove, along with tens of thousands of our fellow New Orleanians that Sunday afternoon.

It usually takes an hour to make the trip to St. James Parish to Uncle L.C. and Aunt Maryann's place. That Sunday, it took us four, even with all lanes of Interstate 10 flowing out of the city. But we made it, and that was the most important thing. We would be safe. It's strange to think of it now, but in the car with Tee and Daddy, we weren't anxious, only fascinated. We had never seen anything like this. Virtually the entire city of New Orleans—half a million people!—was leaving in a single afternoon. It did not occur to us that we wouldn't be coming right back in a day or two.

As we motored out of the city, WWL radio host Garland Robinette took to the airwaves to sound the alarm. "I know the powers that be say not to panic. I'm telling you: Panic, worry, run. The birds are gone. Get out of town! Now! Don't stay! Leave! Save yourself while you can. Go . . . go . . . go!"

We were among the lucky ones. We had cars, and a place to go. An estimated one hundred thousand New Orleanians stayed behind, most of them too poor to own a car, or too sick, elderly, or otherwise unable to get out on their own. The City of New Orleans had an evacuation plan in place for them in which city buses would collect them all and take them to shelters north of town. But the plan broke down, and the evacuees ended up stranded in the Superdome while the buses that were to take them to safety ended up underwater. Around sixteen thousand helpless people suffered for days in the stink, filth, and violence of the Dome, and another twenty thousand endured similar misery at the nearby Morial Convention Center.

That night, Katrina roared ashore in Plaquemines Parish, south of New Orleans. As the savage winds and torrential rains of Katrina's outer bands began lashing our refuge in St. James Parish, we saw on the news that Katrina had jogged slightly to the east. Uncle L.C.'s place was seventy miles to the west of New Orleans. The thought hit me that if the wind and the rain assault was this hellacious so far inland, I could hardly imagine what New Orleans and the Mississippi Gulf Coast were suffering.

The power went out, and we who were still awake listened to the battery-operated radio for news of the outside world. It was our only connection. All the area radio stations combined their broadcasts and put them on the emergency broadcast network. We sat in the darkness, and then the bruised gray of that Katrina dawn, and waited, and worried, and prayed for our city and its people.

EARLY THAT MONDAY MORNING, we had reason to believe the worst had passed. What we did not know then was that as the Angel of Death passed over, she sent a massive surge of water barreling up the Intracoastal Waterway and the Mississippi River Gulf Outlet (MRGO), two massive, government-built canals that funneled the tsunami straight into the city. The MRGO (pronounced "Mister Go"), a 1960s-era shipping shortcut between the Gulf and the city, converges from the southeast with the Intracoastal Canal to form a single channel—the Funnel—six miles west of the Industrial Canal, which runs through New Orleans and connects the Mississippi River to Lake Pontchartrain.

The same Katrina surge that sent a wall of water nearly three stories tall crashing into the Mississippi coastal cities of Gulfport and Biloxi rocketed up the Intracoastal and the MRGO, converged at the Funnel, and crashed into the Industrial Canal—which forms the eastern border of Pontchartrain Park. As the LSU hurricane scientist Ivor van Heerden would later observe in *The Storm*, his gripping account of the disaster, "The federal powers that be had inadvertently

designed an excellent storm-surge delivery system—nothing less—
to ring this mass of water with a simply tremendous load—potential
energy—right into the middle of New Orleans."

At four-thirty that Monday morning, rising water was leaking
through gates on both sides of the Industrial Canal, flowing into
Gentilly and New Orleans East. But the worst was yet to come. The
surge rolled across Lake Borgne from the east, through the depleted
marshes, and assaulted the MRGO levees, which gave way in parts
of St. Bernard Parish. At the same time, the surge blasted and overtopped the Intracoastal's levees protecting New Orleans East, which
began to flood. Meanwhile, to the west, residents of the Lakeview
district saw walls of the 17th Street Canal shuddering and threaten-
ing to give way under the pressure from rising waters coming in from
the lake.

Sometime before seven a.m., the outer edge of the storm surge
slammed into the Industrial Canal, sending a shock wave and walls of
water along its length. On the north end, billions of gallons of water
poured into Lake Pontchartrain. The wave pushing southward could
not find an outlet into the Mississippi River because the floodgates
had been closed. There was nowhere for the water to go. It overtopped
the Industrial Canal floodwalls on both sides. The Lower Ninth Ward
began to fill with water—and when the worst of the surge came an
hour or so later, the levees began collapsing in the face of Katrina's
blitzkrieg.

The fate of Pontchartrain Park was sealed shortly after nine a.m.,
when the eastern walls of the London Avenue Canal, a drainage canal
running through Gentilly two miles east of my family's home, began
to bulge outward from the surge rushing in from the lake, and finally

gave way. The flood cascaded downhill, drowning the eastern half of Gentilly and submerging Pontchartrain Park, the bottom of the bowl, under as much as twenty feet of water—among the most severe flooding in all New Orleans. Then came multiple 17th Street Canal wall breaks, inundating Lakeview and sending the flood gushing into Mid-City, and minutes later, the western wall of the London Avenue Canal cracked, delivering more water into Gentilly. By the time the winds stopped, there had been over fifty separate breaches in the levee system protecting New Orleans.

Katrina left New Orleans later that day, but for three days the water kept relentlessly gushing into the city from swollen Lake Pontchartrain. By then, 80 percent of New Orleans was underwater. Except for the French Quarter and the Garden District, both built on the city's highest ground, every neighborhood in the city took on water. Nearly fifteen hundred people were dead. Half the houses in the city had four feet of water in them, or more. There was no electricity or clean water in the city; looting and the breakdown of civil order would soon follow. Tens of thousands of New Orleanians were stranded in the city with no way out; many more evacuees were displaced, with no way back in.

Historian Douglas Brinkley described the shock and terror of what it felt like to be in the city's ruins in Katrina's immediate aftermath: "All at once, ten thousand years of civilization had been stripped away."

And the government—city, state, and federal—had no idea what to do.

Incredibly, had it not been for a front moving southeast from the Midwest, weakening Katrina and pushing its eye slightly to the east, the destruction in New Orleans would have been even worse. But this was already inconceivably bad—and for the people of Pontchartrain Park, it was the apocalypse. The entire neighborhood sat entombed by filthy water up to the eaves of houses, and even higher. The place sat in that water for weeks.

Night after night at Uncle L.C.'s house, still without electricity, Daddy sat listening to the radio and staring at the wall, saying that our little half-brick house was strong, that it surely had withstood the flood, and that we would be able to rebuild. He had no comprehension of how bad things really were. Three days after the levees broke, Garland Robinette, who had heroically broadcast through the entire storm, even after gale-force winds blew out his studio's windows, expressed the fear and rage of the entire city, both captive and in the diaspora, when he tore into the federal government for its inaction in the face of the city's unspeakable suffering. During his broadcast, which I listened to from St. James Parish, Mayor Nagin exploded in a live call-in interview with Robinette. He tore into the feds, saying, "They don't have a clue what's going on down here."

Daddy was in denial. Family friends who had somehow evaded checkpoints and made it back into the city called to tell us that things were worse than we could imagine. Jonathan Bloom, a childhood friend from Pontchartrain Park, was the first to call with news of our neighborhood's fate.

"I've made it into the Park, Wendell, and the whole place is a lake," he said. "Pontchartrain Park is gone. Don't let your parents come back here alone. When they see this, it might kill them."

We stayed together as a family at the house that week, holding on to each other with all we had. It's at times like this that you really see the best of family. I tried to get into the city to see what was happening, but the roads were blocked; it was impossible to get out of St. James Parish. So I went back to Uncle L.C.'s and sat with the family, listening obsessively to WWL. We heard the reports of chaos in the city, of people trapped in the Superdome and at the convention center, hungry, thirsty, sick, abused, but it was difficult to imagine these things actually happening in our city—in America.

Nighttime was the only time our mobile phones worked. I would call my friends in New York City and back in L.A., telling them that they didn't understand how bad it was down here. "Wendell, we know," they would say. "We're watching it all on TV." I found this so hard to believe. We had no power at my uncle's place and had no realistic sense of what was going on just downriver from us, until we located a generator later in the week and restored electricity to Uncle L.C.'s house.

Just before the power returned, people I knew at HBO, the cable network that produced *The Wire*, phoned and said they were concerned about me. They offered to help my family and me get out of Louisiana. I thanked them for their offer, then walked back into the house and turned on the television. Then I saw what for me were the first pictures of the disaster, the horrific images that are now an indelible part of American history.

My city was in ruins. My people were in mortal danger. I could not believe that these images had been seen all week long, all around the world, and still so little was being done to relieve the suffering. I broke down in sobs.

When the water receded, National Guardsmen found old Mrs. Baham in her house, drowned. Mr. Baham had tried to climb a tree in his front yard to escape the rising water, but wind had pulled the tree down. They found his body entangled in its branches. These were two of the nine people in our neighborhood lost to Katrina. My folks grieved over not having pushed the Bahams harder to evacuate with them.

NOT EVERYONE who stayed perished. Leonard Morris, who was in his eighties, was planning to leave with his family when he ran into his fishing buddy. When his friend said he was going to ride out the storm at home, Mr. Morris sent his family on and remained behind. Even though he was elderly and suffering from cancer, Mr. Morris and his buddy used the friend's fishing boat to rescue six or seven people on their street who had stayed behind.

A week after the storm passed, I knew I had to head up to Baltimore and get to work. HBO had been terrific to us, sending bedding and clothing so my parents, who had lost everything except what was in their suitcases, would have something to wear. Tee told me to get back to work. I flew back home to L.A. to gather some things, then went to Baltimore to begin shooting.

As soon as I could, I flew back to Louisiana to help my folks find a house in Baton Rouge. As my father's leg was still broken, I was pushing him around in a wheelchair. We had so many mixed emotions heading north into Baton Rouge from Uncle L.C.'s place.

"Why are we doing this?" Daddy said. "Why are we looking at

houses? Can't we stay at L.C.'s a little bit longer? You know we're going back home."

"Daddy, there won't be any little bit longer," I said, my heart breaking.

The realtor took us to a large four-bedroom house in a comfortable subdivision. I thought it was great. You had to move quickly on Baton Rouge real estate in those days; so many displaced New Orleanians were resettling in Baton Rouge that houses were not on the market long. My folks gave me the thumbs-up, and I picked up the phone and started the process of getting the mortgage.

The hour-long drive back to L.C.'s was somber. "I don't know if we'll ever get back home," my mother mused.

"No, don't think of it that way," I said. But I feared she was right.

The Baton Rouge place was a nice house, but it wasn't home. The worst part about their lives in Baton Rouge was their lack of friends. One of the benefits of your golden years is having lifelong friends around you, folks who understand the difficulties, the fears, the anxieties, and the ever-present specter of decline and death. My parents were afraid that everyone was gone, or soon would be, and they wouldn't have said good-bye.

"We have to find out where everyone is. We'll get that list together, and after that, I want to start seeing them," Tee said to me. As she located friends, she would invite them over. Others she would travel to visit. The thing that allowed my mother and father to wake up every morning and carry on with life was their quest to find the lost and reestablish contact, and to begin repairing their shattered world.

Their Catholic parish in Baton Rouge, St. Louis King of France, was very welcoming. It was a white Catholic parish that suddenly had these new African American members. The locals were kind, though it was plainly awkward.

"Those people are being really nice," Tee told me. "I know it's uncomfortable for them. It's uncomfortable for us. And I really thank them. But that's not my church. I need to get back to my church."

Sitting in Baltimore on the other end of the phone line listening to my mother long for home, I resolved that if I had to move heaven and earth, I was going to get Tee and Daddy back into their real home. I found it unbearable to think of their loneliness and their fear that they would never see their friends again. It made me think of what it must have been like in Europe after the war.

I FLEW to Baton Rouge every two or three weeks, when I had a break in filming. We had some small triumphs to celebrate, almost all of them involving bumping into someone from New Orleans. I once was at a Walgreen's on Perkins Road getting medicine for my parents when I ran into the daughter of one of Tee's friends. Her mother had survived the storm and was living on the West Bank, across the river from New Orleans. She gave me her mother's phone number, and I raced back to the house to give it to Tee, as if it were a winning lottery ticket.

The first Thanksgiving in the Baton Rouge house, three months after Katrina, gave me a sense of what life must be like in war-torn countries, when people are turned into refugees in their own land. Having to leave everything you own behind when you run for your life, losing your family and friends on a moment's notice, not knowing where anybody is, or if you will ever see them again. But Tee had insisted that her family, and as many of her friends that she could find, come to the new house to celebrate.

"We may have lost everything, but we have each other, and that's the most important thing. We have a lot to be thankful for," Tee said.

At dinner, we went around the room, and each person shared what he or she was thankful for in the aftermath of the storm. It was a simple gesture, but it meant the world. It reminded me that if you have the love of your friends and family, you can find in that the faith and strength you need to move on.

When my turn came, I said that I was thankful that we had survived, that we were still together, and that we had shelter. I said I was thankful for my parents, and everything they did to give me a wonderful life in that home that we lost. Whether we would ever be able to go back or not, I told them, I would always have the memories of the life they gave me there. Katrina stole so much, but she could never take that.

"Y'all have given me so much over the years," I told my mother and father. "I am so thankful that I will be able to help y'all now, to repay you in a small way for all you did for me."

My mother wrote me a beautiful letter afterward.

"Wendell, I really appreciate everything you've done for the family," she wrote. "You have been there for us in two of the darkest hours of our lives, when we lost your brother Stacey, and when we lost the home where we had been for fifty years of our life. You have been there for the family, to make sure we're back on our feet. I just want to thank you."

Thanksgiving dinner and Tee's generous thank-you note after the gathering set the tone for our family's immediate future: We were going to be thankful, we were going to be resilient, and if we could, we were going to rebuild. After all, *can't* died three days before the creation of the world.

In early 2006, Mayor Nagin's Bring New Orleans Back commission made public its plans for redeveloping the city. Urban planners revealed a map with green dots, representing green space, over neighborhoods where displaced residents should be discouraged from rebuilding. The idea was to allow these areas to return to nature. New Orleanians, both those in the city and in the diaspora, reacted with outrage. Folks were afraid that moneyed interests were going to take advantage of the catastrophe to mount a land grab. Daddy, Tee, and I realized that if we didn't get back down and start fighting for Pontchartrain Park, people who didn't have our best interests at heart would take our home.

I made my mind up that no matter what, I was going to get my mother and father back home. Their roots were too deep in New Orleans, and in Pontchartrain Park; they were withering outside of it. They wanted to be home. They *needed* to be home. And they could only be in the little half-brick house on Debore Drive that had been their home for half a century.

I'm going to make this happen, I thought. *If they walk into that house and die on the spot, I will have done my job.*

In October 2005, nearly three months after Katrina chased us out of Pontchartrain Park, my parents and I returned to see what was left of our family home. Jonathan Bloom warned me once again to prepare Daddy and Tee for the sight of it. "It was like someone put black detergent in there, filled it with water, and shook it for days," he said. "It could kill them."

HE WASN'T EXAGGERATING. We had heard of one elderly evacuee who had returned, took one look at what was left of his house, and dropped dead of a massive heart attack. For many New Orleanians, the loss wasn't just a house. It was their entire neighborhood, it was every familiar connection, all gone. Everyone was trying to hold everything together, but in all the chaos and pain, they had so little to lean on. Most or all of the people who would have held them up through any normal crisis had been scattered all over the country, many virtually disappearing without a trace.

Two years after the storm, the National Institute of Mental Health sponsored the first study of Katrina's psychological fallout on residents of New Orleans and the Gulf Coast region. It found that about half of those studied had an anxiety mood disorder, with more than 30 percent suffering from the more serious post-traumatic stress disorder. New Orleanians, the study found, were suffering far more than Katrina victims from elsewhere. This had to do with the relative poverty of those most affected by the storm, but also with the grinding struggle with FEMA, with contractors, with the city's dysfunctional bureaucracy—and the fact that most of those having to endure it were among the poorest and least educated in the nation.

Daddy and Tee were neither poor nor uneducated, but they were very old; he was eighty and she was seventy-five. Both had known hardship growing up, and Daddy had survived the Battle of Saipan.

But back then, they still had their lives ahead of them. They had buried a son, but as painful as that was, they had their friends to help them get through the dark thicket of grief. Now, in the late winter of their years, they had to endure the destruction of a home and a neighborhood that symbolized their entire life's work and achievement, and the obliteration of a tightly knit community that had given them comfort, meaning, and blessing.

Ron came home for the journey back to Pontchartrain Park with our parents, to see what was left of their dream home. We brought along Tee Mae, the family matriarch, as well. Motoring back into Gentilly after the storm was like entering a foreign country. As we drove up A. P. Tureaud Avenue, the only sign of life was a corner bar called Bullet's, which stayed open to offer food and drink to people in the storm, even when its first floor was underwater. As the city began to dry out, Bullet's became a communal place where people could see one another and share information. It was like an oasis in the desert.

We drove on, passing Dillard University, whose fifty-five-acre campus borders the London Avenue Canal. Dillard was once a place of dignified beauty, known for its majestic white-columned buildings, grand live oaks, and sprawling green lawns. As we turned onto Gentilly Boulevard and laid eyes on it, there was nothing left but a field of brown and gray. The live oaks were barren. There was nothing green or alive to be seen.

Tee knew then that Pontchartrain Park was going to be far worse than she had imagined.

The only image I can compare post-apocalyptic Pontchartrain

Park to is Hiroshima after the atomic bomb. The devastation was so complete, so definitive. We stopped at a Red Cross station on the perimeter before going in and got food, drink, and supplies, including hazmat suits, because the water that flooded the area had been so toxic. Making our way over to our beloved Debore Drive was like homecoming in Chernobyl. Everything—everything—was gray from caked-on mud left behind by weeks of stagnant water. There was so much debris in the streets that we had to drive on sidewalks. The silence was absolute; not a soul was around. All the trees were destroyed; those left standing had been stripped of their leaves. This is what I imagine nuclear winter is like.

Months later, when I began rehearsing my role as Vladimir in the Classical Theater of Harlem's production of *Godot* (which, in 2007, we would reprise in New Orleans), I didn't have to work to place myself in the desolation imagined by Beckett. I had been there with my family. I had seen it, smelled it, felt its wrath, and absorbed its numbing lessons amid a silence that seemed eternal.

At last, we pulled up to our house. The grass was gone, and mud was caked above the doors. But it was still standing. There were no cars. There were no people. If there was movement, even two blocks away, you could hear it. The stench of mold, chemicals, mud, sewage, stagnant water, and decay was overwhelming.

As silly as it sounds, we tried to open the front door with a key, which didn't work. So Ron and I broke down the door.

The inside was worse than our direst imaginings. Much worse. The interior looked as if a bomb made of mud and ink had gone off inside. All the furniture had been overturned and thrown into piles by the water. The refrigerator was on its side, and when we opened its door, the smell of rotten meat nearly knocked us down. Katrina had not merely sacked the house; she had defiled it.

My father started to cry. "This is where we raised our family, Black. And it's all gone."

My mother stood by silently and cried too. We all did. Everything we had associated with that house, every object, was gone, either washed away by the flood, disintegrated by the toxic brew in which it had been steeping for weeks, or so fouled that it likely could never be recovered.

Standing on that filth-gilded street that had once, in my family's imagination, been paved with gold, I knew without the least doubt that I had lost everything that told me who I was. The spirit had gone out of the house that had been the embodiment of our family's life, leaving it a corpse putrefying under the relentless south Louisiana sun. It felt that the only thing any of us standing there had left was our lives, our memories, and each other. And then the sense came over me that if we didn't regain at least some of what was stolen from us, we would lose our lives too. Given how old Daddy and Tee were, this was not an abstract threat. In that moment, with the old man's sobbing the only sound in the sepulchral silence, I felt as if I were standing at my mother and father's open grave. There was nothing keeping them from stepping forward into the void and letting the desecrated earth swallow them whole.

Standing in the driveway, a few feet from the filthy front door, Daddy broke down. "I don't want to go back," he declared. "It's too much."

But we had to go back. There was no way forward except to go back. The road to the Pierce family's future, if we were to have a future, ran through Pontchartrain Park. If we didn't take it, if we didn't push on through the debris and the despair, we might as well die.

I thought of Aristile, and what he had come through. I thought of Mamo and Papo, and what they achieved against odds that must have seemed impossible. I thought of Daddy and Tee, and all the older folk who raised me in Pontchartrain Park, and how the tenacity of their hope drove them forward. I thought about the experience of all Africans in the American Diaspora, how they—how we—had everything taken from us. We lost our ancestral homeland, we lost our gods, we lost our freedom, and often we even lost our families. We were poor and abused, beaten and lynched, told we were nothing, humiliated every day of our lives.

And yet we came through all these things. Not only did we survive them; we conquered them. Every Negro spiritual, every blues lament, every jazz composition is a song of victory. Every true poem, every real drama, and every authentic novel written by an African American is a proclamation of triumph. Every performance by an African American actor, dancer, or musician that faithfully expresses our people's journey and forges a bond of recognition and understanding among all peoples about humanity's collective pilgrimage—each one is to defy death, to deflect its sting, and to deny it the last word.

That desolated house, which had cradled my brothers and me, was now a tomb. The neighborhood founded in one of the deepest valleys in the city of New Orleans, and that Tee and Daddy and their generation cultivated into a lush and fertile garden, was now a desert. The water had long since receded, but it had left behind nothing but dry bones.

Everything within me screamed: *These bones must live!*

And then a light appeared in the darkness. Staggering around the ruins in our hazmat suits and masks, like explorers on an alien world, Daddy found his wallet, which he had left behind in the rush to flee the storm. He opened it and found that everything in it had been destroyed—except for a single item. It was a photograph of my late brother Stacey. The borders had been eaten away by the poisoned water, but Stacey's face looked upon us with perfect clarity. And he was smiling.

"Oh my God!" said Daddy. "I've still got Stacey! I've still got my son!"

That was the sign we needed. Finding the image of his dead boy, the firstborn son whose memory he and my mother mourned every day, caused a new birth of hope in Daddy's heart. If Stacey could come through the flood, so could he. So could we all.

We doubted our strength to go on, but we made our minds up to do it anyway, one step at a time. Daddy, Tee, Ron, and I decided to come back every single day and clean as much as we could manage, for as long as we could manage.

And so we did. It was an excruciating experience, like waking up every morning to go to your own wake. My father said we should just throw everything away, but Tee and I said no, we couldn't afford to do that. We were going to bring every single relic we found inside the house outside, lay it in front of him and my mother, and let them decide what to hold on to and what to let go. If everything really is lost, I told him, you might lose any hope that you have a future.

In those early days of recovery, Daddy and Tee had a second sign of hope. On the day of our Katrina exodus, a neighbor of ours, a man I will call Mr. Willis, had told them he was going to stay. We were sure we had lost Mr. Willis, just as we had lost the poor Bahams. One day, as we began to clean the house, I heard my mother outside scream, "Oh my goodness, you're alive!" It was Mr. Willis, returning home.

It turns out that after the storm had passed that morning, Mr. Willis had gotten into his truck and driven uptown to check on his rental properties. When news went out on WWL that the levees had broken, he sped back toward Pontchartrain Park to retrieve his adult son, whom he had been caring for as the younger man fought drug addiction.

Mr. Willis never made it back to his house. Authorities had already closed his exit from the freeway, and in fact were launching rescue boats from the off-ramp. He had no idea what had happened to his son. Had he drowned? Was he perched on a roof, waiting to be saved? Had he swum to the levee and walked out? How could Mr. Willis possibly know?

Days later, FEMA tracked Mr. Willis down and told him that his son had been found; he had been sent to Washington, D.C., and was housed in a shelter there. After his rescue, FEMA saw that he had substance abuse problems and put him into a rehab program.

"What I thought was the bleakest day of my life turned out to be a blessing," Mr. Willis told us. "The help I never could get my son before the storm, he was getting now. I lost everything, but I think I gained the life of my boy."

Mr. Willis had no flood insurance and no money to rebuild his ruined house. That did not stop him. "I'm going to go out and get a board, and I'm going to put it up," he told my parents. "Next day, I'm going to go get another board, and put it up."

What a balm that man's hope was to us. He had faith that all would be well, that he would live to see his home restored, and that he would have a role to play in that resurrection miracle. Mr. Willis's hope validated the impossible dreams Daddy, Tee, and I carried in our heads. Because Mr. Willis believed, that made it easier for us to believe. We could not have known it that October day in 2005, standing in the mud-covered wreckage of our lives, but a few years later, Mr. Willis and his wife would return to their rebuilt Pontchartrain Park home. In that terrible moment of our first return, Mr. Willis helped us see what he could see, and that shared vision cleared the path forward for us too.

That vision made going forward possible, but it did not make it easier. We had to sift through the house like archaeologists excavating our own hearts. Piece by piece, I carried the shattered remains of my family's life outside to my mother and father. We had to mourn each picture, each office file, each chair, and each pot.

I came to understand the deeper meaning of that process in a conversation I had with my mother as she eyed a particular grime-glazed haul I had laid at her feet.

"These glasses are still good to drink out of," she said. "We could still use these plates."

"Tee," I said, "this has sat in toxic sludge for three months. You don't want to use this again."

"Wendell," she said with a deliberate focused pause, "this was given to me on our wedding day. We're going to keep it."

This is how the entire process of recovery and restoration went with them. In my training as an actor, I had been taught that inanimate objects can have a powerful emotional hold on your life and had used that insight in creating characters. I drew on that training to help me be more sensitive to the pain and the grief my parents were suffering as we worked on the house. It's one thing to practice on a stage this kind of imaginative empathy with a fictional character. It's something else to do it with your mother and father, in the ruins of the family home.

The place finally became clean enough for them to enter safely and help with the sorting. Every now and then, you'd hear a wail from the back of the house. *Oh my God. Oh, Lord have mercy. Ohhh*. I heard the cry of a young couple grown old, a man and a woman who had gotten married, started a family, and brought up their children in a modest little home they could call their own. Now, as stooped and frail old people, they had to pick through what was left, through the molded, soured, rotting piles, confronting reminders of their own mortality and the impermanence of all things. The photos that had survived, the mementoes they had collected over the years, the framed diplomas their sons had earned and given to them as certification that their sacrifices had meant something. The report cards they saved. That trophy from Little League. The baptismal garb. The anniversary gifts. The love letters.

We recovered many things, and said good-bye to many more. The item whose loss I mourn more than anything else: the final notice on his mortgage, the one that affirmed that Daddy had paid for his home in full. That he owned a piece of land and the house built upon it free and clear, like any other American man.

Every little thing that could be saved felt like rescuing one of their own children. Everything that could not be was like losing a member of the family. I thought I knew how an inanimate object could be so meaningful, and endowed with so much emotion and purpose, but I had not realized until I wrestled with the ghosts of my family's past how profoundly real that is. What the fall of 2005 taught me was my own version of *The Piano Lesson*. The truth of August Wilson's art was made manifest in those long days full of hurt, hope, and homecoming.

As we made progress, I watched my mother's spirit rise in her. I began to see the young couple that had bought the house in Pontchartrain Park and were setting out to fill it with the things they needed for everyday life. One day, I found myself shopping with my mother for curtains, dishes, and furniture.

"I've always wanted a brass bed," Tee said. "I'm going to get a brass bed this time."

I bought my mother a brass bed, and I rejoiced in the opportunity. I was not really buying a place for her and my father to lay their heads at night. I was sharing in her dream, making it real, participating in a side of her that I had never before seen, that had been submerged by the years of teaching school, day in and day out, and the routine of raising three boys. This was who my mother had been before she had my brothers and me. I can hardly express how pleased I was to meet her.

I met Daddy in the same way. Standing in the backyard one day, I heard him say, "We got to get a workbench out here. I got to get my tool chest." And there he was, the young Army veteran, husband, and new father, building his own castle in America. Katrina had made him a castaway, but now that he had his feet back on solid ground, Daddy remembered what he had always known: You can't get lost in America.

In January 2006, my parents got a federal rebuilding loan. A few weeks later, I hired a contractor to rebuild the house from the inside out. The normal procedure would have been to tear down the outside walls and construct them from the ground up, but I knew that if my parents ever saw the walls go down and an empty lot, it would mean a breach in the levee from which they might not recover. It cost me a little more to do it that way instead of demolishing it and building new, but it was important to make sure that the family home was regenerated from within.

Ron had a buddy from West Point who had a construction company in New York. He sent one of his men down to supervise our construction every couple of weeks, to check on the rebuilding process. It took a year.

Just before Christmas 2006, Amos and Althea Pierce returned to their gleaming home in New Orleans for good. "We're back now," Daddy said, with the voice of an angelic herald bringing tidings of great joy. For my mother to be able to cook Christmas dinner in her home again was a feast that offered a foretaste of heaven. We finally, as a family, knew that a crushing burden had been lifted. We had wondered if it would ever really happen, if it was possible to rise out of Katrina's waters and live again.

But we had. We honest to God had.

We ate and drank and laughed and rejoiced at the feast of Christmas, celebrating the birth of a child born in a stable in an obscure corner of the Roman empire. There we sat on that night divine, giving thanks to God for the rebirth of our own family's life in what, however little known or cared for by the rest of America, had always been the Pierce family's Promised Land. *The thrill of hope*, says the Christmas carol, *the weary world rejoices*. And so did we all, with a peace that passed the understanding of any soul who could not know what it means to miss New Orleans.

"Thank you, Wendell," my mother said to me that night. "Thank you for this." It had begun as a gift to them, my own way of saying thank you for all the sacrificial gifts of love Tee and Daddy had given to my brothers and me over the years. But it ended up being a gift to me as well. It was a gift whose meaning the poet T. S. Eliot captured in his poem "Little Gidding," when he said that we will not end our searching journey through life until we

> *arrive where we started*
> *And know the place for the first time.*

ON THAT CHRISTMAS NIGHT, in that tiny half-brick house on Debore Drive, feasting with my mother and father in the joy of our restoration, I knew in a way I never before had what mattered most in life. By the sweat that arose on my brow and the tears that ran down my cheek as I mined the fragments of the past, day after day, until both my hands and my heart were raw, I gained wisdom and strength and vision.

And I gained an awareness of the power I had to use my talents and resources to find, to bind, and to restore. I had helped recover the past and build from it a future for the people I loved more than my own life. If I had within me that power, did I not also have a responsibility to use it for the good of others in my community?

In giving my mother and father their home back, I had taught myself the first bars of the melody that would become my song.

At the table, Daddy and Tee admitted to me that they really had wanted to be back there all along, because this house was the last place they wanted to be on this earth. They had never told me that before: that they wanted to die at home. And now I had made their final dream possible.

In time, nearly all their lost friends would return from the Katrina diaspora. But on the peace of that Christmas night, it was only us three. Behind the walls of that new abode called forth out of the wasteland with faith, hope, love—and with hard, hard labor, not all of it the work of hands—a father, a mother, and a son had returned home together, and rested in what Eliot called

> *A condition of complete simplicity*
> *(Costing not less than everything)*

EIGHT

GODOT: WHAT'S THE GOOD
OF LOSING HEART NOW?

If there is a city in America where art and culture are more intimately woven into the bonds of civic resilience than New Orleans, I have not yet been there. And I've been all over.

Albert Murray taught me that culture emerges from a people's confrontation with and assimilation of experience. Murray and August Wilson further taught me that the peerless creativity of Diaspora Africans on the North American continent is the fruit of their affirmation of life in defiance of suffering and oppression. For Africans in America, the music they created under conditions of unspeakable pain both expressed their sorrows and their joys, and gave them the means to carry on. Their music—blues, jazz, Negro spirituals— were how they imposed aesthetic form on their experiences and redeemed the hard times through which they lived.

These insights give us a way to understand the history of music in New Orleans—and more broadly, the art that came from New Orleans culture—as a social phenomenon of extraordinary importance to the survival of the community. In this sense, art is not merely entertainment; it is life itself.

Consider the amazing story of how New Orleanians created jazz. In the late eighteenth century, when the Spanish ruled the colonial city, masters gave their slaves Sundays off as a day of rest. Hundreds of slaves came together in an open area outside the old city limits to drum, make music, dance, and be free Africans for a day. Historical eyewitness accounts of the scene told of slaves in wild, elaborate dress, and many in no clothing at all. This place, unique in North America, was called Congo Square, and it sits in what would come to be called the Tremé neighborhood.

The Spanish and French Catholics who ruled the city took a relatively relaxed attitude toward African slave culture. Historians speculate that the structures and spirit of their Roman Catholic faith were more easily syncretized with traditional West African religion. Whatever the case, in the 1700s, Europeans, Creoles, and free people of color began coming to Congo Square on Sundays to watch the Africans make music on drums and stringed instruments. Congo Square was also a place of commerce; the Code Noir, or Black Code, allowed the Africans to sell whatever they could and keep the money. When the Protestant Americans took possession of New Orleans in 1804, they tried to suppress Congo Square, but it was useless.

The enslaved musicians communicated with each other through the music on the square, exchanging information in rhythms and melodies. This was a practice that music historians believe launched the jazz practice of "trading fours," in which jazz band soloists alternate four-bar segments with the drummer.

Over time, the music of Congo Square absorbed the influences of all the peoples of the city. European melodies merged with African rhythms. The slaves—and after Emancipation, the freedmen—took up European musical instruments, like brass horns. Whites fascinated by the new music joined in. By the late nineteenth century, a new and distinct musical tradition—jazz—had been born.

It was a musical style that celebrated improvisation within form, one that extolled individuality within the sure foundation of the collective. As Albert Murray said, a form of music as liberated and as liberating as jazz could not have existed except in a condition of freedom. But the slaves were not free, nor, really, were black New Orleanians after the Civil War. Ah, but here's the thing: *Their spirits were free.* They had an inner light that hard times and hard men could not extinguish. It came pouring out of those desperately poor, miserably burdened African Americans in the rhythms and melodies of jazz, which migrated out of Tremé, out of the Crescent City, and changed world music and culture forever.

And as the product of a cultural mélange happening nowhere in the world but on Congo Square, jazz was a uniquely American art form. It is, in fact, the manifestation of the American aesthetic. There is the order of the song, and the notes of the melody, and the chords forming the architecture of the piece, but you have freedom to find your own way within those boundaries. This is America, man, and as Daddy said, however far you roam, you can't get lost in America.

Black New Orleans incorporated the marching band tradition of jazz into a practical form of self-help: social aid and pleasure clubs.

The clubs came out of the late-nineteenth-century tradition of black benevolent societies, a form of social insurance freed slaves developed to protect themselves against calamity in the absence of conventional insurance (which wasn't available to them). These informal civic organizations, usually centered around neighborhoods, allowed poor and working-class African Americans, through pooling their resources, to pay medical bills and bury their dead. The roots of this practice lie in a West African tradition of communal responsibility.

Eventually the benevolent societies came to be known as "social aid and pleasure clubs": It is just like New Orleans to give "pleasure" as much emphasis as "social aid." By the early twentieth century, the clubs were known all over town for their "second-line" parades. They began as jazz funerals. When a club's member died, the club marched solemnly behind the family and a dirge-playing jazz band to the cemetery. After the burial, the band led mourners out of the realm of the dead and back to the land of the living with raucous up-tempo numbers. "Oh, Didn't He Ramble" and "When the Saints Go Marching In" are traditional favorites. This is the New Orleans cycle.

The "first line" includes the band and the social aid and pleasure club members. The "second line" consists of mourners and everybody else who joins the band as it parades through the streets. Second-line marchers—if "marching" is the word for the high-stepping and buck-jump dancing—often twirl parasols or hold handkerchiefs high as they roll. If you have ever been to New Orleans in the July heat, you understand how practical those props are in this ritual.

In his 1954 memoir *Satchmo: My Life in New Orleans*, Louis Armstrong recalled the joy he took as a young musician, then called Dipper, playing in second-line marches with fellow band members from the Colored Waifs' Home:

> In those days some of the social clubs paraded all day long. When the big bands consisting of old-timers complained about such a tiresome job, the club members called on us.

"Those boys," they said, "will march all day long and won't squawk one bit."

They were right. We were so glad to get a chance to walk in the street that we did not care how long we paraded or how far. The day we were engaged by the Merry-Go-Round Social Club we walked all the way to Carrol[l]ton, a distance of about twenty-five miles. Playing like mad, we loved every foot of the trip.

The first day we paraded through my old neighborhood everybody was gathered on the sidewalks to see us pass. All the whores, pimps, gamblers, thieves and beggars were waiting for the band because they knew that Dipper, Mayann's son, would be in it. But they had never dreamed that I would be playing the cornet, blowing it as good as I did. They ran to wake up mama, who was sleeping after a night job, so she could see me go by. Then they asked Mr. Davis [one of the Home's counselors] if they could give me some money. He nodded his head with approval, not thinking that the money would amount to very much. But he did not know that sporting crowd. Those sports gave me so much that I had to borrow the hats of several other boys to hold it all. I took in enough to buy new uniforms and new instruments for everybody who played in the band. The instruments we had been using were old and badly battered.

That second-line parade gave the poor people of Satchmo's old neighborhood the opportunity to have a great time dancing in the street, as well as donate cash to help the Waifs' marching band.

Satchmo said no matter how old he got and how far he had gone in the world, he never tired of watching those New Orleans social aid and pleasure clubs parade, calling it "an irresistible and absolutely unique experience." Eventually the clubs took to parading for its own sake—Zulu, the best-known club, even parades during Mardi Gras—or for reasons having nothing to do with death. We have come a long way from the time when social aid and pleasure clubs were critical to the survival of the community. Folks have come to see only the pleasure part. But the social aid element was where it originally came from.

You can still see that principle informally at work today. The second line literally walks commerce into a neighborhood. This is the tangible, pragmatic impact of culture. The band leads the crowd to one member's house or business and stops for a while. If you look behind them, you'll see a candy man, a guy selling beer and soda, or a woman on her stoop selling barbecue. When the parade stops, people have their lunch or a drink with a neighbor. And if it stops at a barroom or a restaurant, and you have a hundred people or more who have been marching and dancing and having a good time for a mile, they'll come into your place and refresh themselves. The second line literally uses art to bring business and life into a neighborhood.

The second line also marked a defining moment in the city's post-Katrina life. On January 15, 2006, exiled New Orleanians came in from all over the country to march in the city's first official second-line parade since the storm. Around the country, naysayers were talking down New Orleans, saying that we weren't going to ever be the same. New Orleanians both living in the city and those trying to move back showed up for the All-Star Second Line Parade, put on by thirty-two of the city's social aid and pleasure clubs. Three brass bands and thousands of New Orleanians paraded for hours through some of the worst-hit black neighborhoods near downtown.

"Neighborhoods that were just totally abandoned, shipwrecks, were alive that day," said Jordan Hersch, a parade organizer, in a public radio interview. "Families hanging out on the porch, smoke in the air from people grilling, having lunch, waiting for the band to come around.

"It was about letting people know that this culture is forceful, and it's meaningful, and it's powerful," he continued. "It is what can bring the city back to life."

Amen. Those paraders were reaching back into our collective history as New Orleanians to find their song beneath the debris and devastation left by Katrina. Their dance and song that day was a conjuring that summoned the past into the present to make way for a future that many doubted New Orleans would have. It was a ceremony of innocence that Katrina's tide could not drown. It was the casting out of the spirit of despair and defeat. It was a rite of resurrection.

MY OWN ARTISTIC CONTRIBUTION to the resurrection culture emerging in post-Katrina New Orleans had consequences for my own life far beyond the realm of art—consequences I scarcely could have imagined when a creative door in New York City opened in Katrina's aftermath, and I walked through it.

In the spring of 2006, theater director Christopher McElroen mounted a production of *Waiting for Godot* in Harlem. Because the plight of post-Katrina New Orleans reminded McElroen of Beckett's play, he set his 2006 version in a waterlogged city. The drama takes place on the roof of a house surrounded by floodwaters (McElroen literally encompassed his set with fifteen thousand gallons of water). I played Vladimir; J. Kyle Manzay played Estragon. The Harlem production ran for five weeks, with *The New York Times* calling it "dazzling," adding, "Who knew this play could still surprise?"

The biggest surprise was yet to come. That fall, New York artist Paul Chan traveled to New Orleans to teach art classes at Tulane University. He had never before been to the Crescent City. Seeing what Katrina had done shocked him to the core. Chan had been to shattered postwar Baghdad and to the bleak postindustrial landscape of Detroit; in both places, he observed signs that life continued, despite catastrophe.

"New Orleans was different," he later wrote.

When he toured the Lower Ninth Ward, seeing the wild vegetation, the desolate roads, and concrete foundations that were all that remained of family homes, he was staggered. To stand within the precincts of a major American city and hear nothing at all, endlessly, was like being frozen in amber. As he waited there for his ride to pick him up, it occurred to Chan that he was standing in a place he had never been, but also one he had been to many times.

"It was unmistakable. The empty road. The bare tree leaning precariously to one side with just enough leaves to make it respectable. The silence," he wrote. "Standing there at the intersection of North Prieur and Reynes, I suddenly found myself in the middle of Samuel Beckett's *Waiting for Godot*."

Why *Godot*? As Chan put it, there was a "terrible symmetry" between post-Katrina New Orleans and Beckett's absurdist drama, a parallel that "expresses in stark eloquence the cruel and funny things people do while they wait: for help, for food, for hope. It was uncanny."

Beckett, an Irish émigré living in Paris, wrote what would become one of the twentieth century's towering artistic achievements, based on his experience in Nazi-occupied France. He and his wife served the underground French Resistance and endured conditions of poverty, hunger, and extreme uncertainty. Everything civilized people thought they knew about the way the world worked had been taken from them—at first by the Great War, and then by this Second World War, which brought the barbaric Nazis flooding over the French border, engulfing the country.

Would deliverance from the Nazis come? How does one get on with daily life in the absence of a reason to hope for salvation? These are the questions at the heart of *Godot*, which Beckett dubbed a "tragicomedy." It's not a tragedy, strictly speaking, because the fault for the suffering of Didi and Gogo is not in their nature, nor is it within their power to change their fate. It's not exactly a comedy either, because though the script is laced with mordant wit, based in the absurdity of trying to make sense of life in conditions of utter ruin, there is no happy ending.

Yet there is hope. Godot might come tomorrow. You never know. In any case, we have to get on with the business of living.

When he returned to New York, Chan began thinking about staging a production of *Godot* in the Lower Ninth Ward. He explored what the writer and public intellectual Susan Sontag accomplished in

Sarajevo in 1993, mounting *Godot* in the darkness and despair of that once beautiful city as besieging Serbian forces lashed it with shelling and sniper fire from the surrounding hills.

Sontag, who died in 2004, risked her life to bring theater to Sarajevo. She was also criticized by some in the West for what they saw as a pretentious stunt, one that, by showcasing a play notoriously bereft of uplift, only made it more difficult for Sarajevans to bear the burden of daily life.

In a 1993 *New York Review of Books* essay, Sontag defended herself from these critics. "In Sarajevo, as anywhere else, there are more than a few people who feel strengthened and consoled by having their sense of reality affirmed and transfigured by art," she wrote.

"People in Sarajevo know themselves to be terminally weak: waiting, hoping, not wanting to hope, knowing that they aren't going to be saved," she continued. "They are humiliated by their disappointment, by their fear, and by the indignities of daily life—for instance, by having to spend a good part of each day seeing to it that their toilets flush, so that their bathrooms don't become cesspools. That is how they use most of the water they queue for in public spaces, at great risk to their lives. This sense of humiliation may be even greater than their fear."

Because Sarajevo was such a wonderful place to live before the war, the degradation war forced on the cosmopolitan city made the despair of its people especially acute. As Sontag observed, "That kind of idealization produces a very acute disillusionment."

All of this could have been written of storm-savaged New Orleans, whose fall grieved its remaining people more than I can adequately say. None of us thought our city was paradise before the storm. There was crime. There was poverty. There was racism, and ignorance, and corruption. But there was also a joy of living, and a style of living, that existed nowhere else in America, and a grace and grandeur that made New Orleans a city of dreams.

The flood took that from us, leaving us with death, destruction, displacement, and a citizenry who, in too many instances, behaved like vultures feeding off putrid carrion. In so many ways, post-Katrina New Orleans was a wasteland in which, to paraphrase William Butler Yeats, the best of us lacked conviction that we knew the road home to the city we had once loved, and the worst were full of a passionate intensity that was determined to prevent us from finding it.

This was Beckett territory. Chan contacted Creative Time, the Manhattan-based art production company best known for erecting the twin shafts of light in the ruins of the World Trade Center, to see if it would be willing to produce a New Orleans staging of McElroen's version of *Godot*—not acted in a theater, but at the Lower Ninth Ward crossroads where he first conceived the idea.

Chan started making twice-monthly trips down South to lay the groundwork for the play. He was determined to avoid accusations of being a drive-by New York artist, condescending to the locals by giving them art they didn't ask for and couldn't relate to. He got to know local folks and asked them to help out with the production if it interested them. One of the most important figures in this respect was Robert Green, Sr., a Lower Ninth Ward resident who had lost family in the storm, and who was then living in a FEMA trailer.

"He was so many things to me: conscience, friend, security," Chan wrote in a 2010 "field guide" Creative Time assembled to document the project. "He knew everyone in the Ninth Ward. That's what community means. He knew the person who owned the gas station up the street, he knew the kids who were running a new barbershop on the second floor of that gas station, he knew the churches in the area. He knew Pastor Hayward at New Israel Baptist Church. A lot of the places that he introduced me to when we were organizing *Godot* were churches, because they were still organizing people when many had left and no one else cared or had the time. We would go to church Saturdays and Sundays, and it helped that I was familiar with Scripture."

I helped with this as well, introducing Paul and his team around New Orleans, lending my perspective on where to go, what to see, and whom to talk to. Paul threw himself into teaching and lecturing anywhere in the city that would have him, sharing his gifts and expertise with local art students and organizers, and working with the arts infrastructure that already existed in the city. He went to churches— one Lower Ninth Ward pastor preached a *Godot*-themed sermon, "Waiting for God to Do"—he went to neighborhood association meetings, and he participated in two potluck dinners in the Lower Ninth Ward. Paul also quietly set up what he called a "shadow fund" to leave behind money to help the work of eleven arts and community organizations whose work he saw and admired during his New Orleans sojourn.

By the time he moved to New Orleans full time in August (to teach art classes for free at Xavier University and the University of New Orleans), his *Godot* production had spread roots throughout the community. The play would truly grow out of organic relationships that Paul, director Chris McElroen, and their company cultivated in the months leading up to the play. The New Yorkers committed themselves to allowing the reactions and the advice of local artists, community organizers, and others to drive their decision making. They did not want to be called carpetbaggers, or in any way to be seen as exploiting the city's pain so they could feel good about themselves.

The team learned quickly that business in New Orleans is rarely straightforward. You have to be prepared to wait, to tolerate inefficiency, and to meet people face-to-face—usually over a meal. And you have to be prepared to listen. Night after night, we met with folks all over the city, telling them what the play was about, why we were doing it here, and asking them how we could do it right.

One of the most important decisions the team made early in the process was to go beyond the Lower Ninth Ward with the play. The Lower Ninth was famous the world over for what it had suffered, but there was intense pain and frustration citywide. Tulane art historian Pamela Franco suggested taking *Godot* to Gentilly, where, unlike the now vacant Lower Ninth, most of the housing was still standing, if gutted by the flood.

Godot is seemingly a simple play to stage, with a small cast and minimal set design. But doing it in a neighborhood that had been devastated by a hurricane (Gentilly), and in one that had been obliterated by the storm (the Lower Ninth), was especially challenging. Plus, most of the production team lived in New York and had to shuttle back and forth, greatly complicating matters. Though the budget was bare-bones, Paul and his team were committed to making every effort to stage a first-rate production for the city.

Months of endless community meetings, potlucks, forums at

schools, homes, churches, bars, and theaters around town paid off. Producer Gavin Kroeber said later that without the volunteers and the active goodwill of so many New Orleanians, the show would not have come off. He credited the post-Katrina politicization of so many city residents and their passion for resurrecting New Orleans culture for drawing such a diversity of local folks to the unusual project.

"I've often wondered how likely it would be for an absurdist play to bring such a breadth of community partners to the table in, say, Brooklyn, San Francisco, Atlanta, or even the 'slow-motion Katrinas' of the American Rust Belt," Kroeber mused in the post-production field guide.

Rehearsals started in October 2007, in an abandoned school in the Upper Ninth Ward. Signs began appearing on trees and utility poles all over town, saying cryptically: *A country road. A tree. Evening*—the stage setting given by Beckett in the play. The town began buzzing about what was coming. We were going to deliver two performances in the Lower Ninth Ward on the first weekend in November, and two the weekend after in Gentilly—in front of a storm-gutted house less than two miles from Pontchartrain Park.

It's impossible not to be nervous on any opening night, but this one was like no other I had ever experienced. This was my city. These were my people. I was going to give everything I had to them, both those living and those who had passed in the storm. Would it be received? An expatriate New Orleanian named Randy McClain gave me reason to believe it would.

McClain and his family had left New Orleans in 2003 for Nashville, but had never forgotten the city. He had been reading about our

Godot production in *The Times-Picayune*'s online edition and wrote
the newspaper a letter that it published just before we opened. In it,
McClain said that his teenage son was an aspiring actor.

"I want him to see how a neutral ground stage can become a place
of social and political comment and a play can be a call to action,"
McClain said in his letter. "I want my son to see theater that touches
lives and does more than just entertain. So, we're driving nine hours,
lawn chairs in the trunk, to see art."

How many Randy McClains could we count on? I had my answer
when I converged on the Lower Ninth Ward on opening night and
saw the headlights of an endless stream of cars, all filled with people
going to see art. On that magical evening, hope floated atop the river
of light flowing into the basin of night.

Waiting for Godot begins with the two tramps, Vladimir (also
called Didi) and Estragon (Gogo), standing under a bare tree.

> *ESTRAGON: Nothing to be done.*
>
> *VLADIMIR: I'm beginning to come round to that opinion. All my life I've
> tried to put it from me, saying, Vladimir, be reasonable, you
> haven't yet tried everything. And I resumed the struggle. So
> there you are again.*

In that first exchange between Didi and Gogo, the play lays out its
philosophical concerns. Do we quit struggling and resign ourselves
to fate—or do we resist? And if we are to resist, on what basis should
we hope that we might succeed? Vladimir concedes that the weight
of the burden is "too much for one man."

"On the other hand," he continues, "what's the good of losing heart now, that's what I say."

The pair spends the first act making small talk, mostly, revealing that they have been traveling together virtually their entire lives and have grown dependent on each other. They repeat lines and gestures, indicating that the course of their lives has been charted out by petty rituals and exchanges meant to pass the time together. They are, we find, waiting for Godot, a mysterious figure whose arrival will make everything right again. Didi's belief that Godot will come makes everything bearable and keeps the thought of suicide at bay. Why kill yourself when there is hope that tomorrow help will come? They meet a wealthy man, Pozzo, who is headed to the market to sell his slave, Lucky. Later, a boy comes to them, a messenger from Godot, saying that he won't be coming today, but will arrive tomorrow.

> BOY: *What am I to tell Mr. Godot, Sir?*
>
> VLADIMIR: *Tell him . . . [he hesitates] . . . tell him you saw us.*

All Vladimir wants at that point is to know that their suffering did not go unobserved by the man who has it in his power to end it. It's as if the assurance that Godot knew what they were going through, even if he didn't rescue them, would be enough to give Didi and Gogo hope to hold on for one more day. Surely if Godot got word of what they were enduring, he would hasten to help them. Surely.

The first act ends with Didi and Gogo vowing to leave this place. But they do not move. In the second act, more or less the same things occur, which caused one critic to quip that Beckett "has written a play in which nothing happens, twice." So much of life, Didi comes to understand, is about playing the same games, over and over, and expecting a different outcome. But this time, Didi has two awakenings.

In the first, Didi delivers the play's most important lines, telling Gogo that they should shut up and act to help suffering Pozzo.

> *Let us not waste our time in idle discourse! Let us do something, while we have the chance! It is not every day that we are needed. Not indeed that we personally are needed. Others would meet the case equally well, if not better. To all mankind they were addressed, those cries for help still ringing in our ears! But at this place, at this moment of time, all mankind is us, whether we like it or not. Let us make the most of it, before it is too late! Let us represent worthily for once the foul brood to which a cruel fate consigned us! What do you say?*

Soon after this, a furious Pozzo departs the scene with a declaration that life is meaningless. "They give birth astride of a grave," he says, of human beings, "the light gleams in an instant, then it's night once more."

This gets to Didi. "I don't know what to think anymore," he confides to Gogo. Didi is tempted to believe that the life he leads has been a pointless exercise in repetition, and that "habit is a great deadener"—meaning that going through the motions is a way to numb oneself to the pain of existence. Yet when Godot's messenger boy arrives with the news that Godot won't come today, but perhaps he will tomorrow, Didi says, as usual, "Tell him that you saw me."

The play ends as the first act did: with Vladimir and Estragon seated under the tree, resolving to get up and go, but not moving.

GODOT, of course, is never going to come. Are Vladimir and Estragon heroes or fools? Is their persistence in the face of absurdity a sign of their indomitable will to live, or of their supreme idiocy? Is there a difference?

Well, what would you say about the people who second-lined through the ruins of their city? An affirmation of life in the face of death—or folks acting silly in a time that calls for solemnity? What would you say about people who drove out to a wasteland to watch a bleak play about the meaning of life, performed in what amounted to a graveyard? Sages or fools?

When you sense that there may not be much of a difference, you are getting close to the point of Beckett's play, and why it resonated so profoundly with Katrina survivors in New Orleans.

"It is ours, it speaks directly to us, in lines and situations that have always been there, but which now take on a new resonance," said *Times-Picayune* critic David Cuthbert, in his review of our production. "There is no great entity riding to our rescue to 'fix' what has been broken. We must do it ourselves, as we have, with the help of compassionate strangers and our own crazy courage. The play brings light, life, and humanity to a dark corner of the city and the ongoing dark night of our souls."

Ann Maloney, also writing in *The Times-Picayune*, conceded that had she seen Godot in the theater, she might "have found it pretentious—too arty. But as we drove home on Sunday night, I felt a camaraderie with the two men who joked, hugged, cried and fought as they dealt with crushing disappointment and a yearning for better days."

Dewey Scandurro, a New Orleans lawyer who attended one of our Gentilly performances, shared this view. He said he had read *Waiting for Godot* many times, first as a French major at Tulane, but he never really understood it until he had lived through Katrina and watched *Godot* performed in the ruins.

When a friend from far away told Scandurro he didn't understand why such a difficult play resonated with New Orleanians, he responded, "Return to your city after it's been laid waste, and *Godot* makes some sense. Wait for FEMA to answer a phone for a month. Watch them turn away Walmart trucks full of water when people at the Convention Center are on the verge of dehydration. Listen to the government explain that they cannot get into the city when your 63-year-old mother was able to get out on roads that were always open. Watch the mayor and governor and parish president go insane on live TV. Read about the New Orleans Police Department spokesman committing suicide in a squad car.

"Chaos. Hopelessness. Absurdity. That play summed up what it meant to live in New Orleans in those days," he said.

Listening to the audiences after the performances, we heard people saying how strange the play was, but how sorry they felt for Didi and Gogo, and how they know what it's like to feel abandoned, because . . . and then the theatergoer would inevitably tell his or her own Katrina story. A few people who didn't know *Godot* thought someone had written it in response to Katrina. From my perspective, the sense of unity in compassion that *Godot* brought to our broken, beaten-down community was a minor miracle. There were people of all races and social classes in those audiences, and it seemed that nearly everyone left feeling that, while they had lost a lot in the storm, there were others who had lost even more—and they wanted to help.

It was profound.

According to Beckett, that's what it means to live in modern times. *Waiting for Godot* deals with the aftermath of a catastrophe that annihilated everything that gave humanity a sense of direction and ultimate meaning, leaving us all in a void. For Beckett, the catastrophe was the two great wars that pulverized the pillars of Western civilization, prying away our illusions like a torturer extracting fingernails from his victim.

I don't see Didi and Gogo's repetitions as pointless, as empty rituals to pass the time until death. Rather, I see their repetitions as attempts to *remember* the past, when things had meaning and they knew where they were going. As foolish and trifling as their games may seem, the men are not surrendering to hopelessness; in fact, they are fighting the battle against despair. They are tempted to believe that they cannot go on . . . but they must go on. So they go on. Even waiting is an act of hope in the face of the void. To refuse death is, however feebly, to affirm life.

"All mankind is us, whether we like it or not," declares Didi. This is the human condition: thrown into the void, confused, uncertain, and forgotten by those outside. The only difference between the people of post-Katrina New Orleans and every other American is that New Orleanians no longer had the illusion that life was always going to be normal, predictable, reasonable. A storm, or an earthquake, or a tornado, or a war can sweep aside everything you know and love, leaving you with no direction home.

What should we do? How can we go on like this? Our city is gone. Godot—that is, the government, FEMA, insurance companies, and so forth—isn't coming to save us. All of us here together in New Orleans—rich, poor, black, white, Uptown, downtown, from Gentilly to the Bywater—have only each other, and our memories of what we have lost.

Here is one big difference between Beckett and the people of New Orleans, including me: We did not lose faith in God because of the storm. God didn't make the levees fail; man did, by building them badly and maintaining them poorly. Far from blaming God for our suffering, or losing faith in His existence, New Orleanians drew closer to Him. Over and over, you would hear people say that we needed God more than ever, and that prayer was the only thing that was going to get us through.

Prayer, and hope. *Hope is a memory that desires.* If we can remember who we were and what we had, and can act in concert to reenact the rituals that defined us, we might find in that the hope to go on, despite the indifference of others to our fate. *Godot* says let's try our rituals—not only the rituals of the church, but the rituals of festival, of family, of sport, of cuisine as well—any piece of ritual that you can remember and bring back can help restore us and make us whole again. We know Godot is not coming, but in the meantime, we're not going to give up the quest to recover our collective memory, and to use it to rebuild the present and create a future.

In the darkest of times, we were never resigned to fate. We call

New Orleans the Big Easy, the place that care forgot, but deep down, that's not true. Our city and its culture mean everything to us. That's why *Waiting for Godot* speaks so powerfully to people in times of extreme difficulty. Living under occupation, Beckett knew what it was like to have everything taken from you, and he reached across the decades and the ocean to connect with people in New Orleans who understood what this means.

His play reached across time and place and spoke to the people of besieged Sarajevo, just as it had spoken to the black sharecropper in the civil rights era, the one who saw the Free Southern Theater's production in rural Mississippi and said, "Godot? He ain't comin'. I know that."

It was important to that sharecropper to recognize that fact. He needed to rid himself of false hope, and he needed to see his own experience of life's hardship, in Sontag's words, "affirmed and transfigured by art." There is power in that.

The search for humanity and purpose in life is at the heart of *Waiting for Godot*, a search that does not end despite the failure of the world to do the right thing. My ancestors did not cease to believe that a better day would come for African Americans, but they never sat idly by waiting to be rescued by Godot. They would not allow themselves to be defeated by slavery, or Jim Crow, or the Ku Klux Klan. They would not succumb to ignorance, or self-indulgence, or moral lassitude. How easy it would have been for them to believe that nothing they did or ever could do would make a difference in their life or in the lives of their children, and their children's children. "Segregation forever!" swore the white politicians, who held all the power in a society that told black folk they amounted to nothing.

My ancestors and so many of those Moses generations—those who led our people out of slavery and the degradation of bondage—refused to believe they amounted to nothing. They refused to believe that their suffering had no meaning, that it would not be redeemed. They persevered, against breathtaking odds, strengthened by their culture: by their faith, by their families, by their communities, by their rituals, by their songs. In fact, it was only in suffering that my people found their song—and gave to America a song of itself.

Waiting for Godot tells us that we are in the same predicament as Vladimir and Estragon. We can find our purpose not in the empty promises of others, but in ourselves, and in our ability to determine our own futures. The only way we are going to find hope is by doing so together. Didi and Gogo, they stay in place. They go on. As we New Orleanians must.

This message, I am certain, struck a chord in the hearts of all the people who saw our production. I do not know what every one of them thought as they left the performance. True, we made a political statement with that production—on opening night, we invited leading local, state, and national leaders, and reserved seats for them, with their names on the chairs, but—surprise!—they did not come. But overall, *Godot* doesn't have a particular political message, a platform, or a specific call to action.

When asked by *The New Yorker* if his *Godot* experience gave him new insight into the possibilities of art in achieving social justice and political change, Paul Chan said it did not. It brought people together, yes, but he was trying to bring about "articulate speechlessness." He went on: "My mind was cleared for something else to happen, which I think is what art does. If you do it right, that's what happens."

People who had never crossed the bridge into the Lower Ninth Ward came in to see this existential play about the isolation of man, the abandonment of man, what it is to lose faith, what it is to lose hope—and how to find it again. In that surreal landscape, where our city used to be, in the presence of men who just got off a shift working on the docks, to a suburban housewife, to some button-down white lawyer driving in from the Central Business District, to a poor black man living in a FEMA trailer—all of us, together, as New Orleanians, in that moment, we were all mankind. We can't lose hope. We've got to find a way. Nobody will save us but ourselves.

We can't go on. We must go on. Pull up your trousers. Let's go! Let's do something!

After the show closed, I couldn't shake the conviction that more was required of me. I couldn't just fly away, back to my life in L.A., and forget about New Orleans. I thought hard about what performing *Godot* in the Lower Ninth Ward and Gentilly had meant to me. I thought even harder about how nearly losing my city revealed the depth and intensity of the love I had for the home I had left behind more than half my life ago. No, I could not simply fly away. But what could I do?

Here's how I found the answer.

LESS THAN TEN DAYS after New Orleans flooded, *The Wall Street Journal* published an account of the Katrina aftermath as seen from Audubon Place, the gated Uptown neighborhood where some of the wealthiest New Orleanians live. Jimmy Reiss, a rich and politically well-connected resident from an old family, came back to the city in a helicopter and hired an Israeli security firm to protect his house from looters.

The newspaper reported that Reiss was headed to Dallas the next day with about forty other Crescent City bigwigs to powwow with New Orleans Mayor Ray Nagin, whose family had taken refuge there, to discuss the future of New Orleans. They were going to insist on a New Orleans with a lot fewer poor people.

"Those who want to see this city rebuilt want to see it done in a completely different way: demographically, geographically and politically," Reiss told the *Journal*. "I'm not just speaking for myself here. The way we've been living is not going to happen again, or we're out."

Papo had seen men like this coming a long time ago. Jimmy Reiss was not a man who had the best interests of people who looked like me at heart.

Reiss was by no means an outlier. In his terrific 2005 book *Why New Orleans Matters*, written that terrible autumn from his outpost in the Katrina diaspora, Tom Piazza recalled talking a month or so after the storm to a "very privileged Uptown white woman in late middle age" who couldn't see what the fuss was all about. She had returned from staying with family in Florida, and her house was undamaged. Everybody in her neighborhood was doing fine. She had not heard from tenants in one of her rental properties, and she had sought a legal opinion, which said she had the right to clean the place out and leave the tenant's belongings on the sidewalk.

"I don't want to," she said, drawing out the word want, "but there are a lot of people looking for places to live." And anyway, the severity of the disaster had been so overstated on the news—all that focus on the Ninth Ward and all that. "The Ninth Ward isn't New Orleans," she said to me. "You can come to New Orleans a hundred times and never even see the Ninth Ward."

So true, I thought—and that kind of savage, self-satisfied, ignorant attitude of large numbers of the criminally oblivious privileged is also a part of New Orleans. God plainly loves them because they have electricity, and it is also plain what God thinks of those who don't. They hold many of the purse strings, and they will be trying with everything they have to determine the future of the city.

Piazza chewed on former First Lady Barbara Bush's remark that things seemed to be working out for the "underprivileged" New Orleanians in the diaspora, who in her view really had not had much to lose.

The "underprivileged" people of New Orleans spun a culture out of their lives—a music, a cuisine, a sense of life—that has been recognized around the world as a transforming spiritual force. Out of those pitifully small incomes and crumbling houses, and hard, long days and nights of work came a staggering Yes, an affirmation of life—their lives, Life itself—in defiance of a world that told them in as many ways as it could find that they were, you know, dispensable.

He was right. The people who were the least able to fight for themselves and their own stake in New Orleans were the ones whose culture had made New Orleans worth fighting for.

Jimmy Reiss was a member of the mayor's Bring New Orleans Back commission, which in early 2006 released a controversial report that called for allowing some flood-prone areas of the city that had been inhabited pre-Katrina to return to green space. The report suggested that if residents of these neighborhoods—most (but not all) of whom were low-income folks—could not demonstrate within four months that they had the means and the intention to rebuild, then the city could buy them out or seize their land under eminent domain and redevelop it.

So now we knew: If we didn't get back in there and start fighting for Pontchartrain Park, those who didn't have our best interests at heart were going to take our homes.

Daddy and Tee were among the first displaced Pontchartrain Park residents to return. I had paid a premium price to hire a contractor to rebuild their house. They moved in a month or two after the *Godot* performances. Rumors flew around the frightened Pontchartrain Park exile community. One story had it that Donald Trump had been through and was going to work with the city to seize our land under eminent domain and turn our neighborhood into an exclusive gated community. After all, this was prime property close to the lake, in a quiet part of town with a golf course at its heart.

"Wendell, you've got to get involved with the neighborhood," someone said to me at the time. "Whatever attention you can bring to Pontchartrain Park to help it get back on its feet would do a world of good. Decisions are being made now."

But what could I do? I was an actor who lived in Los Angeles and worked all over the country, and even overseas. What role could I possibly play on a stage like Pontchartrain Park?

Then again, had I not just played a literal part on two stages that actually were storm-ravaged neighborhoods, just like Pontchartrain Park? Was there a connection?

I had emptied myself out in playing Vladimir, channeling into my performance all the hope and the anger and the confusion that all of us in New Orleans had been feeling, doing all I could to connect with the hometown audiences. When human beings make art, we say collectively, "These are our values; this is what is important to us." On those street corner stages in the Lower Ninth Ward and Gentilly, all of us—the cast, the crew, the audience—shared an intense and cathartic communion, and in that moment, many of us reflected on who we were, what we stood for, and where we were going, together. On those nights of live theater in the wasteland, art intersected with life in an electrifying way. This, Albert Murray had taught me so many years earlier, is where culture is born, and reborn. Folks who saw the show told us, many of them with tears rolling down their cheeks, how much the play meant to them, and how seeing it had given them hope.

It was a resurrection moment. As an artist and a New Orleanian, I had had the privilege to be part of it. I had hoped *Godot* might change something for the better in the city, but I didn't know what. Now I could feel *Godot* changing me. When I ran through the darkness toward the stage lights in those performances, the audiences heard my voice before they saw my face. *"We're going to change things,"* I had said. *"I'm coming . . . for you . . . for all of them"*—that is, for all those who perished in the flood.

MAYBE, just maybe, I was being called to stay for all the people, living and dead, who had given me so much. Especially our fathers and mothers of Pontchartrain Park.

Visiting Daddy and Tee on those evenings, I would listen to the stories they would tell about the neighborhood in the old days, and it dawned on me that as young men and women, they had done something revolutionary. The simple act of daring to own your own ordinary home was a courageous act. They must have had their doubts and fears. They knew it was dangerous, that moving to Pontchartrain Park might cost someone their life. I remembered Daddy's story about how he had bought his first gun after they moved in and white thugs began to punch black housewives. If they were doing that in the daytime, Daddy said, no telling what they would be willing to do at night.

My mother and father had staked their claim, and they weren't going to back down. Neither would their neighbors. Thinking about all that generation had gone through to get to Pontchartrain Park, and all that Papo and Mamo's generation before them had endured to make a better life for their descendants, it struck me as blasphemy to allow our neighborhood to be taken from us. What a slap in the face to our ancestors if we let that happen.

I reached out to Troy Henry, a childhood friend from the neighborhood who had become a successful New Orleans businessman. "We owe it to our parents to do something to bring back Pontchartrain Park," I told him. He agreed, and he helped me come up with a plan to bring back the neighborhood association and to make sure that residents had the right to redevelop the area ourselves.

IN JANUARY 2007, I put out a call to the neighborhood, inviting folks to come to a picnic on the playground. At the time, only about 40 percent of the houses were inhabited. It was like living on a frontier. Yet people loved Pontchartrain Park so much that some even came home from around the country to be at that meeting, to learn how we could organize to save our legacy and our future. Nobody was going to come in and save Pontchartrain Park; all we had was each other.

When I saw that a hundred fifty or so people had gathered on a playground smack in the middle of a devastated urban landscape, eager to discover what they could do to help themselves, for the first time I knew that one person could have a major effect. That one call to action was heard by so many. As I rose to speak to the crowd, I realized that the younger ones among us have luxuries that our parents did not have. They were just trying to build a decent life for themselves. They not only battled bureaucracy, ignorance, and everyday racism, but also had to fear for what the violent hooligans from across The Ditch in Gentilly Woods (which, after 1970s-era white flight, was now all black) might do to them. This playground where we were gathered, our parents put their lives at risk so we, their children, could grow up playing here, like any normal American kids.

How could we in good conscience let it go?

"I grew up in this neighborhood," I began. "It has been brought to my attention that there's an effort underway to make Pontchartrain Park different from what it was before the storm. I'm not sure what's going to happen, but I'm putting out a call to action: We are going to restore Pontchartrain Park ourselves."

I talked about the legacy our parents had left for us here, and how we had a responsibility to them and to ourselves to fight for it. Katrina had revealed to me the value of this place, and I was committed to moving back to defend it.

"This is a call to service," I said. "This is a call to exercise our right of self-determination."

This wasn't mere rhetoric. The threat was real. Tulane University's architecture school had just created a course on urban renewal in "Pontilly," as they had renamed the Pontchartrain Park and Gentilly Woods neighborhoods. The funny thing was, Tulane had never before shown interest in our part of town. I had seen how much of Pasadena, California, where I live for much of the year, had been bought up by Caltech, and how seemingly half of West Baltimore, where I had shot *The Wire*, was now owned by Johns Hopkins, which acquired the real estate under similar distressed conditions. Everybody knew that Pontchartrain Park had a bull's-eye on it.

Out of all the neighborhoods in the devastated city it could have chosen, the Tulane architecture school picked Pontchartrain Park as the focus of an urban redevelopment class. Now we saw graduate students photographing Pontchartrain Park and asking all kinds of questions of neighborhood residents about life there.

Some suspected—I among them—that the university's interest

was really in owning the property and that it was using an academic project as a false front. This was all speculation, of course, but if Tulane could acquire Pontchartrain Park, it would be in a position to petition the state to close Southern University at New Orleans and reopen it as a satellite Tulane campus. Plus, Tulane would own five hundred houses, and a golf course.

It would be a sweet deal for Tulane. For the rest of us, not so much.

Troy and I formed the Pontchartrain Park Community Development Corporation for the purpose of restoring the neighborhood. Our hope was for it to be a haven for home-owning families, especially African American ones, to keep our parents' dream alive for a new generation. Oddly enough, when the New Orleans Redevelopment Authority (NORA) granted our company redevelopment rights to the neighborhood, it seemed to me that Tulane lost interest in Pontchartrain Park as a laboratory for redeveloping New Orleans. I felt that my cynicism about Tulane's motives was vindicated. We got to work. Our goal: to build three hundred solar-paneled, geo-thermally heated houses there.

Eight hard years later, we are not where we wanted to be on the road to Pontchartrain Park's comeback, but we are making steady progress. The route to building new homes has been winding, full of detours, switchbacks, potholes, and washouts. In all candor, it has been a very New Orleans story. Unfortunately, one of the most resilient aspects of life in the Big Easy has been its rough-and-tumble politics.

Troy ran for mayor in 2010, but lost to Mitch Landrieu, son of former New Orleans mayor Moon Landrieu. I was told the worst thing you can do is come in second in the mayor's race, because the victorious political machine is going to spend the next four years trying to keep anything you do from succeeding, because your opponents want to neutralize you as a political threat for the next election.

In New Orleans, politics are as pervasive as they are murky. Plus, competence and efficiency are not virtues we have come to expect in our public servants and agencies. It is difficult, therefore, to say whether obstacles suddenly arising in your path come from bureaucratic ineptitude or political malice. It took NORA two years of hemming and hawing to transfer four properties to us. It tells you something, though, that when U.S. Senator Mary Landrieu was publicly commending us for trying to bring a grocery store to the Lower Ninth Ward food desert, which hadn't had a decent food store for decades, her brother Mitch was meeting with the bank about the grocery store project, trying, I suspect, to kill the deal.

As with the Tulane project, I can't prove my suspicions, but I do know this: Before the deal's financiers went into the meeting with the mayor, they were committed to financing the grocery store; when the meeting was over, they dropped us. The project's developer moved on to take on another opportunity elsewhere in the city. It's hard to believe that this wasn't about politics. Where our store was going to be in the Lower Ninth, there is still nothing but an abandoned building.

I also had a letter of intent to open a food store on a blighted corner of North Broad and Bienville in Mid-City, in an area designated as a food desert by the city. Then the developer stopped returning my phone calls, and the next thing I knew, the city awarded $2 million in grants to turn the site into a Whole Foods. Imagine that: attempting to meet the grocery needs of poor and working-class people with a premium supermarket mocked as "Whole Paycheck" for its high prices. Where is the sense in that? But my business partner and I noticed a pattern: Projects we were involved in that had been moving along well suddenly stopped, and we saw that Mayor Landrieu was involved in some way.

To have had that incredible *Godot* moment of hope in the desolation of the Lower Ninth Ward, and then to see a project as worthwhile and as necessary as a grocery store go down because of city politics—was a beat-down. Our absurd struggles with NORA and various bureaucracies to get houses built in Pontchartrain Park are worthy of a Beckett play. Friends of mine have told me that I have done all I can, and that I can't go on like this. It's not worth it, they say.

But I have it on good authority that *can't* died three days before the creation of the world. I'll go on, for as long as I can. What's the good of losing heart now?

When Nelson Mandela died in 2013, I read in his obituary a quote of his that resonated deeply with me: "It is always difficult until it's done." It made me think about all the times I've wanted to give up, to focus on my career, to lay down the burden of rebuilding Pontchartrain Park. It seems impossible that this will ever get done. But we're not going anywhere but forward.

In January 2014, I bought a house in the neighborhood, across the park from the street where I grew up. If I am asking others to move to Pontchartrain Park after the disaster, then I need to do it myself, I figured. Because of the nature of my work, I am constantly shuttling between New York, Los Angeles, and New Orleans. My house in my hometown sits only a few blocks away from my dad. I tuck him into bed at night, and instead of going into my room down the hall, I drive to the other side of the park. I love waking up in the morning there, watching the old neighborhood come back to life.

The golf course is open once again. Southern University's campus has expanded. All the churches are praising God on Sunday mornings, just as they always did. Major League Baseball rebuilt the baseball stadium nearby. The neighborhood school is brand-new. And slowly but steadily, we are moving families into houses. When it's fully restored, Pontchartrain Park will be filled with young families as well as original stakeholders who have been there forever. It will look like the neighborhood I grew up in.

For the first time, we have four or five white families living in Pontchartrain Park. In 2014, the basketball coach at the University of New Orleans bought a house in the neighborhood. My father's reaction? "This is America, man, this is what it's all about." I never thought I'd see the day when an eighty-nine-year-old black man would be so happy to have a young white basketball coach and his family move into the neighborhood, and to declare that this liberty is what he fought for.

And so, when people smirk and ask *What good has art ever done for anybody?* I can point to everything my partners and I have accomplished in Pontchartrain Park. For me, the catalyst was *Waiting for Godot.* Hurricane Katrina woke me up to how much I loved New Orleans, and how much I owed her and her people. *Godot* showed me the power art has to galvanize people to change their lives, their communities, and their world. It happened to me.

We will never know the change that the New Orleans production of *Godot* created in the city and beyond. Years after the show, I still hear from people who tell me they were there and it was one of the most powerful moments of their lives, or people who have never been to New Orleans but who heard about the play and want to know more.

It is impossible to measure the change art creates in the world, but that does not mean it has no impact. Did the 2006 All-Star Second Line Parade build new houses, create new jobs, or move a displaced family back home? Not directly. But if it gave the people who saw it, marched in it, or just heard about it reason to believe in the rebirth of New Orleans, and to do their part to participate in the city's resurrection, then yes, the parade made a difference.

Who's to say that someone in the audience for one of the *Godot* performances left saying to themselves, *Yes, we must go on*—and then in some way, however small, acted to defend the city and its culture, or to rebuild it, to restore it, to make those dry bones live?

How do we know what seeds are growing today in the hearts of young people who saw *Waiting for Godot* and sensed, somehow, that their lives would never be the same? We shall see.

I can answer only for myself. Pontchartrain Park gave a young boy who grew up there, in a loving community of faith, family, and high expectations, the confidence and nurturing he needed to become an artist. Art gave the man the means and the inspiration to do all that he could to give back to Pontchartrain Park the gift of itself.

NINE

TREME TAKES ME HOME

In the end of 2006 and early 2007, at the same time that my emotional life focused on what was happening in New Orleans, my professional life centered around wrapping up *The Wire,* then in its final season. David Simon and the cast and crew had been so loving to my family and me in Katrina's wake. David threw a Katrina relief concert in Baltimore, bringing up the subdudes and the Iguanas, two of his favorite New Orleans bands. It turned out that David was privately thinking about New Orleans as much as I was.

One night on the *Wire* set, David called me aside and said his next project would be set in New Orleans. "I'll let you know more about it later," he said. "I might want to run some things by you about New Orleans." *Oh, man,* I thought, *he can't write a series about New Orleans without including me.*

Later, David handed me a couple of script pages from this planned show. "Here's a scene about a trombone player, just a couple of ideas I have," he said.

The trombone player character? He was an easygoing but still struggling musician named Wendell. That's how David Simon told me about *Treme*.

"David!" I said.

"Yeah, I'm writing this with you in mind," he replied.

To have any writer say he's writing a series with you in mind is an honor. To have a writer of David Simon's caliber write something about your hometown, and do it with you in mind, is a gift from God. I couldn't believe it. I was moved to no end. It turned out that David had been thinking about a New Orleans show for years, since coming down for Mardi Gras one year and falling in love with the place. The narrative in the proposed show, a multiracial ensemble drama, would begin in late 2005, three months after the storm, with the show's characters—a hodgepodge of New Orleanians of different races and social classes—struggling to rebuild their shattered lives. David's passionate interest in social realism and complex urban drama added depth and urgency to the concept.

After *The Wire* wrapped, the actor Ray Romano called to say that he was creating a cable TV series called *Men of a Certain Age*, and had written a part with me in mind. It was an hour-long drama about three buddies in their late forties, facing middle age. My character was a stressed-out husband and dad who couldn't handle working at his father's car dealership. We got together, and he showed me an early draft; it was literally written in crayon, with stick figures. A pleasant joke to spark my interest. Ray's production company had the deal all ready to go. At that point, *Treme* was only in the pilot stage; HBO had not green-lighted production, but the possibility was strong.

Two shows, each created by an accomplished, successful artist, each of whom created a part with me in mind. I am a man who is blessed by the generosity of my friends. But I had a choice to make.

Finally, I called Ray to tell him I couldn't take the role. I was going to gamble on *Treme*.

"It's not about a great television job," I told him. "You have to understand, *Treme* is a depiction of my city and my life. It's so clear that I have to do this. It's not just choosing one job over another."

(The role eventually went to Andre Braugher, who won a Peabody Award and was twice nominated for Primetime Emmy Awards for his work on the show. Despite critical acclaim for the series, TNT canceled *Men of a Certain Age* after two seasons.)

Looking back, I believe *Treme* was divine intervention. Yes, it was a great television show, one that meant the world to me. *The Times-Picayune* called it "the screen depiction that New Orleans deserves, has always desired, but has been denied." That I was able to play a part in a historic artistic event in the life and times of my beloved city is an honor I will carry in my heart all the days of my life.

Treme sent the message that in New Orleans, our culture, what we create, what has inspired and delighted generations of people around the world, was our polestar. It was the solid ground on which we were going to rebuild our collective house. It was going to be our answer to those who wondered aloud why anyone would want to bring back New Orleans. With our culture, we were going to remind America why New Orleans matters. (And by the way, *Why New Orleans Matters* author Tom Piazza signed on as a *Treme* writer from the beginning.)

More than that, though, *Treme* was a gift from God because it allowed me to live in New Orleans for the final years of my mother's life. God gave me that part in *Treme* to spend time with Tee and Daddy, to prepare for her passing, and to reestablish myself as a New Orleanian who works to help his neighborhood and his city.

There is no substitute for being there. *Treme* made it possible for me to be there when it mattered most. A month before Tee died, she told a friend how much I was on her mind. "Audrey, I'm ready," she said. "But Wendell's not. He's not ready for me to go, and that worries me."

I knew Tee was sick, but I did not know how sick. I didn't want to see it. My mother broke the news to me at home.

"Wendell, I'm dying," she said.

I brushed it off.

"No, Wendell, I'm *dying*," she repeated. "I want you to stay close to your brother. I want you to know that."

One night, as I was keeping vigil during her final decline, a doctor friend came over to sit with me at Daddy and Tee's as my parents slept. I poured us a couple of drinks. We didn't speak of Tee's condition. All I could say was, "These are the times."

A few hours later, I was kneeling in my mother's bedroom, holding her dead body in my arms. Althea Lee Edwards Pierce left this world on October 22, 2012. She was eighty-two.

We've got to be ready for the times. I had been there for four years shooting *Treme*, four years to prepare for this moment. So I could be strong for Daddy. So I could be strong for myself. So I could fulfill my mother's wish.

We filmed the last episode of *Treme* in early 2013, halfway through its fourth season. On the last night of shooting, I turned to David Simon and said, "This was more than a job. This was more than a TV show. I was brought here to spend these last years with my mother. And you gave me that gift."

For my part, I was able to help him on the front end of *Treme* production, guiding him to people in New Orleans that he had to meet. One of the first I sent him to was Karen Livers, a veteran actress who is steeped in Crescent City culture. If you know Karen, you'll end up knowing everyone worth knowing in town. She's friends with artists, writers, Mardi Gras Indians, musicians, bartenders, chefs, the social aid and pleasure clubs, and all the characters who make New Orleans so colorful.

Though *Treme* was about the city of New Orleans and its struggle to rebuild after Katrina, David and series co-creator Eric Overmyer chose to focus on what David called the city's "culture bearers." The show took its name from the historically black neighborhood that was the home of Congo Square, where Africans and Europeans and Creoles, slaves and masters and free people of color, came together and created jazz. The Faubourg Tremé was where what the world knows and loves as New Orleans culture was born. David wanted to avoid what some folks derisively call "N'Awlins"—the kitschy version of the city that so many tourists come wanting to see, but that has only a tangential relationship to the real place. Our show would not be *N'Awlins*; it would be *Treme*.

To help Team *Treme* get it right, I advised David to hook up with my great friend Lolis Eric Elie, whom he had met at a past Mardi Gras. Lolis is a New Orleanian to the marrow. The son of Lolis Edward Elie, one of the city's preeminent civil rights attorneys, he was at that time a columnist for *The Times-Picayune*, as well as the author of several well-regarded books about food. He had just completed, with filmmaker Dawn Logsdon, *Faubourg Tremé: The Untold Story of Black New Orleans*, a prize-winning documentary about the historic neighborhood. David not only reconnected with Lolis, but hired him as story editor for *Treme*, a gig that turned into a television career for my friend.

I was terrified at the beginning of *Treme*, because I knew that if there was anything false about New Orleans in the series, I would never hear the end of it. I constantly took cast members around town to clubs, to restaurants, and to second lines, helping them with their character research. They met real New Orleanians—people like musician Kermit Ruffins, chefs Donald Link and Susan Spicer, and many others who were invited by David to appear on the show. Combine this with David's love of New Orleans music and his sense of storytelling, and you have a fictional television series that combines the relevance of a documentary with the poignancy of a poem. The series aired on HBO from 2010 through the end of 2013. By the end of its run, *Treme* had become an inextricable part of the culture it celebrated.

My experience with *Treme* deepened my appreciation of the art that came out of New Orleans. I realized that so many New Orleanians are people who are artistic though they lack the privilege of art being their occupation. Still, they create. That a working man would give a year to constructing a Mardi Gras Indian suit, a grandiose costume resplendent with brightly colored feathers and intricate, hand-stitched beadwork. That a schoolteacher would work a year organizing her walking krewe (a parade club that marches but has no floats) for Carnival season. That a high school musician would work out physically to prepare to march with his band in a parade every night for a two-week period, to play music and make his city dance and shout for joy.

Before *Treme*, I knew how much beauty and how much fun the end result of these labors were. No one from New Orleans can fail to appreciate that. What I did not know until after *Treme* was how deeply art, and the love of art, imbues the everyday lives of the city and its people. It wasn't just entertainment. It wasn't just for fun. It was for love, for beauty, for transcendence.

You could not get a better example of art and life imitating each other, at least for me. Katrina's near-destruction of my family's life, and the challenge of rebuilding that life despite the constant fear that most of the people, places, and things we loved were washed away forever—this was what hundreds of thousands of New Orleanians were coping with, and what the characters on *Treme* wrestled with too. Where does hope come from, then? How do you find the strength to go on? What makes life worth living when almost all of the things that made life worth living before are gone, or nearly so?

Some fans of *The Wire* were disappointed with *Treme*; they wanted to see *The Wire* in New Orleans. There was crime and political intrigue in New Orleans, just like in Baltimore, and David addressed that in *Treme*, though in a different, less gritty way. If the main concern of *The Wire* was how culture, especially the culture of bureaucracies, tears individuals and society apart, the central theme in *Treme* was how culture holds people together and helps them endure. In *Treme*, we achieved that.

There are, however, many similarities between Baltimore and New Orleans. Both are port cities filled with robust working-class people and culture. Both suffer from deep and abiding poverty. Both have suffered from white flight and the economic losses that brought about. Both love crabs—steamed, then spiced, in Baltimore; boiled in spices in New Orleans. And both have hearts that serve as cultural magnets: the French Quarter and the Inner Harbor.

Culturally, we have a lot more going on in New Orleans than they do in Baltimore. And African American culture in New Orleans is more southern, and therefore more friendly. But then, in Baltimore, black folk are more aware of their history than we are in New Orleans. They have Frederick Douglass, and a historical memory of insurrection in the nineteenth century. We remember the civil rights movement, but not much before that.

Treme showed a nation that thinks of New Orleans only as little more than a party town that our culture is not just about entertainment and letting the good times roll. We showed the parades rolling, but we also showed *why* parades matter. We showed the gumbo pot bubbling on the stove, but we also showed why gumbo makes a difference in the lives of everyday folks. Culture—art, music, food, religion, all of it—is what gives all people everywhere a tangible sense of what they share as a community. There may be no better place to highlight that universal fact of humanity's life than in New Orleans, where the culture is so singular, and so powerful.

It's like this. I would call my mother up sometimes and ask her how her day was, and she would start talking about the string beans and pork chops she had made Daddy for dinner. For Tee, as for so many New Orleanians, to have cooked and eaten a delicious mess of string beans, cooked down in salty bacon, paired with a couple of succulent chops, was pretty much the definition of a good day.

BECAUSE OF THE WAY it showcased our culture, *Treme* drew people to New Orleans. I know this for a fact. Once I was at Jazz Fest, hustling across the Fair Grounds, late to see Allen Toussaint play. Someone in the crowd stopped me and said, "Aren't you the guy from *Treme?*" Yes, I said, but I really have to go.

"No, please stop for a second," she said. "I'm from Cleveland. The only reason I'm here is because I saw *Treme.*"

It happened at a restaurant in the city, when a waiter told me he didn't want to say anything at first, but the reason he moved to New Orleans to live and to work was because of *Treme*. He told me that he had been walking on the Appalachian Trail, not really knowing where to go when he finished, and stopped at a hotel overnight. He saw *Treme* on the hotel television and knew where he was headed next. He just had to be a part of New Orleans.

In New Orleans itself, *Treme* became group therapy for the entire city struggling to come back after the devastation of Katrina. There were watch parties all over the city on Sunday nights. Those who had gone through the flood were reminded of the pain, but also of the virtues of life in New Orleans. Most of all, they were reminded of what we were all fighting for: our culture. Amid all the skepticism both inside and outside the city about whether New Orleans was worth saving, or could be saved at all, *Treme* answered week after week why our city and its culture were so important. *Treme* reminded us that the lives our culture would save would be our own. *Treme* told people who believed that we were nothing but a corrupt, crime-infested, fading good-time town that, to paraphrase Oscar Wilde, we may be flat on our backs, but we are looking up at the stars.

At its best, *Treme* helped us remember that pain and suffering and injustice need not have the last word, because even out of something as monstrous as slavery, something as angelic as jazz can arise to redeem the time. I'm biased, but I really do believe that *Treme* played a part in helping my storm-bedraggled city rediscover its song.

My character turned out not to be named Wendell, as in the original *Treme* draft, but Antoine Batiste, a trombone player and the epitome of the journeyman musician in New Orleans. He is someone who puts his hat out on a French Quarter street and plays for tips in the afternoon, and winds his day down in a nightclub playing with a well-oiled band. He ekes out a living doing what he loves to do, adapting to any situation.

Like jazz, his life is improvisational. He is a likable ne'er-do-well who struggles for constancy in his profession and relationships as a father, ex-husband, and partner to his live-in girlfriend. His personal life reflects the turmoil left behind by Katrina, yet when everything else is out of order, the music is the one thing that makes sense to him. It is Antoine's true north.

It took the storm and flood to shake Antoine out of his lackadaisical, devil-may-care approach to life and awaken to the awesome responsibility he has as a culture bearer. When he becomes a middle school music teacher, Antoine is surprised to find within himself a new maturity, one that helps him accept his task of teaching the city's musical tradition to the next generation.

In New Orleans, high school marching bands are a big deal. Band programs offer some of the poorest and most desperate kids in the nation a way out of the poverty and chaos that threaten to engulf them. Through the love of music and the city's culture, Antoine discovered a way to love the kids whose education had been entrusted to him. This helped him to become a better father and partner; it helped him to become a better man.

In season three, Antoine takes one of his students to meet Lionel Ferbos, the living incarnation of New Orleans jazz tradition, at the Palm Court Jazz Café, where he played every Sunday night until his retirement in the spring of 2014, at the age of a hundred two. Mr. Ferbos, as I knew to call him, lived in Pontchartrain Park and had played jazz trumpet for an incredible eighty-seven years. In that episode, Mr. Ferbos, playing himself at the Palm Court, explained to Antoine's student the importance of jazz in the culture of New Orleans.

That scene is now a precious historical document; Mr. Ferbos passed away two days after he turned a hundred three. The Archbishop of New Orleans celebrated his funeral mass at the Corpus Christi–Epiphany Catholic Church, in the Seventh Ward, the heart of the city's old Creole establishment. Hundreds of musicians and mourners second-lined behind the hearse to the cemetery.

What the storm did to Antoine—reminding him of his responsibility to preserve and pass on the cultural legacy of New Orleans— it did to me as well. All it takes for a tradition to die is for a single generation to refuse it or ignore it. Katrina woke me up and fired me up. I wanted to come home and play a part in the reclaiming of our city—and its rebirth. Our ancestors created something known and loved the world over; we cannot let it go. In the same way, we children of Pontchartrain Park cannot let die the neighborhood legacy created by our parents. My New Orleans homecoming, and the art and activism I have produced these past few years, made a better man of me. When *Treme* viewers trace the moral arc of Antoine Batiste's character, they are also, in a real way, following the moral arc of my own.

Of course there are big differences. I'm a professional actor, not a journeyman street musician. Antoine emerged from research David did with the trumpet player Kermit Ruffins, trombonist Stafford Agee, and saxophonist Donald Harrison, Jr. Antoine also came out of a busker on Royal Street I know only as Wolf.

Wolf never had a case for his horn, carrying it on his arm like Antoine did. Every horn player I know says that Wolf was one of the defining members of the street brass band renaissance in the 1980s. You could always pick Wolf out of a crowd, they say, because when he would do a solo, he would crouch down into a squat, almost in a fighter's stance. But I had never seen him.

Keith Hart, who taught me trombone—I learned how to do all the right moves, but Stafford Agee played the music off screen—told me one day, "Wolf is the guy, but he's fallen on hard times." Wolf became a mythical character to me, like John Henry or Paul Bunyan, living and playing somewhere on the streets of New Orleans. He was the mystery musician who carried his horn in the crook of his elbow, who was so soulful that when he squatted with his 'bone on his shoulder, you knew he was going to take you somewhere special.

After we started shooting *Treme* in 2010, people would ask me whom Antoine was based on. A combination of people, I would say, but he's mostly Wolf. The purity of his love for music and the brilliance of his musicianship was clear, but he had a tumultuous personal life that meant you could never really count on him. That was Wolf, and that was Antoine.

So one day Doreen Ketchens, among the great clarinetists of New Orleans, was playing on Royal Street and I took a friend to see her. She plays the clubs all the time, but when she hits the street, the other buskers all defer to her. Doreen is the real deal, continuing the legacy of Sidney Bechet, Pete Fountain, and Dr. Michael White.

Standing a ways down Royal Street listening to Doreen play, I said to my friend, "See how great she is? That's real New Orleans music."

Then Doreen finished her solo, and *whomp!* there was a mighty trombone blast. "Oh my God," I told my friend, "Can you hear that? That's real New Orleans right there! Let's get closer."

Sure enough, the trombone player squatted and tightened like a fist, and nearly knocked us all out with the power of his playing.

"Wolf!" I shouted. "It's Wolf!"

"Yeah, what?" he said, then started playing again.

After he finished, I went to him, introduced myself, told him about the show, and said, "I think I'm playing you."

"Yeah," he said, "I heard."

Before we walked on, I told him that I had to keep in touch with him.

"I'll be in touch with *you*," said the lone Wolf.

I reported back to David that I had met the real Wolf and exhorted him to put him in the show. We finally did, in the season-two re-creation of the jazz funeral for Dinerral Shavers, the real-life snare drummer who was shot to death on Dumaine Street by a street criminal in 2006. In the final season, when Antoine is doubting his music, he plays late into the night at a jam session. Kidd Jordan walks in, and Donald Harrison, Jr., walks in . . . and there, in the musician's scrum, is Wolf.

Wolf tells Antoine that he's no damn good, so they have a cutting contest, an improvised battle between two jazz soloists. It makes me so happy to think that *Treme* viewers had the opportunity to bear witness to Wolf's genius. He is one of the grassroots innovators, a street musician who helped start the modern brass-band rebirth in New Orleans—and we were able to get him on film in a way that gives him the honor he deserves.

This is why *Treme* was more than a TV show. We documented the culture of our time in New Orleans, in a way that will be there to be explored and studied for decades to come. New Orleanians who were children during the post-Katrina aftermath will one day be able to screen *Treme* for their grandchildren, and tell them, yes, baby, that's what it was like. They will have a cultural document.

And if anybody doubts the importance of New Orleans, the vitality and uniqueness of our culture, and its relevance to the meaning of life, let them come to *Treme*. Every one of us who had anything to do with that show—its producers, writers, actors, crew members, and guest stars, as well as all the people throughout the city who welcomed us and made production possible—all should think of *Treme* as our gift to New Orleans, to America, and to the future.

Delmond Lambreaux (Rob Brown) is the other professional musician in the *Treme* cast of characters. He is the son of Albert Lambreaux (Clarke Peters), a laborer and Big Chief of a Mardi Gras Indian tribe (more on this in a moment). Delmond is a refined, sophisticated artist who has taken what he was given in New Orleans, moved to New York City, refined it, and elevated it. He is now a modern jazz star, but he is alienated from his father and his roots, and struggles throughout the series to reestablish contact, and to make New Orleans his own.

Delmond is a familiar example of the New Orleans artist who leaves home to further his training, because he knows there really is no other way. They told us on our first day at NOCCA that this was how it was going to be, and they were right. Nobody ever really leaves New Orleans in his heart, but the family and friends they leave behind sometimes make it hard to maintain a connection. Like Chief Lambreaux, they may look down on those who leave as having been disloyal to their roots. And truth to tell, there really is a danger that success in the wider world can blind an artist to what he owes to the culture that raised him up.

Delmond reminds me of Wynton and Branford Marsalis, Donald Harrison, Jr.—his late father was Big Chief of the Guardians of the Flame, a Mardi Gras Indian tribe he founded—and trumpeter Terence Blanchard, who grew up with me in Pontchartrain Park, and, of course, pianist and singer Harry Connick, Jr. They all became part of the 1980s migration of New Orleans jazz musicians to New York, pioneered by Wynton. They were all from New Orleans, but to some extent, they were no longer of it.

That was Delmond. It took the storm, and trying to care for his stubborn father from afar, to awaken him to the richness of the music, culture, and tradition in New Orleans, and to bring him back home. In Delmond's past was his future. He learned that his artistic freedom and creativity did not have to come at the expense of his family and his tradition, but that they could exist together. This really happened to Donald Harrison, Jr., who served as a *Treme* consultant and appeared in nine episodes. After his father's death in 1998, he returned to New Orleans and became Big Chief of his dad's tribe. That was the true story behind Delmond's story.

Delmond's biggest challenge is to figure out how to be inspired by his father's legacy rather than be crushed by it. Big Chief Albert Lambreaux symbolizes the deep pride so many African American men in the city developed within their own communities, in part because they were denied pride and the attention and opportunities they deserved outside their communities.

When *Treme* begins, Chief Lambreaux returns to his storm-devastated neighborhood, and to the now abandoned bar where his Indian tribe used to practice. The Mardi Gras Indians are an African American New Orleans social tradition going back to at least the mid-nineteenth century. Each "tribe" is composed of men from a certain neighborhood, or "ward," gathered around a leader, known as the Big Chief. On Mardi Gras Day and on St. Joseph's Day (March 19), they "mask"—that is, don extremely elaborate, colorful costumes made of beads and feathers—and march and dance through the streets, chanting and drumming. Lore has it that the tribes model themselves after Native Americans in homage to those who offered refuge to slaves escaping the city and plantations.

In the event that two tribes' paths cross, they will engage in a ritualistic, highly theatrical battle in the streets. In the old days, these meetings were frequently violent, as they were used to settle scores. In modern times, though, the battles are entirely symbolic and offer an opportunity for opposing tribes to show off their own costumes (called "suits") and prowess. The greatest compliment a Mardi Gras Indian can be paid is to be told that he is "pretty."

It's an "only in New Orleans" institution that looks frivolous to outsiders, but that has profound, abiding meaning to its participants, and to the black community. The sense of brotherhood among the Indians is powerful, and the craftsmanship that goes into the creation of their hand-sewn suits—which the men make themselves—is breathtaking. The chants they use have been handed down from generation to generation.

In *Treme*, Chief Lambreaux's dogged determination to bring back his lost tribe members to the city is his declaration that the colorful tradition must be saved, no matter what. It's not really about feathers, chants, and Mardi Gras rituals involving fake Indian tribes; it's about the survival of the community—the real-life tribe. Indian masking on Mardi Gras is the way they know who they are, and what it means to be part of their culture. Chief Lambreaux knows that by fighting for his tribe, he's fighting for the soul of his people.

As Big Chief, Albert Lambreaux has to be steadfast. He tries to demonstrate steadfastness to his adult children and to all the members of his community. He tells them by his words and his actions that if they don't understand this pride and protect this legacy, no one else will. It takes strength to stand fast in the face of life's storms. I mentioned earlier, in talking about my late uncle L. H. Edwards, the 1931 Sterling Brown poem "Strong Men." It reads, in part:

The strong men keep a-comin' on
Gittin' stronger. . . .

That poem—my favorite—*is* Chief Lambreaux. That poem is my father. That poem is Ellis Marsalis and the legacy of all those musicians. The poem discloses the particular quality of Chief Lambreaux's character: He's protective of his community and its cultural traditions, and he demonstrates how those cultural traditions can rebuild family and community scattered to the winds. He is a craftsman who is proud of his construction work. He is rebuilding his community both spiritually and materially. When he finishes restoring his home, Chief Lambreaux can lie down and let his spirit fly away.

He is the embodiment of all those men—some known, most unknown—who have built and sustained their families and tribes, no matter how materially impoverished they were. We may have little money, but we are rich in spirit, culture, and family—but that is a wealth that must be reinvested by and in each generation if it is to remain.

This is what drew Donald Harrison, Jr., home to become chief of his father's tribe. He plays jazz all around the world, but on Mardi Gras morning, he puts on the new suit he's been sewing all year and hits the streets with the Guardians of the Flame. This is what drew Branford Marsalis and Harry Connick, Jr., back home to create the Ellis Marsalis Center for Music. And this is what drew me back home to perform in *Waiting for Godot*, and to dedicate myself to rebuilding Pontchartrain Park. Like Delmond, we rallied from afar to the side of our fathers and our tribes in the hour of their despair, and we found new purpose in old traditions.

Even *Treme*'s carpetbagging developer Nelson Hidalgo (Jon Seda) recognizes the beauty and worth of New Orleans's culture. Even amid the craftiness and carpetbagger planning, in the midst of pillaging for self-gain, he realizes the beauty of the food and the music and the culture of the city.

Nelson personified the kind of wheeler-dealer who rushes in behind every disaster. They come saying they mean to do good, but they really mean to do well—for themselves. This sort of character flocked to post-Katrina New Orleans like vultures on a carcass. They knew that the hurricane's flood would be followed by a flood of reconstruction dollars rolling in from the federal government and insurance companies, and they were determined to ride that wave all the way to the bank.

The carpetbaggers infiltrated the restoration process on the political end. Once they gained the confidence of a particular political leader or bureaucrat, they became "experts" tasked with developing programs that were most beneficial to them.

You saw that in New Orleans after the storm. Those without the city's best interests at heart decided that we had to disperse the poor, to break up this concentration of poverty. Thus, they tore down the housing projects. What they were really after is to make sure those precious plots of land so close to the French Quarter and downtown didn't have poor people in them.

In Pontchartrain Park, we put together a plan to bring back a neighborhood in which almost every resident owned their house, and which was one of the most stable neighborhoods in the city. But thanks to political machinations and misguided policies, we have been forced to turn away cash buyers for redeveloped Pontchartrain

Park houses because city policy requires our Pontchartrain Park Community Development Corporation to sell to people who have an income that is lower than the average median income. It means that most will have been in public housing. I recognize that those folks need a place to live, but when you won't let in people who have the means to return to their own community, something is seriously wrong. We had a man who wanted to buy a house right across the street from his grandmother, but we couldn't sell it to him because he made too much money in the eyes of federal housing law. This is the kind of logic that led to New Orleanians qualifying for government aid to raze their homes, but not to renovate them.

Nelson Hidalgo reflected the culture of political corruption and economic exploitation that will forever keep New Orleans and Louisiana down if we never overcome it. What redeems us is, again, our culture: our music, our cuisine, our architecture, and our traditions. Take the culture out of Louisiana and I would agree with people who say New Orleans is not worth saving. It's Newark with oppressive humidity. It's Cleveland with a better football team. Lafcadio Hearn, a nineteenth-century writer who left Cincinnati for New Orleans, summed it up best in a letter, this quote from which we used in the *Treme* pilot:

> Times are not good here. The city is crumbling into ashes. It has been buried under a lava flood of taxes and frauds and maladministrations so that it has become only a study for archaeologists. Its condition is so bad that when I write about it, as I intend to do soon, nobody will believe I am telling the

truth. But it is better to live here in sackcloth and ashes than to own the whole state of Ohio.

DAVID SIMON put the Hearn quote in the mouth of Creighton Bernette, a Tulane literature professor played by John Goodman. Creighton is a big, bluff man, a passionate connoisseur of New Orleans culture who is radicalized by Katrina. In the *Treme* pilot, he explodes in an on-camera interview with a British TV journalist who questions his view about the cause of the city's destruction (that the hurricane was a natural disaster, but the flooding of the city was a "man-made catastrophe of epic proportions").

Creighton's wife, Toni Bernette (Melissa Leo), is a civil rights attorney. Her character is based on Mary Howell, a legendary New Orleans plaintiffs' lawyer who made her considerable reputation fighting police brutality and corruption, and representing clients as diverse as whistleblowers and street musicians. Toni symbolizes those New Orleanians who bravely take on the thankless battle of forcing a city that would prefer to let the good times roll than to do the hard work of democratic self-accountability. The Toni character constantly puts the question to the viewer, at least the ones in New Orleans: Are you going to be part of the solution, or are you going to be part of the problem?

NOPD Lieutenant Terry Colson (David Morse), an honest cop whose conscience drives him to cooperate with the FBI in taking down police corruption, is walking the same straight path as Toni. He sacrifices his career to do the right thing. How could he say that he loved New Orleans if he did otherwise? How could he live with himself? Even when Colson's family leaves New Orleans for Indiana, he stays behind to work for reform in the police department. He knows how much this matters to the city.

If New Orleans is ever going to be saved, it will be saved in part by good men and women in public service like Terry Colson. The headlines are reserved for bad cops and crooked bureaucrats, but the good public servants have been there all along. They just need to find the courage of their convictions, and to realize that lawyers like Toni Bernette—and her real-life double, Mary Howell—are not the enemy.

Unlike her fictionalized TV version, Mary Howell, happily, did not have a husband who committed suicide. But John Goodman had signed on for only a year of *Treme*, so Creighton was going to have to leave the scene somehow. Creighton became a combination of post-Katrina residents who went online to become grassroots activists and advocates for New Orleans—ordinary people who were shaken by the disaster out of their silence.

The chief inspiration for Creighton was a computer science professor and blogger named Ashley Morris. He was a big-boned, larger-than-life wild man whose profane, often witty blog rants about New Orleans after the storm drew a large local following. One of Morris's most popular Katrina aftermath jeremiads, one that dropped three f-bombs in the five-word title alone, began like this:

> I'm so glad all you Chicagoans have figured out exactly how
> to fix New Orleans. Look at your own nasty city and explain

why you can't deal with snow other than to throw tons of salt
on the road, and why you can't buy a beer for under $5. Fuck
you, you fucking fucks.

It went downhill from there. Or uphill, depending on your point
of view. Ashley, well known to David Simon as a fan of *The Wire*,
dropped dead of a heart attack in 2008. He never saw the homage that
David paid him by putting many of his actual blog lines into Creighton's mouth, in the character's YouTube rants. Morris's f-bomb ex-
travaganza was, word for filthy word, the sign-off of Creighton's
YouTube debut.

Creighton's despair over the fate of his city led to his suicide. He
took the Algiers ferry over to the West Bank and, at the midway
point, jumped overboard into the Mississippi. This too has a real-life
analogue: The New Orleans suicide rate after Katrina tripled, and the
rate of serious mental disorders reached what government health officials described as an epidemic level never before recorded in the
United States—all this, with the mental health treatment infrastructure in collapse. As sad as Creighton's fate was, this too was a big part
of the city's experience after the storm.

On the day he took his own life, Creighton savored all the things
he loved the most about living in New Orleans. He went to Audubon
Park, to Casamento's for oysters, to Café du Monde for beignets, and
Liuzza's by the Track for gumbo, a barbecue shrimp po'boy, and a
cold Abita Amber. At last, he went to the foot of Canal Street and
caught a ride on the Algiers into oblivion. Creighton's last day was
an elegy for the Crescent City, and a tragic reminder that for all its
power to heal and to renew, culture cannot save us all.

LaDonna Batiste-Williams withstood all that Creighton Bernette did, and much, much worse, but held on with the tenacity of one of the alligator snapping turtles that have lived in the Louisiana swamps since time out of mind. LaDonna—portrayed by Khandi Alexander, who gave one of the great performances in American television history—represents that indestructible force within the people of New Orleans that helps the city come back time and time again. We said it best on the *Treme* season-three poster: *Hurricanes. Floods. Exile. Crime. Corruption. Betrayal. Greed. Neglect. Is that all you got?*

LaDonna survived the storm, the flood, the death of her brother Daymo at the hands of the criminal justice system, a rape and beating, the collapse of her family, and the burning down of her neighborhood bar, Gigi's—but she never gives up, and never gives in. I also see in LaDonna a symbol of African American resilience: *Slavery. Poverty. Jim Crow. Segregation: Is that all you got?*

MOST PEOPLE who come to New Orleans to see the culture never go outside the French Quarter, Uptown, or a few other select sites on the tourist map. Those funky little corner barrooms like Gigi's, the ones few outsiders ever visit, are true incubators of New Orleans culture. They are the town squares for their neighborhoods. From those bars, the Mardi Gras Indians came, and the social aid and pleasure clubs as well.

These barrooms are places where the diverse cultures of the city cross, and creatively cross-pollinate. Even the businessman from the

Central Business District will come have a drink with the man who works in his mailroom, because they both love that piano player, and besides, the red beans and rice that joint has on Mondays is something else. In New Orleans, it started at Congo Square, where black and white, rich and poor, came out to see the slaves sing and dance, and where that fertile social intercourse gave birth to jazz.

The culture is more fluid in New Orleans than in most places, but also more stable. This is a poetic paradox of life in the Big Easy. Today, you can walk two blocks from a neighborhood where the working poor live, and suddenly you're on St. Charles Avenue, one of the grandest boulevards in the world, and you think, *How about that, the descendants of former slaves and descendants of former slave owners haven't moved.* You have a bar on every corner, and a church on every other, and those two worlds yield to each other as easily as Saturday night gives way to Sunday morning.

When you listen to the Library of Congress recordings of Jelly Roll Morton, all nine hours of them, you can hear the Rampart Street and St. Charles Avenue, the church and the barroom, the rich and the poor. The grandiose and the grassroots, all rubbing shoulders (and other things too) with each other, because New Orleans is so small. It's hard to keep these combustible elements mixing without the occasional explosion, but places like Gigi's, with their cold beer and warm hearts, presided over by happy geniuses like Miss LaDonna, are where New Orleans lays its burdens down on a barstool, puts a dollar in the jukebox, and solves its problems over a plate of red beans and rice.

Davis McAlary (Steve Zahn) is one of those quixotic white guys you run into all over New Orleans. He's an Uptown blueblood rebelling against his posh upbringing, not for the sake of rebellion, but because he honest to God loves the music of black New Orleans. He can sit with his mother and father wearing the blue blazer that he bought at Perlis, the old-school Uptown clothing store, and later that night take his bohemian Aunt Mimi (Elizabeth Ashley) to a bounce concert in the hood. Davis's passion for the city overwhelms him, but his chronic inability to get his life together is deeply representative of New Orleans's self-sabotaging dysfunction. That "Take it easy, bro'" attitude of his has its charms, but it also has a serious downside.

The real-life Davis is Davis Rogan, a tall, shambling DJ and musician (a better one than his *Treme* version, it must be said), a fifth-generation New Orleanian who wrote all the songs for Steve Zahn's character. His manic reputation has gotten him thrown out of many a Big Easy bar. In one club on Frenchmen Street, they used to have a sign posted that said, "If your name is Davis Rogan, please leave." David Simon once said of him, "Like New Orleans, Davis Rogan is always one bad move away from falling on his ass. And yet, on at least every other occasion, he's the cat that drops from the tree and lands on his feet."

What the real-life Davises understand that some in their social and economic class do not—I'm talking to you, Jimmy Reiss—is that if you eliminate the grassroots community that you think of as the source of our problems, you also eliminate the community that is the source of so much of our greatness. Jacques Morial, playing himself in a season-one episode of *Treme*, tries to explain to Davis McAlary what's really at stake when the feds and the city establishment push for a smaller city—one without poor people.

"The culture of New Orleans, that's what's at risk," Morial says. "If they knock out the infrastructure that sustains the culture, then it's gone forever."

This is what happened with Louis Armstrong, Kid Ory, Jelly Roll Morton, and all the artists who created jazz a century ago. The establishment thought, "Oh my God, we've got to get rid of this slum"— and bulldozed the Back o' Town neighborhood where they all came from. That's where the Superdome is now. And here we are, after Katrina, facing the same thing. The same mentality that tore down Pops's house, Jelly Roll's house, Sidney Bechet's house, is alive and well in New Orleans.

The 400 block of South Rampart Street is home to three of the most important buildings in jazz history. First is the Eagle Saloon, once a venue that hosted early jazz greats like King Oliver, Jelly Roll Morton, Sidney Bechet, Buddy Bolden, and Kid Ory; second is the Iroquois, a Negro vaudeville theater where young Louis Armstrong won a talent show by dunking his head in flour and doing a whiteface routine; and the Karnofsky Store, a tailor shop owned by the Jewish family who took young Louis Armstrong under their wing.

In 2011, John Hasse, the American Music curator at the Smithsonian Institution, told *The Times-Picayune*, "There is probably no other block in America with buildings bearing so much significance to the history of our country's great art form, jazz." Yet there these buildings sit, across the street from City Hall, derelict and in danger of collapse. The Eagle should be our La Scala, our Carnegie Hall, and that block ought to be the Lincoln Center of New Orleans. But decades of neglect have left all three buildings barely standing.

Fortunately, the properties received historical landmark status in 2009, which will likely preserve them from destruction. That's the hope, anyway. How a city that celebrates its culture in so many ways can neglect it so grievously in others is one of the most frustrating mysteries about New Orleans life. As Creighton Bernette, *Treme*'s oracle, said in the first season, "Down here in the city of misrule, we are always our own worst enemy."

And yet people keep coming. Texas-born Janette Desautel (Kim Dickens) migrated to New Orleans to become a chef but, like so many of the city's chefs, saw her small restaurant capsized by Katrina. Her story line somewhat parallels Delmond Lambreaux's, in that she heads to New York to hit it big, cooking with chefs like Eric Ripert and David Chang (as he did with top musicians, Simon loved to bring in culinary rock stars for *Treme* cameos). Though Janette, whose character is partially based on Bayona's Susan Spicer, loves not having to deal with the craziness of post-Katrina New Orleans, she longs to be back. When an investor lures her home with the promise of opening her own splashy, top-tier restaurant, Janette takes the bait.

The hopeful chef learns in time that the investor is really a cynical businessman who wants to crush what is best in her for the sake of commercial success. What saves Janette, in the end, is the integrity of her art, which redeems her from this deal she made with the devil.

Treme was the first time a fictional television show really explored the culinary world in a sustained way—especially, of course, the New Orleans food scene. Having Lolis, with his encyclopedic culinary knowledge, on staff was a godsend, as was hiring Anthony

Bourdain to write the restaurant scenes. During *Treme*'s run, there were blogs dedicated to discussing what Janette was cooking, how she was cooking it, and what everyone in the show was eating on particular episodes. We featured Crescent City restaurants, from the high-end places like Galatoire's and Bayona, down to the more democratic joints, like Mosca's and Li'l Dizzy's. We also celebrated favorite local eats, like the lemon ice at Angelo Brocato's and the fried pies from Hubig's (which, sadly, burned to the ground in 2012). I am immensely proud of the fact that *Treme* captured on film what it meant to be in New Orleans, living and eating (a distinction without much difference in the Big Easy) in the first decade of the twenty-first century.

Treme's other artists who found their way to New Orleans are the musician couple Sonny (Michiel Huisman) and Annie (Lucia Micarelli), whom we meet busking on the street in the French Quarter. Those two symbolize the adopted New Orleanians who come to town for Mardi Gras or Jazz Fest, fall in love with the place, and never leave. This has been happening for three hundred years. It even happened to country people like the Edwardses, my own family, some of whom found their way down the river and never left.

After Katrina, this phenomenon exploded. People from the world over saw what had happened to us and came to help. Sonny and Annie were there before the storm—Sonny helped rescue stranded people—but they did not abandon New Orleans. They are accomplished enough musicians to want to move past the standards tourists want to hear and are approaching a crossroads in their personal and professional lives. Annie, the greater talent of the two, leaves Sonny and his drug habit to make a run at greatness. Sonny, who will never be better than second-rate, drifts in and out of despair before finally finding safe harbor with a life and a wife away from the music scene.

When Annie finds her musician mentor Harley (Steve Earle), who teaches her how to channel her experience of living in New Orleans into her music, she sets anchor. Harley's murder by a street criminal reminds her of the harshness of life in this chaotic city, but the gift he gave her, of helping her find her song, will restore her and redeem his memory. This too is a story told over and over, from generation to generation in my city.

Everyone who has ever loved New Orleans, whether they were born here or got here as fast as they could, knows that that love costs, sometimes not less than everything. But if you can be faithful, if you can hold on through all the hurt and heartache, you may find resurrection in the life of a spirited culture like no other on earth.

So that is how *Treme* explains New Orleans. The final *Treme* episode aired on December 29, 2013. It was a bittersweet moment for me. God knows I was sorry that the good times I had making the show had come to an end. I was sad that a series that served as a rallying point within the Crescent City community had ended. And I was regretful that we would not have the opportunity to tell more stories about the life and times of the people of New Orleans.

It was hard for me to say good-bye to Antoine Batiste. There was a whole world inside him that we were just beginning to explore. They had a saying in 1910 when Anton Chekhov's play *Three Sisters* first opened in Moscow: "Let's go see how the sisters are doing." The idea was that the sisters lived before the curtain rose, and they would live after the curtain came down. That's how I felt about Antoine: that his life would go on, and that he would live forever through the lives he would influence as a high school music teacher. As with portraying Bunk Moreland, I was never fully satisfied that I fleshed out Antoine's character, but in both cases, I'm grateful that I was able to have the opportunity to try.

BUT MOSTLY I was proud and grateful that I had been part of the creation of an enduring work of art celebrating the soul of my city. *Treme* will endure not only because David Simon and his cast and crew made a television drama of exceptional quality, but also because, like so much imperishable art, *Treme* told a universal story about the power of the human spirit.

In *Treme*'s third season, we filmed a scene re-creating the *Waiting for Godot* production in which I had starred. Melissa Leo, portraying Toni Bernette, sat in the bleachers and cried. Her tears were tears of recognition: that we have come through the storm, and survived. For so many New Orleanians, each Sunday night during the season was a time when we gathered around the campfire, so to speak, and saw acted in the lives of these fictional characters the story of our lives. It was a cathartic experience, but also an edifying one, because it reminded us of what mattered to us, who we were, and who we could become again.

Memory and desire, life and the people who live it, all came together for an hour each week in a drama that reminded us of why the sacrifices we made to come home and rebuild were worth it. In *Treme*, we used the art of television drama to declare to the world (and maybe even to ourselves) that this city will never drown, that there's no use in losing heart now, because the strong men and women of New Orleans are just gittin' stronger.

TEN

TEE AND THE
JOYFUL MYSTERIES

Back in 2004, as a friend returned home from a trip to Africa, I told her that while she was away, this guy Barack Obama delivered the keynote address at the Democratic National Convention, and it was a knockout.

"You can see it online," I said. "You've got to watch this thing." On and on I went.

I knew Barack Obama was going to be a big deal, and I was right. Obama, who was at the time a Democratic candidate for the open U.S. Senate seat in Illinois, spoke of the fundamental unity we Americans share amid our diversity.

"It's what allows us to pursue our individual dreams, yet still come together as a single American family," Obama told the convention crowd. "*E pluribus unum*—out of many, one."

Obama warned that there are those who thrive on dividing American against American, for the sake of political gain.

"Well, I say to them tonight, there's not a liberal America and a conservative America; there's the United States of America," he proclaimed. "There's not a black America and white America and Latino America and Asian America; there's the United States of America."

That was it. I was hooked. This is the vision we need to renew America. It was electrifying.

Could this Obama one day become our nation's first black president? Shirley Chisholm, an African American Democrat, made history with her 1972 run for the White House. Jesse Jackson made his historic first bid for the presidency in 1984, but despite his surprising primary showings, there was never a real chance that a man as controversial as he had been, and who was as far to the left as he was, could win office in a country in the grip of the Reagan Revolution.

Obama was different. For one, he may have been a community organizer, but he had an Ivy League pedigree. He was a member of the establishment and knew how to talk their language. For another, he was from a younger generation, one that was poised to build on the foundation built by the Rev. Jackson and the civil rights movement. Barack Obama, who emerged politically in the post-Clinton era, had the political and cultural sensibility to take the progressive fight into the future.

In 2007, I was living in New Orleans again, working to reconstitute the Pontchartrain Park Neighborhood Association and getting a fast, harsh education in practical politics. I realized that if we were going to get things done in Pontchartrain Park, we residents—about fifteen hundred of us—were going to have to get politically active. If we didn't organize and find our collective voice, we would have no leverage to fight the city and well-connected developers when they came to grab our land. Politics, I learned quickly, mattered. If we homeowners didn't get involved to protect our own interests, we would by default surrender the battlefield to those who do not have our interests at heart. Simple as that.

This is how I came to volunteer for the 2008 Obama presidential campaign. Nobody knew how much things needed to change in America more than the people of New Orleans, who had suffered like nobody else under the incompetence of the George W. Bush administration. It was intolerable to think that America could stand four more years of a Republican in the White House.

What's more, it was impossible for me to believe that Hillary Clinton would be the change agent the country needed. Had she won the Democratic nomination and then the presidency, that would have meant at least twenty-four years of the White House being in the hands of members of the Bush or Clinton dynasties. That's not change.

Finally, the opportunity to be part of a campaign that, if successful, would result in the first black president was not to be missed. Ours was a nation that enslaved my ancestors. It fought a civil war that ended slavery, but spent the next century treating us like second-class citizens, keeping us poor, uneducated, and oppressed. Yet we endured, from generation to generation. And now we had the real possibility of triumph: that the country that brought us here as chattel would elect one of us as its president.

How could I, the great-grandson of a slave, not be part of that? This might be a fulfillment of the hopes that Mamo and Papo, and Tee and Daddy, tendered in their hearts through the long, hard years of struggle. I was too young to march for civil rights during the movement, but this was something I could do in my own time and place. For the first time in my life, I felt the kind of hope that was alive in the 1960s, before it all fell apart. Barack Obama became the Robert F. Kennedy of my political imagination.

My brother Ron and I put ourselves at the Obama campaign's disposal. Ron went to Iowa, and I went on the radio. I had a contact within the campaign who sent me a schedule of black radio stations around the country that I was to call to rally support for Obama's election. It felt great to be active in changing my country for the better. What I was working toward at the local level in New Orleans, I was also working toward nationally. This is the difference between being a subject—willing to be passive pawns in a game controlled by others—and a citizen who makes himself a player.

The American people responded to the message of change. You couldn't get a better example of people needing to see change than what we had gone through in New Orleans. The entire country was suffering the effects of an economic hurricane that had wiped out tens of thousands of families and businesses. We couldn't keep going like this. If we didn't get change now, we were going to be in trouble.

On Election Day, I was at my home in California, where I was registered to vote. I woke up early and went to the firehouse down the street from me in Pasadena to cast my ballot. Pasadena is like Uptown New Orleans: well off, heavily white, heavily Republican. I was standing in one of two lines at the firehouse, one of the few African Americans there that morning, when a little old white lady leaned in and said to me, "There's going to be a lot of people like us today."

"People like us?" I said.

"Republicans voting for Obama," she replied.

"I've got to tell you, I'm not a Republican."

"Isn't this the Republican line?"

"No, they do it by zip code."

The poor woman looked horrified. She had revealed her political disloyalty to a Democrat!

After voting, I went straight to the airport and flew to Chicago, to be at campaign headquarters on the big night. They put me to work doing more radio calls for the get-out-the-vote effort. That night, when the returns started coming in, you could see David Axelrod and David Plouffe, the Obama campaign's top strategists, deep in conversation in a conference room. At 6:48 Chicago time, the TV networks called Pennsylvania for Obama—a state that we had been told would be a bellwether.

The shot echoed around the room. All of us had the same thought: *Get to Grant Park!*

I hustled the two blocks away from the Michigan Avenue campaign headquarters and joined the river of people, tens of thousands strong, flowing into the downtown park. Some were waving flags. Some were holding *Yes We Can* signs. Some were weeping tears of joy. Everyone was jubilant. Somebody had given me a pass that let me go to the front of the crowd, down by the stage where, win or lose, Obama would soon speak.

At ten p.m., all 240,000 of us in the park were watching the CNN broadcast on the big screens set up on the stage. The polls had just closed in California. And there it was! The banner headline: "Barack Obama Elected President." The crowd erupted. Tears ran wild down my cheeks. I thought of Papo and Mamo, and all they had endured to get to this moment. I thought of Daddy and Tee, and the fears they faced down to help our country arrive at a night like this. I thought of those who sat humiliated at the back of the bus, dreaming of a day when a man who looked like them would one day be president.

And I thought of all those who died to protect the right to vote. "There's blood on that ballot box," the saying goes, and never did those sacred words feel truer than on that glorious November night in Chicago.

There were so many good-hearted folks in the crowd that night who knew what a special meaning this event had for African Americans. They would say to me, "Hey, man, great night"—meaning for my people. I would say to them, "Yes, this is good for my people, but this is good for *all* of us."

Then, above us on the big screens appeared the face of John McCain, the vanquished Republican candidate. He was conceding the election to Obama, and damned if his speech didn't catch me off guard.

"A century ago, President Theodore Roosevelt's invitation of Booker T. Washington to visit—to dine at the White House—was taken as an outrage in many quarters. America today is a world away from the cruel and prideful bigotry of that time," the Republican said. "There is no better evidence of this than the election of an African American to the presidency of the United States. . . . Let there be no reason now for any American to fail to cherish their citizenship in this, the greatest nation on Earth," he continued. "Senator Obama has achieved a great thing for himself and for his country."

It was one of the most eloquent speeches in American political history. Everything that was in my heart—the heart of a forty-four-year-old black Democrat from Louisiana—was coming out of the mouth of a seventy-two-year-old white Republican from Arizona. It was a strangely, wonderfully American moment, and it made me flush with patriotism.

At last, the president-elect emerged, taking a victory walk around the stage with his wife, Michelle, and their daughters, Sasha and Malia. Then, alone on the stage, Barack Obama said his first public words since learning that he would become America's first black president.

"If there is anyone out there who still doubts that America is a place where all things are possible, who still wonders if the dream of our founders is alive in our time, who still questions the power of our democracy, tonight is your answer," he said.

"It's the answer," he continued, "that led those who've been told for so long by so many to be cynical and fearful and doubtful about what we can achieve to put their hands on the arc of history and bend it once more toward the hope of a better day."

THOSE WORDS from President-Elect Obama called to mind the 1965 speech Dr. Martin Luther King, Jr., delivered in Montgomery, Alabama, after completing the long march from Selma to petition the governor to respect voting rights for Negroes. The march began on March 9 in Selma with white lawmen savaging the peaceful protesters crossing the Edmund Pettus Bridge, tear-gassing them and beating them in front of television cameras. Bloody Sunday, as it came to be called, shocked the conscience of the nation.

One week later, President Lyndon B. Johnson addressed a joint session of Congress in a nationally televised speech. He took the side of the Selma marchers. "Their cause must be our cause too," Johnson said. "Because it is not just Negroes, but really it is all of us who must overcome the crippling legacy of bigotry and injustice. And we shall overcome."

LBJ had had enough. On March 17, he submitted the Voting Rights Act to Congress. Four days later, the march resumed, under federal protection. By the time the protesters reached the Alabama state capitol, their number had grown to twenty-five thousand. In his address to the crowd, Dr. King said that the civil rights movement does not seek the victory of the black man over the white man, but aims at achieving peace, equality, and justice, a common victory for "man as man."

"I know you are asking today, 'How long will it take?'" Dr. King continued. "How long? Not long, because the arc of the moral universe is long, but it bends toward justice."

It bent, in fact, toward that bright, shining moment in Chicago. Standing with more than two hundred thousand of my fellow Americans on one of the greatest nights in our country's history, I swore that I would take my mother and father to Barack Obama's inauguration if it was the last thing I ever did.

"I DON'T WANT TO GO," my father said. "It's going to be too cold."

"Daddy," I said, "you may watch it on TV, but you are going to watch it from a TV in D.C."

Thank God I insisted that my parents go, and have that memory of being with them at that special time in the life of our country, especially African Americans. We could not have imagined it at the time, but Tee would lose her fight for life two weeks before Barack Obama was elected to his second term.

I rented a suite of rooms for my folks and Aunt Tee Mae. We flew into Washington from New Orleans on a Sunday night, two days before the inauguration. Riding in a hired SUV from Dulles Airport, we had to take the long way around the National Mall because of security. Though there were five of us in the car, including the African American driver, there was silence, and tears. We all knew what we were in Washington for, and what it meant.

Suddenly, from the front seat, Daddy began to laugh. It was a deep, throaty guffaw. He was overcome by something. I wasn't sure what to make of it. I looked at my mother and Tee Mae, and we decided that because he's hard of hearing, he might not have heard us talking about where we were.

"Daddy," I said, in a strong voice. "Daddy, look, there's the Lincoln Memorial. And look over there, Daddy, it's the Capitol."

He wasn't listening. This old black man who came up in segregated schools, who fought a world war in a segregated army and was denied the medals he won, and who still cried every time he heard the national anthem, just swept his hand around and said, "You know what? A black man over all this! I never thought I'd see the day."

On New Year's Eve 1862, black worshippers gathered in an African Methodist Episcopal church in Boston in an all-night prayer vigil, awaiting word from Washington that President Lincoln had signed the Emancipation Proclamation. The good news arrived the next day. Since then, we have commemorated that event as Watch Night. On the eve of Barack Obama's inauguration, it felt like Watch Night all over again. I could barely sleep.

When I turned on the television in the hotel and saw people gathering on the Mall at five a.m., I shook my folks and Tee Mae awake. "Come on, come on, wake up, let's get down there!" I said. By the time the ceremony started, a million people had gathered on the Mall. It was bitterly cold, but it seemed that we could hardly feel a thing. Not on this day.

Obama put his right hand on the same Bible that Abraham Lincoln used when he took the oath of office, said those sacred words, and just like that, America had a black president. I was emotionally overwhelmed by it all. I had always been proud of my country, but unlike Daddy, I had never wept at the national anthem. When the inauguration ceremony ended with the "Star-Spangled Banner," I cried. For the first time, the anthem struck my ears as a hymn.

Forty-five years earlier, the National Mall filled with 250,000 marchers, most of them African American, who had come to Washington demanding jobs and freedom. They heard Dr. King, standing on the steps of the Lincoln Memorial, tell them that he had a dream "that one day, this nation will rise up and live out the true meaning of its creed: 'We hold these truths to be self-evident, that all men are created equal.'"

On that day, in 2009, four times that many Americans stood on the Mall to see a black man—who was only two years old when they marched on Washington—fulfill one of Dr. King's dreams. The arc of the moral universe stretched across half a century and the length of the Mall, from the Lincoln Memorial to the west front of the U.S.

THE WIND IN THE REEDS

Capitol. And I was able to stand with my mother and bear witness to the dream become a reality.

I DON'T THINK ANYTHING could have made my folks happier (or more surprised) than an African American winning the White House, but the New Orleans Saints winning the 2010 Super Bowl came close. A few months after their victory, President Obama hosted the Super Bowl champions at the White House for a short ceremony. I am known in New Orleans as a Saints superfan. A friend of mine on the president's staff who knew that invited my folks and me to be there with the team, and off we went.

It was great to watch my parents listening to the president as he spoke on the podium. The sparkle in their eyes, the smiles on their faces, and the tears rolling down their cheeks told the story: Born into rural and urban poverty in the Jim Crow South, they had lived long enough to vote for America's first black president, and here they were, in the White House, sharing the East Room with him.

As President Obama left the podium and exited down the center aisle, I called out to him. I introduced myself—we had never met—and introduced him to my parents.

"It's a pleasure meeting you," he said to them. "Wendell's doing great work down there in New Orleans. You should be proud of him."

"Oh, we *are* proud of him," said Tee.

"Mr. President," I said, "my father fought in World War Two."

Said the President of the United States to Amos Pierce: "Thank you for your service."

As we left the White House, Ron joined us. It was a beautiful afternoon. We had a nice stroll across the street to the W Hotel so we could have lunch as a family. In that simple, peaceful act was a perfect coda to this profoundly moving episode.

These two elderly people had lived through some of the most dangerous, violent racial times in America. My father fought for this country and its freedoms even though he was forbidden to enjoy them fully. And now, he had just met the man who was the fulfillment of all he had fought for, suffered for, and dreamed of. Both my parents had done their part to make America a better place, and gave a lot to make sure that a day like today was possible.

And now, let's take a nice stroll in this beautiful sunshine, and have a quiet lunch as a family, just like any other American family. We were free. We were together. Tee and Daddy had triumphed.

It was as if something had come to completion. I was so happy to have been able to give my mother and father that gift. It felt like generations of black struggle and suffering had been for a purpose. My mother, the granddaughter of a slave, who as a child on the bayou saw the Ku Klux Klan burn her neighbor's property, had lived to visit the White House as the guest of the first black president.

All in one lifetime. America!

At that time, good things were happening for me with *Treme*, which had begun filming that spring. Then, bad news: Doctors diagnosed my mother with breast cancer. She responded well to chemotherapy and went into remission, but the chemo drugs took a heavy toll on her heart. On Mardi Gras weekend in 2011, and again in 2012, she was rushed to the hospital with congestive heart failure.

My fear for Tee's life was eclipsed only by my anger that six years after Katrina, we still didn't have a hospital for our half of the city. The Lindy Boggs Medical Center, damaged by Katrina, never re-opened and was sold to developers. The Methodist hospital in New Orleans East was all but destroyed by the storm, and builders of a new hospital planned for the site had not even broken ground. With her heart giving out, we had to speed across the city to the nearest hospital, which was Uptown—and both years, a Carnival parade blocked our route.

In April 2012, my mother's kidneys failed and she went on dialysis. That's when her final decline began. That autumn, I flew home from Los Angeles to celebrate her birthday with friends and family at a fancy French Quarter restaurant. By then, it was clear that she was not going to get better. Every moment was going to be precious.

The weekend after her birthday dinner, Tee fell at home and called out to my hard-of-hearing father, but he never heard her. She lay on the floor for hours, unable to get up, until finally Daddy found her and sent her back to the hospital. She didn't tell me what had happened until she was back home. I caught the next flight from Los Angeles to New Orleans.

When I arrived at their house, I found my mother sitting in her bed. I began cleaning the room and said to her, "Tee, we're going to get some food in you. We're going to make it all right." She was barely eating then.

She looked at me and said, calmly and levelly, that she was dying, and that she wanted to focus on me. Tee told me that she wanted nothing more than my happiness, but it was time to settle down.

"I want you to go back to the Church," she said.

"But I haven't left the Church," I replied, puzzled.

"But I want you to *go* to church," she said.

Think of that. This woman grew up having to sit in second-class pews in the back of the church and in segregated catechism classes. She knew that a family member had been molested by a priest and that it had ruined his life. And still, her last wish for me was to go to church. She had no doubt in her soul that there was so much more to the faith than the fallibility of the men running the Church. God was there. *Your heart will not rest until it rests in Him, son. Go to church.*

On what turned out to be the last week of my mother's life, my brother Ron was thinking about flying in from Washington to visit. I had taken Tee to the hospital yet again when she began to fail, but tests showed nothing wrong. She rebounded—she was a little fire-cracker, even to the last—and we went back home.

I asked Tee if I could shoot a smartphone video postcard for Ron, to show him how well she was doing, and to ease his mind. I did and e-mailed the clip to my brother. He didn't come, and missed the chance to tell Tee good-bye.

I still feel guilty about that. I should have told him to come at once. But I couldn't see what was happening right in front of me. That is, I couldn't see it, because I couldn't bear to see it. On a Saturday night, I checked my mother out of Touro Hospital in Uptown, loaded her into the car, and drove toward home.

"Let's not take the expressway," I said. "Let me drive you through the city."

We took small detours through New Orleans, driving through Tremé so she could see a street festival. Wending our way back to

Pontchartrain Park, my mother gazed out at the city that had been home for most of her life, silently taking it all in. She knew.

I put her to bed and went into the living room to watch TV with my father. Around eleven that night, she was in bed, peaceful, but squinting slightly and rubbing her stomach.

"Tee, if you're not going to lie down and sleep, come on in and watch the television with us," I said.

Because she was so weak, I put her in a low wheelchair that I had rented.

"*Ohhhh, ohhh, ohhh!* Lord, have mercy," she moaned, rubbing her belly. "Hold my hand hold my hand hold my hand."

Daddy was sitting next to her. He began to cry. "What's the matter, Black?" he said.

"Ohhh, hold my hand, you just don't know, you just don't know," she said.

He was sobbing now.

"Stop that crying, Amos," she said. "Just hold my hand."

Daddy took one hand, and I kneeled down to take the other.

"Lift me up," she said. "Lift me up."

I stood, positioned myself behind her, and slid my hands under my mother's shoulders.

"No, no, no, not you," she said. "Lift me up, Lord, just lift me up."

She called out to her dead sisters. "Gladys and Yvonne, lift me up."

"Let me get you a pain pill," I said. I gave her the medicine, then went to lift her from her wheelchair. She slipped down to her knees. *Oh, God,* I thought, *I'm dropping my mother.* She was like a rag doll. I carried Tee to the sofa, and she fell fast asleep.

She slept there all day Sunday, and into the night. Around one-thirty on Monday morning, I woke her. "I don't want you to sleep here the whole night," I said. "You should be in bed."

I picked my mother up as if she were a child, cradling her in my arms. "Ohhh, that was a good one," she sighed, and I laid her in bed.

"Promise me you'll eat something in the morning," I said. "Look at me. Promise me."

But she was already asleep.

Then, the next morning, I got up around nine o'clock. My father was in the bathroom. I poked my head into her bedroom to check on her. She was right where I put her. Her eyes were wide open. I said, "Tee, you up?"

She was gone.

I didn't holler, and I didn't start crying. Calmly, I called the paramedics and asked them what to do. They told me to put her on the ground. I gave my mother CPR until they arrived. I never imagined that I would be able to hold my mother's cold, dead body, and feeling no fear, I would blow into her mouth, then press down on her chest, trying to restart her heart. *"Whooo, whooo,"* she seemed to say, but it was just my air passing over her vocal cords.

My father, who is profoundly deaf, had not heard any of this. When he emerged from the bathroom and saw the paramedics hunched over his wife, he said, "What's going on? What's going on?"

Then he screamed.

One of the paramedics told me my mother was dead.

I went to my father, looked him in the eye, and said, "Daddy, she's gone."

Sixty years of marriage had come to an end that morning. My

mother died in the home where she loved her man, raised her boys, and reclaimed the life Katrina stole from her.

The EMTs pronounced Tee dead and left Daddy and me there to wait for the undertaker to pick up her body. We sat with my mother for an hour or so alone in their bedroom as the house filled with others who had heard the news that spread through the neighborhood like wildfire. We said her favorite prayer, the rosary. The undertaker put Tee's body on a gurney and began rolling her out the same door through which she had carried me in as a newborn almost half a century earlier. As she passed, I leaned over, whispered, "Thank you for what you've done for me," and kissed her on the cheek. It was complete.

After what seemed to be the longest day, that night I drove down to Loyola University's concert hall to catch part of Wynton Marsalis's performance. I stood alone at the side, listening to the music. At one point during his set, Wynton left the stage to come over to the alcove where I was standing, embrace me, and offer his condolences.

Toward the end of the concert, Wynton started to introduce his "New Orleans Function," a set from his 1989 album *The Majesty of the Blues*, meant to evoke the way New Orleanians deal with death through music and communal ritual (that is, the jazz funeral). As he addressed the audience, Wynton began to talk about a man and about his mother, who had just passed. He then revealed my identity and pointed out that I was there in the hall with them all.

The audience gasped. Wynton invited me to join him and his band. I tried to beg off.

"We go all over the world, but we are family," Wynton said from the stage. "I want you to come on up here and know that we're family, and we love you. We are going to hold you up and lift you up, and let you know how much you are loved.

"You come on up here and be with us," he said. "This is for your mother."

How could I say no? I walked onto the stage, and Wynton's band, which included his father, Ellis, began playing the traditional jazz funeral dirge, "Just a Closer Walk with Thee." The tears, they ran down like a mighty river. Head bowed, I pulled out my handkerchief and dabbed my eyes as each musician played a solo to show respect to my mother.

Do you see this, Tee? Do you see what you meant?

And then, as tradition demands, the tempo picked up, and the song changed from mourning to celebration, from death to life. "Oh, Didn't He Ramble," they played. My spirit rose, buoyed by the music and the love of my people. Holding my handkerchief, I raised my right hand high, waved it to salute Tee, and began to dance, second-line style. I did a little jig off the stage, to the warm applause of the hometown crowd. Wynton led his band in an impromptu second line through the hall.

That's how we sent my mother home. It was a thing of beauty.

There was one more homegoing for Althea Lee Edwards Pierce. Tee had always said that when she died, she didn't want a big funeral. She would joke, "Just put me in a sack and throw me in the woods."

More seriously, she told us in the family that when the news of her death reaches us, we are to go to mass as soon as possible. That's what I did. After learning that the Catholic Church approved of cremation, she told us that she wanted to be cremated and her ashes to be scattered on the water. "Bayou Lafourche," she said. "Take me home."

As she lay dying, Tee wrote a will specifying exactly how she wanted to be sent off. Tee instructed all gathered on the banks of Bayou Lafourche to say the Our Father, the Hail Mary, and the Glory Be. Anybody who wanted to give a eulogy could have two minutes, no more. Wendell and Ron get five minutes each. Then sprinkle her ashes in the bayou, and sing "Going Home."

And that's exactly what we did. At her funeral mass, when it came my turn to say a few words, I spoke about my mother's touch. So many times when I was growing up, Tee would rub my back. It made me feel so good, so loved, so cherished. In her final days, I said, when she was suffering so terribly, I hoped that my hands rubbing her back brought her a measure of the comfort that she gave so selflessly to me as a boy.

It turned out that the Church accepts cremation, but it insists that the ashes be interred in an urn, in the earth, as if you were burying a body in a coffin. If Tee had known that, she likely would not have gone against the Church. All I had to go on, though, was her will. *O Lord, forgive me, but I am going to honor my mother's wishes*, I prayed.

When we held the funeral mass, the priest asked, "Now, where are you going to inter the body?"

"Out in the country," I answered. Well, what would you have said?

A small gathering of family stood in the front yard of the old Edwards home in College Point, across a country highway from Bayou Lafourche. We were uncomfortable; we weren't sure what to do. After brief prayers, we walked across the road to the water's edge, where Ron and I climbed into a canoe I keep out in the country. Ron held the red vase containing her ashes close as I paddled to the middle of the bayou. The family stood on the bank singing "Going Home," just as Tee had asked them to.

Ron passed the vase to me, and I upended it, releasing my mother's earthly remains into the still, murky water. *Ashes to ashes, dust to dust*, I thought. There was such a sense of finality in that gesture. I hoped that she was there to see it; we had given her exactly what she wanted. It was the last thing that I could do for my mother: fulfill her wishes to be back home. Bayou Lafourche was her whole world: family, love, childhood, all of her memories were anchored in this rural patch of Assumption Parish, and on that stretch of Bayou Lafourche.

My father stood on the bank, wailing. My nieces cried as they sang. And then it was over.

I hope you're happy, Tee. I did what you wanted me to do. I'm going to miss you dearly.

My father and I visit that spot whenever he wants to go to the country. At night, he prays: "Lord, I hope you don't hold this against me, but I want you to take me so I can be cremated and be in that bayou again with her, and walk into the sunset."

That first winter without Tee was hard. She was always on my mind. On good days, I felt like she was watching over me. On bad days, I felt like a motherless child.

She made her presence known in a strange and wonderful way one evening a few months after her passing. I was at the Independent Spirit Awards ceremony in Santa Monica when Ava DuVernay approached me. Ava is an African American film director who was a

2012 Sundance Film Festival sensation, and who earlier that night won the John Cassavetes Award for the best independent film made for less than $500,000. She told me that, on the morning of the first Obama inauguration, she found herself talking to two ladies from south Louisiana. One of them said, "Oh, my son is an actor. There he is over there, Wendell Pierce."

"Wendell, I spent those six hours of that morning with your mother and aunt," Ava told me that night. "You mother is so proud of you."

"Thank you for telling me that," I said. "We lost her last fall."

"Oh, my."

From that connection, and our shared happy memory of being with Tee at the inauguration, Ava later cast me to portray the Reverend Hosea Williams in her film *Selma*, which tells the story of the march that changed America. Reverend Williams, along with civil rights organizer John Lewis, led the six-hundred-strong march across the Edmund Pettus Bridge, and was severely beaten by police in the Bloody Sunday attack—a scene from history reenacted in the film.

There is a long, winding, but unbroken trail leading from the Edmund Pettus Bridge to the U.S. Capitol, where a black man took the oath of office as President of the United States. The path from the inauguration to Tee's son standing on that historic Selma bridge in front of Ava's cameras was shorter and more direct, but for me, a serendipitous blessing that blurred the lines between art and life.

That is the tangible part of her legacy. There are moments when I literally feel like an extension of my mother, living out everything that she taught me and shared with me. When I accomplish something today, I feel that I'm doing it for her, and that she is doing it through me. She was working on me till the day she died, and when she left, it was as if she gave me her blessing: *There, Wendell. There, son, everything you are, and everything you are doing, is my gift to you.*

Now that I'm caring for Daddy in the final years of his life, I feel him giving me more of himself in the time he has left. It's a painful transition for both of us, knowing that his days are short. But no matter how contentious things may have been between us at times, I feel his presence with me and in me.

I came to see that his hostility was simply his attempt to protect me from the possibility of artistic failure. In 1988, when I made my Broadway debut in Caryl Churchill's *Serious Money*, I took Daddy and Tee to the opening night party at the World Trade Center. It had been only seven years since I left New Orleans to pursue my acting dream, and now I was an actor on the most prestigious stage in the world.

"Daddy," I said, "you remember when you wouldn't take me to those auditions? I want you to remember this night, too."

"Oh yes, son," he said. "I'm so proud of you."

He was. I'm sure of it. It means the world to have my father be proud of me. The pride I have in being the son of a man with the strength, integrity, and steadfastness of Amos Edward Pierce, Jr., is boundless. In all I do in this life, I hope to honor the name that is his legacy to me.

TEE HAD BEEN GONE just over a year as I approached my fiftieth birthday. I was still grieving hard. Her death was without a doubt the most profound experience I had ever gone through. I had buried my brother, and I had rebuilt our family home after Katrina annihilated it and our neighborhood. But nothing was as devastating to me as losing Tee.

She was such a force of life that trying to understand that she was no longer here in the flesh was difficult to grasp. How could she die? It made no sense. Since the day I kissed her good-bye as they took her body out of our family home, I had been haunted by a vision in which my arms are outstretched, trying to grasp her spirit, anything I could hold on to.

Grief. There is no way around it. You think you can't go on, but, like Vladimir and Estragon, you go on.

As my half-century mark loomed, all I could think about was Tee. If I could have anything in the world for my birthday, I thought, it would be to spend one moment with her again.

I remembered her devotion to the Blessed Mother—that is, to the Virgin Mary. Tee prayed the rosary all the time and was so well known for it that she was often asked to lead the rosary at Catholic funerals. When I was a boy, she would take my brothers and me during Lent into Daddy's home office, kneel down with us, and pray the rosary.

I have always gone to mass, though not every Sunday. I cannot imagine not having the Church in my life, though I am not nearly as devout as my mother. I came from such a strong black Catholic world in New Orleans that I did not realize until I went to school in New York City that there are so few of us in America. It is impossible for me to separate being Catholic from being an African American and a New Orleanian. Wherever I am in the world, when I see a stranger make the sign of the cross, all my sense memories from childhood come rushing back. *Me too!* I think. *We are connected.*

The sign of the cross, and the rituals and sacred objects of Catholicism, are tangible things that connect us with God and each other. You can see them, hear them, smell them, feel them, and taste them on your tongue at the climax of every mass. This is how I connect religion to art: not in the sense that art provides moral and theological instruction (though it might), but rather in that it is a kind of sacrament that induces within you an experience of transcendence, of connection with the eternal, and of unity with all humanity.

Despite all of the disagreements I have with the Church, it is the way I come to God. My friends ask me why I like confession. The answer is because that priest connects me to Jesus. It goes all the way back to the Apostles, who laid their hands on the head of a man who laid his hands on the head of a man who, in an unbroken succession of ordinations, arcing over two thousand years, laid his hands on the head of the man on the other side of the screen in the confessional. Whether you believe Jesus was divine or not, when you talk to that priest, you are talking to the man who talked to the man who talked to the man who talked to Jesus. That is powerful to me.

Catholic spirituality has always taught that we don't approach the all-holy God directly, but through mediators. God chose to become a man, Jesus Christ, so that we, in our imperfection, could know Him. In the same way, Catholics believe that we can relate to God as He manifests through creation: through the sacraments, certainly, but also through beautiful art, through the majesty of nature, through feasting at the table, through works of mercy, and through acts of love.

The early Christians developed a strong devotion to Mary, the mother of Jesus, because they saw in her a way to relate to her son. Catholics are sometimes accused of worshiping Mary, but that's not true. She was the mother of God, but she was not God. We think of her, though, as a tender mother and a portal to an encounter with the living God. Many Catholics over the centuries have struggled to relate to God the awesome Judge, but they have seen in Mary a more gentle and approachable aspect of the divine. For some, God may seem far away and hard to get to, but the Blessed Mother, she's like your own mama.

It's like that with Tee and me. I have never had the strong faith she had, but I saw it in her, and felt it radiate from her. Tee made faith real. I may agonize over what I believe about God, and He may seem foreign to me sometimes, but Tee, I knew her. I loved her. I am a child of God, but I am also a child of Tee. God manifested Himself to me through her love, through her sweet voice, through her luminous face, through her tender caress and abiding care for me.

Tee knew God and loved Him with all her heart. I know Tee and love her, and her memory, with all of mine. Therefore, in the emotional logic of Catholicism, I love God through my mother, and I have faith that she is with Him now, interceding with Him for Daddy, Ron, and me. Death cannot separate us from the love of Tee, or of God. That chain will not be broken.

As I've said, my birthday happens to be December 8, the Catholic feast of the Immaculate Conception of Mary. Tee used to point to me and joke, "That's my little immaculate conception."

And so, the thought occurred to me that for my fiftieth birthday, I should seek out the devotion Tee had to the Blessed Mother. I am not an especially pious man, but I was devoted to my mother as my mother was devoted to Mary. If I connected the two, I might have a little piece of my mother again.

I thought of the places in the world I could go on pilgrimage. There was Lourdes, where the Virgin appeared in the 1800s to the French peasant girl Bernadette Soubirous and showed her a healing spring where there have been miracle cures. There was Mexico City, where the Virgin came to the Indian convert Juan Diego and left behind a miraculous cloak with her image, which can be seen today in the cathedral. She is venerated there as Our Lady of Guadalupe.

And then I recalled a 1950s movie I had seen as a child, *The Miracle of Our Lady of Fatima*. It was a fictional retelling of the Virgin's appearance to three shepherd children in Fátima, a Portuguese village some seventy miles north of Lisbon, in 1917. I had forgotten everything I knew about the apparition, but I remembered those children, and Our Lady.

Fátima it was, then. On impulse I bought a plane ticket to Lisbon and booked a hotel. "Are you sure you want to do this?" my friends asked. "It's your fiftieth birthday. We could have a great time here."

Nope. I was going to spend this birthday with Tee, in Fátima. I was hoping for a spiritual experience. To be honest, I was hoping to see my mother one more time.

I did no research in advance; I was going on instinct. When I checked into my Lisbon hotel on a Friday, I told the concierge that I knew there was a church in this town called Fátima, and asked if he could book a car and driver for that Sunday, December 8. I thought it was a nice touch that my birthday was on a Sunday that year.

I had a couple of days to bide my time in Lisbon, waiting for Sunday. This was my first time in Portugal, and I wanted to do something classically Portuguese. On Saturday night, I found a great restaurant where they featured a woman singing fado, a mournful style of music marked by aching melancholy and *saudade*, the Portuguese word for longing. Fado, in other words, is the Portuguese blues. I went into the Bairro Alto, a neighborhood that has been there since the fifteenth century, and settled in at a table at O Faia, an intimate, cavelike restaurant.

The lights dimmed and a singer appeared. When she opened her mouth and began her song, I knew at once that I was in the right place. I had never heard anything so beautiful, so painful, so filled with yearning. Her fado expressed so exquisitely what I was feeling in those days: my grief over my mother, my longing to see her again, my hope that she was at peace, and the bittersweetness of reaching a milestone in my life but without my beloved Tee at my side.

It felt, in that moment, like the fado singer was channeling all the sorrow in the world and turning it into a work of art so beautiful and pure and true that it was difficult to bear without going to pieces. So I went to pieces. All alone, on the other side of the world, in a restaurant surrounded by strangers speaking a language not my own, I wept. The singer struck the rock of my heart with the staff of her song, and a torrent of emotion surged through the breach.

I'm not the only brokenhearted person who has ever been alone in a Lisbon fado restaurant and come undone. People gave me my space. The waiter discreetly and respectfully removed my plates between courses. I had my head bowed and was crying. It was as if the staff at the restaurant was saying, without words, *Welcome to Lisbon. We understand, brother.*

There were four singers that night, and the best came last. Her name was Anita Guerreiro, and she was like a vision from another era. She was in her seventies, but had raven-black hair, pulled tight in a bun. In her black dress and shawl, she had a haunting, forlorn look. Hers was the face of unconquerable dignity, refusing to bow to life's defeats. She sang like a dark angel, with a voice that seemed to encompass every imaginable sorrow, lift it high, and transfigure it through the power of her artistry.

The singer opened up a channel in my imagination and I began to talk silently to my mother. I thanked her for my life, for all she taught me, for giving me the inner strength to survive within my demanding profession. To never lose my dignity and the willingness to fight for it. To strive to be the best actor I can, and the fiercest fighter for justice. To savor relationships, especially within the family, and always to love the simple things in life. To be a man of vision, and to search for a stronger faith.

It was as if she were sitting across the table from me, and I was having the conversation with her that I wanted to have during those last days of her life but was too afraid to have. It was so clear to me what she would have said had she been with me in that restaurant in the flesh. Tee was a woman who lived her life with complete clarity. What she believed was what she was. That was plain to me now.

By the end of that night, I could not wait to get to Fátima the next morning.

I HAD NO IDEA what to expect in Fátima. I had a romantic notion that I would walk out into the field, just as the shepherd children had, and my own blessed mother would appear to me. My driver parked the car and directed me to what had once been the field of the apparition, but what was now a vast plaza anchored by a huge basilica in honor of the Virgin.

To my shock, there were at least 150,000 people on the plaza that gorgeous December day. They had all come because that year the Feast of the Immaculate Conception fell on a Sunday. This meant that they would see the statue of Our Lady of Fátima carried from inside the basilica in procession through the crowd—a parade that normally happens only on October 13, the anniversary of the final apparition and miracle.

As I stood in the crowd of the faithful, I was moved by their devotion. It was palpable. All my life I have struggled with my faith, so much so that I took "Thomas" as my confirmation name. I hoped that like the questioning Apostle, my doubt would one day find satisfaction and be dispelled. It had not happened yet.

When I was young, I worried about the eternal fates of my best friends, Carlton and Jay. Carlton was Baptist; Jay was Lutheran. They were not communicants of what the Nicene Creed we recited at mass each week called "one holy catholic and apostolic Church."

"When I go to heaven, I can't play with Carlton and Jay?" I said to my mother.

"Oh no, that's not true," she said. Still, that's where I started challenging what the Church taught.

It's not that I don't believe in God. It's just that I struggle with doctrine. I connected with God through the love of my parents, whose belief was so unshakable. When I left home, no matter where I was in the world, I could go to mass on Sunday morning and hear the

Gospel read, and know that was the same Gospel Daddy and Tee were hearing back in New Orleans. I could call them on Sunday night and talk about the Gospel reading. The church, and the experience of Sunday mass, was the manifest connection I had with my parents so far away. That's what kept me going for so long.

Now here I was, a middle-aged man, a doubtful, not-so-good Catholic spending his birthday alone in a one-horse town in a foreign country, a place people go to only because three children a century ago made the fantastical claim that the mother of God appeared to them and gave them messages for mankind. I was not there looking for God, or Mary; I was there looking for Tee.

At first I was put off by the scene. On the long car ride to Fátima, I had looked forward to having a private moment on this spiritually hallowed ground. Instead, I had to spend my birthday with well over a hundred thousand strangers. But seeing the love in their eyes for the Blessed Mother changed me. To be present for the mass, and to know exactly what was being said at all times even though I didn't speak a word of Portuguese—it made me think of Tee, and how much she loved the Blessed Mother and her faith.

It was as if I could hear her voice saying, *Look around you, Wendell—we are not alone.* My eyes encompassed the plaza, and everywhere I looked, I saw the love of children for a mother. Like me, they made a pilgrimage to this place out of love for her, and what God had done for them through her. They were strong in faith—that much was clear—and I was not. But my faithful mother, she shared the strong faith of those people, and she had borne me to this place as surely as I had carried her to her bed on the night she died.

The doors of the great basilica opened. The statue of Our Lady came down the basilica steps atop a golden platform covered with flowers and riding on the shoulders of eight men. This Virgin is veiled in white and has her hands folded in prayer. The statue is as tall as a young girl—taller if you count the crown on her head, inside of which Pope John Paul II placed the assassin's bullet doctors removed from his body. The pope, now a saint, credited Our Lady of Fátima with saving his life. Riding through St. Peter's Square in his open car in 1981, John Paul saw someone in the crowd holding a Fátima image. He inclined to see it better at the instant the would-be killer fired his pistol. Had John Paul not leaned in for a closer look at Our Lady, the bullet would have killed him.

And then, something magical happened. As the statue was carried into the crowd, all those people took handkerchiefs out of their pockets and waved in salute to the passing Queen of Heaven. It was New Orleans, on the other side of the ocean. It was the world's largest second line! I sobbed openly, because I knew that this moment was the reason I had been summoned to this faraway place. As the statue of the Blessed Mother passed by me, it hit me like a bolt of lightning: Now I was finally, and truly, saying good-bye to Tee.

Because organizing my mother's funeral fell to me, I had never been able to be quiet in church, in solitude, and pray for the soul of my mother. When we arrived at the church for Tee's service, there were people there already who thought that I needed to be held and comforted, and who surrounded me with that love and attention. In truth, I needed to be alone with her soul.

Here it was a year later, and I had to cross a continent and an ocean to spiritually say good-bye. It happened in a foreign Catholic country that looked like my piece of the world here in New Orleans: a vast throng of people giving my mother, so to speak, a second-line fare-well. I was allowed to be alone with my mother in the midst of all those people, in the midst of their pure devotion, floating on a sea of love, entirely alone and entirely together.

I felt my mother's presence so strongly in me, and around me. She was telling me to keep the faith. *I believe, Tee. Help me in my unbelief.* It was a sublime moment, a moment of revelation, when faith was stronger than doubt, and I saw religion and art, mother and son, the individual and the collective, bleed into one, saturated and sustained by love.

Art made that insight possible. There was an actor in my class at Juilliard, Kevin Dwyer from San Francisco. When he found out that I was a Catholic, he was astonished; a black Catholic from the South is a novelty to many people. "Man, that's why I became an actor: because of the Catholic Church," he said. "Think about it: the procession, the ceremony, the pageantry. It's so beautiful, and those rituals bind us together and teach us who we are and what to do."

I had never thought about it like that, but he was right. In fact, Catholicism is why I became an actor as well. It wasn't the mass, though; it was a Passion Play, a reenactment of the last days of Jesus. As a Catholic child, I knew the facts of the narrative well, but its truth and power didn't come alive in my imagination until I saw and heard actors telling the story onstage and did my part when it was done in church.

On that day in Fátima, I saw the beauty and the power of art and religion, how it can work like nothing else to enlighten, to unite, and to change your life and the lives of others. I had seen art do that before in many instances, not least in our *Waiting for Godot* performance in New Orleans. But now I saw it in a new and intensely personal way.

Art and religion are both ways of knowing, pathways to and channels of the transcendent truths of our existence. Art makes abstract truths—Love, Justice, Selflessness, and so on—concrete and accessible to all. Religion teaches us that these abstractions truly exist, that they are not simply ideas in somebody's head. Religion needs art— ritual, music, painting, sculpture, architecture, poetry—to communicate its truths to the people.

Art needs religion—that is, a confident belief that there is a realm of truth and spirit existing beyond what we can see, and that can be known. Art that does not speak to our hopes, dreams, and experiences, art that does not help us find ultimate purpose and ultimate meaning, art that does not establish communion—communion between individuals and their communities, and communion between humanity and the realm of ideals, of God—is dead.

Pope Benedict XVI once said that the greatest arguments the Catholic Church has for itself are not books of theology or collections of sermons. No, the Church's greatest treasures for demonstrating the truth of its claims are the saints it has produced and the art it has birthed. Why? Because to see goodness or beauty made incarnate makes it real in a uniquely powerful way.

She may never be canonized by the Church, but my mother was a saint. I am an artist, and God channeled that gift in large part through the love and encouragement of my faithful mother, who no doubt prayed countless rosaries for me. Could it be that Tee and I were both on a pilgrimage up the same mountain, on different but parallel paths, moved forward by the power of love? Religion and art, at their very best, are the tangible manifestations of love. When they combine and express themselves in the culture of a people, a light appears in the darkness, and we find the faith and the hope we need to continue the journey, together.

On that day in Fátima, I saw that Tee had given me everything I needed to go on, and had been giving it to me all along. She had filled me up with everything she had been given, as she herself had been filled by Mamo and Papo and the culture of College Point. Now that she had given all she had to give, she was free to go on.

And so, at last, was I. *At this time, at this place, all mankind is us.* I had spoken that line from *Godot* while standing at that crossroads of humanity in the Lower Ninth Ward. Now it rang in my heart again, in Fátima, called out of myself by the beauty and force of the collective ritual. That's what Tee revealed to me. And it leads to the next line from the play: *Let us do something.*

What a moment of passage that was for me. It was a catharsis, a purification of my soul. Mine was just a face in the crowd that day on the plaza at Fátima, but if you could have seen what was in my heart, it would have been a beacon of light and love. Riding out of the hills back to Lisbon, I felt a renewed sense of meaning in my art and purpose in my life. *Let us do something.* I left Portugal reborn, free to be the actor, the activist, and the man that I was supposed to be.

"Now, I can look at you, Mr. Loomis, and see you a man who done forgot his song," says Bynum, the seer in August Wilson's *Joe Turner's Come and Gone*. "Forgot how to sing it. A fellow forget that and he forget who he is. Forget how he's supposed to mark down life."

Like Herald Loomis, the character I played, I had forgotten my song. Now I had remembered it, had reconnected with truth, with

authenticity, with universality, and with love, and came back from
rambling dancing to a joyful tune.

I did not become a regular churchgoer, or at least I have not yet.
Unlike my mother, I struggle with the doctrines. In that, I am more
like my father. In my childhood, when we would drive out West as a
family, Daddy would gaze at the mountains and say, "Man, I can't
understand how someone can look at that and not believe in God."
That was the extent of my father's theological understanding, and for
him, it was enough to give him a relationship to the divine.

For Daddy, the landscape is an icon, a window into eternity.
Art does that for me. I believe that Daddy, Tee, and I are singing the
same song, in three-part harmony, and it is a song of love, praise, and
unity.

In a 1997 speech to the National Black Theater Festival, August
Wilson spoke of how in the Diaspora, Africans met the unspeakable
adversity of their life as slaves in a strange land without losing their
spirit.

> Undaunted, and within the scope of the larger world that lay
> beyond their doorstep, they had begun to build a culture, to
> set down rules, and to urge a manner of being that corre-
> sponded to their temperament and sensibilities. Life was to be
> lived in all its timbre and horrifics, with zest and purpose. To
> live hard is still to live, and it was this life, worthy of the high-
> est of possibilities, that was to be cultivated and celebrated.
> And it was this culture that I learned in Pittsburgh in my
> mother's house.
>
> It was this culture that the African fought valiantly, at

great cost, to preserve. He fought to preserve it not because it was fashioned out of pain and suffering but because he stood solidly on these shores as a testament to the resilience of his spirit and the nobility of his ideas. And it was this culture that I carried with me when I went searching for a way to dedicate my life.

Amen and amen. I learned this culture in Pontchartrain Park, by way of College Point. I learned this culture in the house of my father and mother. It gave me a past, and it gave me a future. All of it is a priceless gift, a treasure hard won by generations who rose out of centuries of slavery and degradation, and who must have thought they could not go on . . . but went on anyway, on that great pilgrimage of life, second-lining away from the grave where our oppressor wanted to bury our humanity and our hope.

The Bible tells us to "walk in wisdom toward them that are without, redeeming the time." New Orleans tells us no, don't walk—pull out your handkerchief, raise high your parasol, and dance. Dance with joy, but dance with purpose. All of us must do something with the gift of wisdom handed down from the ancestors, with the legacy of fortitude and resilience, and through the transcendence of our art. We must change our lives, and change the lives of our communities. You don't learn to live in love and truth and to walk in wisdom, mercy, and justice for yourself alone.

You must make your life into an icon, a work of art through which all these good things flow and make themselves known to others. In this way, we are all called to be artists, the creators of our own lives. Many times we do not have it in our power to stave off catastrophe.

There are no soliloquies and no songs that would have turned the hurricane away from my city. But we do have it in our power to control our own response to these catastrophes, and through our will, not only to endure in the face of trial, but to prevail.

That's what the southern novelist William Faulkner once prophesied that man would do: prevail. It is, he said in his 1950 Nobel acceptance speech, the duty of the artist to help humanity by making art that speaks to the soul "capable of compassion and sacrifice and endurance."

"It is his privilege to help man endure by lifting his heart, by reminding him of the courage and honor and hope and pride and compassion and pity and sacrifice which have been the glory of his past," Faulkner said. "The poet's voice need not merely be the record of man, it can be one of the props, the pillars to help him endure and prevail."

Faulkner was a man of the American South of the twentieth century, but he spoke that day to a global audience, about what is universal in all times and all places. All great artists do; all those who aspire to artistic greatness must. Nobody knows like the African American how art and culture can help a people endure and prevail, and can redeem the time. It has been my blessing to be the heir to a great culture and its artistic tradition. It is and always will be my duty to use the days God has measured out for me to share that blessing with the whole wide world.

As Louis Armstrong, the greatest artist New Orleans ever produced, famously sang, "I know I'm not wrong, and this feeling's gettin' stronger." Yes, indeed. Strong men gittin' stronger, every day.

ACKNOWLEDGMENTS

This was a personal journey. A journey filled with fear, uncertainty, joy, and fond memories. But there is one person who cleared the path and was steadfast as we ventured forward. That was Rod Dreher. We came together from disparate walks of life but found common ground in love of family, faith, and that sometimes elusive place called home. His wisdom, creativity, and now his friendship will be eternally cherished.

I owe a great debt to all the members of my family who shared their time and personal memories without reservation. Especially my father, Amos, who has become my best friend these past years in the absence of my mother, Tee. If I could be half the man he is, I would be among giants.

I want to acknowledge all the people of Pontchartrain Park, past and present, who fought for, and continue to fight for, the ability to live a full and expressive life in the comfort of a loving community.

Last, I want to thank New Orleans, that northernmost Caribbean city, the last bohemia, which instilled in me a truthful culture that identifies my membership in that most beloved tribe that thrives in the Crescent City.

—*Wendell Pierce*

When I agreed to meet Wendell Pierce for lunch one summer day in New Orleans, to talk about collaborating on this book, I was skeptical. We come from very different cultural and political backgrounds. What we discovered over that long lunch was that we shared more than we realized. Both of us are from south Louisiana, and both of us left home to pursue the creative life. Tragedy struck in the middle of the journey of both our lives, and through it we discovered that our dear old state, sunlit despite its vices, meant more to us than we previously imagined. When Wendell told me some of the stories of his family that day, I understood that the task of telling those stories was a sacred mission. Driving home across Lake Pontchartrain, I prayed that Wendell would not choose me as his collaborator, because I did not want to be responsible for helping him do justice to this history. But he did choose me, and in so doing, opened up a world of faith and family, toil and triumph, that I had never known. Getting to know the Pierce and Edwards families, both in person and through the stories told in this book, and gaining a much deeper appreciation of the African American experience changed my heart profoundly. I hope it has made me a better man. I am grateful beyond telling to Wendell for taking a chance on a white boy from the Feliciana hills, and to his family—especially Uncle L.C.—for the graces that have come to me through their lives and their love for one another. I thank my agent, Gary Morris, and Wendell's agent, Laura Nolan, for having the inspired idea to pair two wandering sons of south Louisiana whose paths would otherwise not have crossed. And I thank Tee for her intercession, which I believe guided both her son and his friend on this pilgrimage.

—*Rod Dreher*